PRENTICE HA

Language Teaching

Teacher Education
General Editor: Christopher N. Candlin

Learning to Read in a
Multicultural Society
The Social Context of
Second Language Literacy

... English teaching

BRUMFIT, Christopher, J.
Language and literature teaching

CANDLIN, Christopher and MURPHY, Dermot
Language learning tasks

CARROLL, Brendan, J.
Testing communicative performance: an interim study

CARROLL, Brendan J. and HALL, Patrick
Make your own language tests

COOK, Vivian
Experimental approaches to second language learning

ELLIS, Rod
Classroom second language development

ELLIS, Rod
Second language acquisition in context

JOHNSON, Keith
Communicative syllabus design and methodology

KENNEDY, Chris
Language planning and language teaching

KELLERMAN, Eric and SHARWOOD SMITH, Michael
Cross-linguistic influence in second language acquisition

KRASHEN, Stephen
Second language acquisition and second language learning

KRASHEN, Stephen
Principles and practice in second language acquisition

KRASHEN, Stephen and TERRELL, Tracy
The natural approach

LA FORGE, Paul
Counseling and culture in second language acquisition

LEONTIEV, Alexei
Psychology and the language learning process

LEWIS, E. Glyn
Bilingualism and bilingual education

LOVEDAY, Leo
The sociolinguistics of learning and using a non-native language

MARTON, Waldemar
Methods in English language teaching: frameworks and options

McKAY, Sandra
Teaching grammar

PECK, Antony
Language teachers at work

ROBINSON, Gail
Crosscultural understanding

SWALES, John
Episodes in ESP

TOSI, Arturo
Immigration and bilingual education

WATERS, Alan
Issues in ESP

WENDEN, Anita and RUBIN, Joan
Learner strategies in language learning

YALDEN, Janice
The communicative syllabus

Learning to Read in a Multicultural Society

The Social Context of Second Language Literacy

CATHERINE WALLACE
Ealing College of Higher Education

ENGLISH LANGUAGE TEACHING

Prentice Hall

New York   London   Toronto   Sydney   Tokyo

First published 1988 by
Prentice Hall International (UK) Ltd,
66 Wood Lane End, Hemel Hempstead,
Hertfordshire, HP2 4RG
A division of
Simon & Schuster International Group

Printed and bound in Great Britain at the
University Press, Cambridge

Library of Congress Cataloging-in-Publication Data

Wallace, Catherine
Learning to read in a multicultural society.
(Language teaching methodology series)
Bibliography: p.
Includes index.
1. English language—Study and teaching—Foreign speakers.
2. Reading   3. Books and reading.
I. Title.   II. Series.
PE1128.A2W22   1986   428.6'4'07   85-19150
ISBN 0-13-527516-4

British Library Cataloguing in Publication Data

Wallace, Catherine
Learning to read in a multicultural society.
(Language teaching methodology series)
1. English language—Study and teaching—
Foreign speakers
I. Title   II. Series
428.2'4'07   DE1128.A2
ISBN 0-13-527516-4

---

1 2 3 4 5   91 90 89 88 87

In memory of

RUTH MARKS

Contents

Acknowledgements

The author and publisher are pleased to acknowledge the following sources, quoted briefly in the text: Peter Abbs, *Ginger and Sharon, Linda's Journey*; Stannard Allen *et al.*, *English for Arabs*, Book 2; Barr, Clegg and Wallace, *Advanced Reading Skills*; Beryl Bainbridge, *The Bottle Factory Outing*; J. D. Bentley, *Toussaint l'Ouverture of the West Indies;* Carol Bergman, *Donnovan*; E. S. Bradburne, *Through the Rainbow*; Dick Bruna, *Poppy Pig*; Josie Byrens, *Never in a Loving Way*; Criper and Widdowson, *Sociolinguistics and Language Teaching*; Farukh Dhondy, *East End at Your Feet*; Paul George, *Memories*; Ginn Reading 360, *Ben and Lad, The King, the Dragon and the Witch*; Goddard and Grattidge, *Beta Mathematics 3*; John Holt, *How Children Fail*; Geraldine Kaye, *Christmas is a Baby*; P. Kinmouth, *Mr Potter's Pigeon*; Ladybird, *Danger Men, Goldilocks and the Three Bears, Little Red Riding Hood, The Little Red Hen*; Willis Lindquist, *Wild Elephant Raid*; Link Up, *Auntie Pat in Hospital, Karen at the Zoo*; S. K. McCullough, *Griffin Pirate Stories*, 'Gregory the Green'; Jane Mace, *Working with Words*; Susan Mayfield, *One Room Living*; V. S. Naipul, *A House for Mr Biswas*; Ann Oates, *Meet Harry King, The Running Man*; Bertrand Russell, *Has Man a Future?*; Manuel C. R. dos Santos, *In Tune*; Scope, Reader 6, *Ali's Coming to England*; Dr Seuss Books, *Hop on Pop*; Paul Scott, *Staying On*; Sparks Readers, *Television Castle, The Wishing Bottle*; Anne Spike, *A Woman's Work*; Peter Trudgill, *Accent, Dialect and the School*; Wight *et al.*, *Make-a-Story*; Kathleen Wood, *All the Long Night; Cosmopolitan, The Guardian*, the *Mirror*, the *Observer*, the *Standard*, the *Sun*, the *Sunday Times*, *Woman*; Dan-Air (baggage ticket), HMSO (Social Security leaflet), Social Democratic Party (leaflet).

(p. 96) Report from the Linguistic Minorities Project, University of London Institute of Education, distributed by Tinga Tinga (Heinemann Educational);

(p. 118) Howell, Walker and Fletcher, *Mathematics for Schools*, Level 1, Book 6, Addison Wesley Publications, London, 1979;

(p. 122) Nobbs, *Modern Society*, Social Studies for CSE, Allen & Unwin, 1976;

(p. 146) Moon, 'Hare and Tortoise', *Jumpers*, Frederic Warne Ltd., London, 1980;

(p. 147) Bradburne, illustrated Cook, 'The Dog in the House', *Red Running Along Book 2*, Schofield & Sims Ltd., Huddersfield, 1973.

Introduction

This book is intended for teachers of reading to adults or children who are learning to read in a second language. Wherever possible, I have quoted examples of actual learner-readers, most of them native speakers of languages other than English. Some of the older learners are literate in their first language; most of the children are acquiring initial literacy through English. At times emphasis is on the individual learner; at times on the classroom or group. Indeed, many linguistic minority learners will be in a multilingual and multicultural reading group, and I have considered the implications of this for the teaching of reading in the classroom. I refer throughout to the Case Studies of learner-readers included in Chapter 9.

In writing the book I have been guided by three related principles: firstly, and most importantly, that reading is to do with language; secondly, that like all other forms of language, the function of written language is above all to communicate—writers communicate a range of facts, feelings, opinions or directives of various kinds to potential readers, who in turn have a purpose in reading, related to their own needs or interests; thirdly, reading—again like all forms of language—makes sense in context. I shall suggest that, as teachers, we might keep these principles in mind from very early literacy teaching onwards.

In my particular concern with the relationship between language and literacy, I have introduced some terms from linguistic description which I believe are helpful in describing this relationship. However, I have tried to keep the use of specialist terms to a minimum, and no prior knowledge of linguistics is assumed.

The first chapter looks at the whole context of the reader who is acquiring second language literacy. We look at the social meaning of literacy and its implications for functioning in everyday life. The second and third chapters look at the role of the text, the reader and the writer in the reading process. I discuss the part played by each of these in our attempt to make sense of the written word.

In Chapters 4 and 5 we turn to the learner-reader and the process of learning to read, particularly for second language readers. I consider ways in which teachers can help to make the interaction between learner, teacher and text more meaningful in the early stages of learning to read, from which students can learn both about the meaning of texts and about what reading itself means. Chapter 5 focuses on the linguistic resources which native speakers, non-standard and non-native speakers respectively bring to the task of learning to read.

Chapters 6 and 7 give practical suggestions for the teaching of reading to second-language readers of varying competence in English and reading. Examples of materials and exercises are included.

Chapter 8 evaluates some of the materials and books available for use in the multicultural and multilingual classroom. Books for both learner adults and children are considered, with a discussion of their content and language. Chapter 9 contains the Case Studies of teacher/learner interactions. Most of the learners are second language learners at a fairly early stage of learning to read in English.

The aim throughout has been to consider ways in which we, as teachers, might try to show learners that reading is meaningful not just as the psychological process of getting meaning from written texts, but as a social activity in the real world.

Although the emphasis is on bilingual learners, it is not suggested that second language readers learn to read in significantly different ways from native speakers. The position I shall take is rather that the kinds of approach which help second language readers will also help those learner-readers who are acquiring literacy in their first language, and that the presence of linguistically and culturally diverse teaching groups can help all learners in such groups to understand more clearly the purposes and process of reading.

I should like to thank a number of friends and colleagues who very kindly read parts of the book while it was in preparation, and whose advice was invariably constructive. They are: John Clegg, Peter Figueroa, Tricia Hedge, Frank McMahon, Ruth Marks, Isabel Smith, Brenda Wallace, John Whapham, Norman Whitney and Edward Woods. Particular thanks are due to those teachers who collected data from their own classrooms: I am most grateful for their permission to quote them, in particular Dorothy Anderson, Caroline Brice, Brendan Kelly, Di Mellish and Harbans Virdi. I have also drawn heavily on the work of several students on a course which is offered at Ealing College of Higher Education, 'Language in the Multiracial Community'. Their studies of language-related issues offer helpful insights into some of the areas dealt with in this book. Finally, and above all, I must thank:

—the students and staff at the Pathway Further Education Centre, Southall, and especially the then Head of the Centre, Shirley Hadi;
—the students and staff at Newfield Junior Mixed and Infant Schools in Willesden, and particularly Pearl Simons and Carol Owen, the then heads of the Junior and Infant School respectively;
—the students and staff at the Friends' Centre, Brighton, in particular the Principal, Janet Price.

I am particularly indebted to my editor, Vaughan James, for his unwavering kindness and support during the preparation of the first edition of this book.

CATHERINE WALLACE

N.B.: In an attempt to resolve the 'pronoun problem', I have referred to the teacher as 'she', the learner as 'he', the writer as 'she' and the reader as 'he'.

1

The Social Context of the Second Language Reader

Social Roles and Reader Roles

In this chapter I shall look at the circumstances in which literacy is acquired and maintained, in particular by readers for whom English is a second language. I shall suggest that for all readers and learner-readers it is important to consider the whole context in which reading takes place. In doing so we must look at what role the reader is assuming in the course of reading any particular text in any situation. Is he reading as a dutiful pupil in the classroom, to please the teacher, perhaps? Or as a potential consumer, to decide which flavour of ice cream to buy? Or in a more private capacity, as someone who is looking for personal pleasure in the enjoyment of a story? Taken together, these reader roles, as we might call them, help to give us both a personal and a social identity. Reading behaviour in literate societies is bound up with a wide range of social, professional and personal roles.

Simply because reading is so much a part of adult life in literate societies the issue of learning to read generates great anxiety. Infant school teachers are under pressure to teach the so-called 'reading skills' as soon as possible; 'reading experts' put forward a range of different models and methods of reading; failure is a matter of considerable concern—even shame, in the case of adult non-readers or poor readers. All this would suggest that reading is difficult, to be learnt only with great effort and persistence with the help of specially skilled people. Yet many children are apparently not taught to read at all, as Clark notes (1976) in her study of young fluent readers. They do not so much learn to read in any formal sense as acquire reading, much as they acquire spoken language. They acquire it in the course of everyday family life. As with speaking, they need some help from the adults around them. Just as parents and other adults, in talking with children, aid the acquisition of spoken language, so may they, in reading to children and talking about reading, guide them into acquiring this new language medium, when they are ready to do so. Reading will not happen on its own; but then neither does talking, as evidenced by the several well-attested cases of children reared apart from humans who have not acquired recognizable human spoken language.

Children learn to talk because there is usually a powerful motive to do so, namely, the wish and the need to communicate with those around them. Admittedly, reading does not work in quite the same way; for while speaker and listener roles takes turns in most conversations, reader/writer roles do not take turns in the case of written communication. Nevertheless, just as children want to talk in order to join in what is going on around them, so are they likely to want to read if reading is part of the behaviour of the other people in their environment.

Another way of putting this is to say that children are socialized into reading. They are motivated to learn to read not only for personal reasons, such as the private enjoyment of stories, but also for social reasons. They aspire to be members

1

of the society of readers they see around them. Frank Smith (1983) puts this neatly when he talks of becoming a reader as 'joining the club'; by this he means that group of people for whom reading is taken for granted as an everyday activity.

But if reading is so readily acquired by some children, why do so many apparently not learn to read to a level of proficiency which will allow them access to a wide range of reading material? One reason is that we, as teachers, make entry into the club difficult: some learner-readers may well get the impression that this is an exclusive club, certainly not open to everyone, to membership of which they hardly dare aspire. While some children find themselves naturally members of the club, others are hammering at the door; still others turn away, convinced from the beginning that they will not be accepted.

In class-conscious Britain, at least, it may be truer to talk not about a single club of adult readers but about a range of different clubs: the readers of the *Sun* newspaper; the readers of *Time Out*; the readers of Mills & Boon romantic fiction; the readers of mail order catalogues. Certainly writers, publishers, newspaper proprietors and advertising agencies have a clear picture of these groups; and in some cases, of course, reader audience is very clearly identified, as with magazines called *Woman* and *18* and *Motorbike*.

Where does the member of a linguistic or cultural minority group fit into this picture? Do, for instance, young Asian women or black teenagers feel part of the same readers' clubs as their white, indigenous peers? If they do not, would they in fact want to be part of the same readerships?

Being a 'reader' is likely to mean something rather different from one social group to another. It will certainly mean something different from one society to another, and from one cultural group to another. Learner-readers from cultural or linguistic minority groups, whose first language and culture is different from the indigenous one, may have different views about what it means to be a reader.

Social roles, actual or aspired to, affect reader roles, whether in a first, second or any other language. A Pakistani Moslem boy, for instance, will be expected to be able to read aloud from the Koran. He will not, however, be expected to understand what he reads, and a gloss is generally provided in Urdu, which in fact is not necessarily his first spoken language, which may be Punjabi. An Indian housewife may not see herself in certain reader roles—for example, as a reader of newspapers or income tax forms, but she may well see herself in the role of 'mother reading to child'. This is not to say, of course, that she may not find herself—in new circumstances and in a different cultural context—taking on unanticipated roles which involve her in different reading activities. Also, as with other kinds of learning, including learning a second language, perceived needs may not match actual needs. However, the question of how the learner sees himself as a potential reader in social, educational and occupational contexts is clearly crucial in assessing literacy needs. We need to be aware of what, how much and in which way our learner-readers expect to read, in line with the way they see their roles, both in their immediate communities and in society at large.

Literacy Versus Reading

Placing reading in a social context leads us naturally to talk of literacy rather than simply of reading. Is there, in fact, a difference? While books concerned primarily with children learning to read tend to talk merely of reading, discussion of adults learning to read is usually described in terms of literacy. Attempts to define either term are full of difficulty. Literacy suggests a concern with the social functions of reading, while learning to read has traditionally been taken to denote the acquisition of a set of skills which are presumed prerequisites to reading itself. In many ways the distinction is invalid, for readers' views of the social function of reading, what it means to be literate, and how literacy may affect their own lives, will determine their approach to the immediate reading task.

The term literacy has social and political implications. Achieving literacy is seen not only as concomitant with certain social and occupational roles but in some countries goes together with political rights, such as the right to vote. Literacy is valued as part of adulthood, of full citizenship. It is clearly partly for this reason that we do not talk of children—or at least younger children—as being illiterate. Illiteracy is a stigma reserved for adulthood. Nonetheless, as teachers of reading we need from the beginning to see functional literacy as the goal; we need, that is, to show our learners that being literate, for children as well as adults, is part of day-to-day life in a personal and social sense. Children need from the beginning to see that reading is purposeful, that it helps us to achieve things.

This should not be taken to imply a merely utilitarian view of literacy. For while children need to be encouraged to see reading as associated with roles with which they can identify in the shorter and longer term, most important of all is the need to see that reading is fun. Southgate *et al.* (1981) point out that reading for pleasure was rarely mentioned by the children in their study of 7–9-year-olds and, as reported to me by teacher Brendon Kelly, in a class of 12-year-olds only two out of 30 children—when asked what was the most important thing about reading—said 'enjoyment', and one of the two was by far the best reader in the class. We need to show children that having fun with reading—reading jokes in crackers or on matchboxes, or reading comic strips in English or in any other language spoken or read in the community—is to be counted as reading just as much as getting through the reading scheme at school. They need, too, to see adults—teachers at school and parents at home—enjoying reading. Fairfield School in Croydon, as described by Walker (1980), set aside time for teachers and pupils to enjoy together the reading of their choice in uninterrupted peace, and this has now become common practice in a number of London schools. Teachers can then also discuss with their learners what they have read—in or out of school—sharing experiences in much the same way as we say, 'Did you see so and so on TV?'

By sharing and discussing literacy experiences—even very simple reactions to notices or advertisements—teachers in school can help to provide a context for literacy. Preparation for reading then becomes not so much teaching the pre-reading skills as making children literacy-aware—aware, that is, of the whole range of contexts for literacy and of uses of literacy, both in and out of school.

Literacy in Context: Home and School

For many children, literacy awareness begins before they go to school. There is considerable evidence that good, young, learner-readers see reading in a social context; that is, they are aware that certain kinds of reading behaviour characterize certain situations, e.g. going round a supermarket. For young children the most important context is the home and family. A number of studies have suggested how important the experience of print can be to the pre-school child. One such study (Taylor, 1981) shows how pervasive this experience can be in families which value literacy. This refers not to explicit didactic programmes, but to a sharing of everyday reading experiences. One father in Taylor's study expressed the opinion that 'occasions when the children were dealing with print' were difficult to pinpoint, but that they were probably going on all the time, when they looked at menus in cafés, when they went shopping, and on buses and trains. Again, this is a matter not necessarily of books but of all the printed or written realia which surrounds us, like signs, labels, posters and graffiti. When it comes to books, Shirley Brice-Heath (1982) mentions how in what she calls 'Maintown' (or middle-class) families, books are not just read but talked about outside the immediate context of reading. Adults, she says 'strive to maintain with children a running commentary on any event or object which can be book-related'. So objects or animals seen in the street, for instance, will be likened to similar objects or animals in the child's reading book. In a doctor's waiting room recently I overheard a middle-class mother point to a picture on the wall and say to her two-year-old child, 'See, the pussy's tongue sticking out—like in your book, isn't it?' Books and reading become in this way a pervasive influence in the lives of middle-class children.

Even when children go to school parents can continue to play an important part—working-class as well as middle-class parents. This was shown by a project on reading carried out in the largely working-class and multiracial London Borough of Haringey. Hewison (1981) describes how every child in two randomly chosen top infant classes at two schools, randomly allocated from twelve multiracial inner-city schools, was heard to read at home. Books were provided by the class teacher. The extra reading practice at home led to a highly significant improvement in the reading attainment of the children (extra reading practice given to a control group of children in school did not show this improvement). Moreover, the children's progress in reading resulted even when parents were not native speakers of English (a large minority in the Borough of Haringey) and were illiterate in English. What happened was that children read to any member of the family who could understand English, and mothers, fathers or older brothers and sisters only stopped the reading when it did not make sense to them, a pragmatic and common-sense strategy.

Literacy and Linguistic Minorities

How does our discussion so far affect learners whose mother-tongue is not the language of literacy of society in general? Here we are not concerned with learners who are temporarily resident in a country. In a British context, such learners have come to be known as 'EFL' learners, who are learning English as a foreign rather than a second language, and have come to Britain usually specifically to improve their English. Many of them will be from other European countries and will be highly literate in their first language.

The purpose of these EFL learners in learning to speak and read English is likely to be very different from that of linguistic minorities who have settled in Britain. These new Britons are learning English as a second rather than a foreign language and are likely to have to function in daily life, work and education primarily through the medium of English. They are sometimes referred to as E2L learners; this is perhaps an unfortunate term as it takes no account of the fact that while they are learners of English they may already have a repertory of two or three other languages and literacies. While aware of its inadequacy I shall, however, use the term E2L as a convenient shorthand to refer to any learner-reader for whom English was not the language first acquired.

Clearly, it is important not to lump together all linguistic minorities, that is, those who have a mother-tongue other than English. There is enormous linguistic and cultural diversity even among those who come to Britain from the Indian sub-continent, for instance, as researches carried out by the Linguistic Minorities Project have shown. This 3-year project researched the variety of languages other than English spoken in England, describing patterns of language use among children and adults in four urban areas. It revealed a great diversity of language use by both individuals and whole communities, including uses of mother-tongue literacy. As Martin-Jones (1984) points out, 'Urban Britain of the 1980s has become a multilingual, multiliterate society.'

For all linguistic and ethnic minorities, however, the development of English language literacy is, if anything, more important than for indigenous speakers of English. Because of certain kinds of disadvantage—including, in some cases, racial discrimination—such minorities may need to be even more alert in the pursuit and defence of the rights and opportunities which full literacy in the standard language can provide.

Biliteracy

To promote the case for literacy in the standard language is not to deny the role of mother-tongue literacy. Quite the reverse; research suggests (cf. Cummins, 1979) that the more fully developed the mother-tongue, preferably supported by mother-tongue literacy, the more readily will competence in the second language and literacy be acquired. The result is bilingualism of a kind that is both socially and cognitively advantageous. Ideally, therefore, one might wish to provide a firm grounding in first language and literacy for all children in the early years of schooling.

However, in the United Kingdom today we are so far from offering such provision for linguistic minority children that with few exceptions (such as the Bradford MOTET Project[1]) mother-tongues other than English are rarely used in schools as the medium or content of teaching. On the whole, even very young children are not encouraged to use any language other than English for speaking, reading or writing, even where the mother-tongue is a very widely used community language and where teachers are of the same language community. This, at least, was the case with the nursery schools in Southall, in West London, described by Francesca Target (1982) in her observations of bilingualism in nursery schools. Practice varied: in one school, while most teacher-directed activity occurred in English, a Punjabi-speaking teacher would occasionally tell Punjabi-speaking children stories in their own language. In another school, where only two out of eighty children spoke English as a mother-tongue, though it was officially recognized that children should not be discouraged from using their mother-tongue in play, a trainee nursery nurse was nonetheless observed on a number of occasions interrupting a group of Punjabi-speaking children playing in the Wendy House and asking them to speak English. Target found little support for mother-tongue development in the spoken medium, let alone through printed material in languages other than English.

Some inner-city schools do, however, give some recognition to community bilingualism, for example, by having bilingual and multilingual signs and messages on the walls. This kind of recognition of linguistic and cultural diversity in communities does at least help to make children aware of some of the different forms and uses of literacy in several languages.

Which Languages for Which Purposes?

When it comes to considering the uses of first and second language literacy respectively, much depends on the context. There will be kinds of reading and writing undertaken in order to maintain feelings of identity with one's own community, ethnic group and family, where readers are taking on what we might call 'private' roles. Then there are more 'public' roles to do with being a member of the wider society, for example as motorist, consumer or taxpayer. Biliterate readers might expect to read in the mother-tongue in their private or personal roles, and in English as members of society at large.

Some views of children and adults

At this point we might usefully consider what bilingual learner-readers themselves feel about the use of more than one literacy.

Many learner-readers, particularly young children, are initially very unclear as to the range of purposes of reading in any language. It follows that they are likely to be similarly unclear as to why they themselves should learn to read in a first or second language. Small groups of bilingual 5-, 6- and 7-year-olds were asked by an Asian teacher, fluent in English and several Indian languages, the following questions:

1. IS READING—very easy/quite easy/difficult
2. CAN YOU READ IN ENGLISH?—No/a little/quite well
3. CAN YOU READ IN ANOTHER LANGUAGE? (for example the language you speak at home)—No/a little/quite well
4. DO YOU WANT TO LEARN TO READ BETTER IN ENGLISH?   Yes/No
   If YES why do you want to learn to read better?
   If NO why do you *not* want to learn to read better?
5. DO YOU WANT TO LEARN TO READ IN ANOTHER LANGUAGE?   Yes/No
   If YES why do you want to learn to read in another language?
   If NO why do you *not* want to learn to read in another language?

6. WHAT KINDS OF THINGS DO YOU WANT TO LEARN TO READ?
   —In English
   —In another language
7. WHAT DO YOU THINK IS THE MOST IMPORTANT THING ABOUT READING?

Harbans, the teacher, spoke to each child individually, simplifying and explaining the questions as needed. None of the 5-year-olds (all girls) could read in their mother-tongue, either Punjabi or Gujerati; most could read a little in English. They all said they wanted to learn to read the language they spoke at home but their reasons were unclear (they tended to say: because they 'wanted' or 'liked' to). Most interesting were their comments on what was important about reading. Examples were:

it makes me helpful;
makes you strong;
makes you grow up.

Being a reader, it seems, is something expected of you: it commands the approval of adults and it is part also of being 'grown up'.

Two of the 6-year-olds, both Gujerati-speakers, said they could 'read a little' in their mother-tongue. Again all the children said they wanted to learn to read in another language than English. This time they were able to give reasons such as 'If somebody asks you, "Can you read Gujerati" I will say yes, because it is good to read Gujerati.' The same boy said that what he wanted to learn to read in English were: 'The books with pictures—easy to read because pictures tell you what to read.' About Gujerati he said: 'Alphabet books in Gujerati and Indian story books.' Another Gujerati-speaker who had some literacy in her mother-tongue was similarly clear about what she wanted to read in her two languages. In English it was: 'Stories and any books', and in her mother-tongue: 'Religious books' (this said in Gujerati). Asked what they thought was the most important thing about reading, one child again gave the answer: 'You grow up.' Other examples were: 'So you can get clever' and 'You might learn with your Mum.'

Of the three 7-year-olds who were asked about their reading, none could read in their mother-tongue (Punjabi or Parsee). They all said they wanted to, however, and two of them related this wish to their role in the family: 'Because if my mummy wants I can read it' and 'When you want to read a story in Punjabi to your grandma, daddy and mummy, you can.'

At the moment many bilingual children brought up in Britain only learn to read the mother-tongue in their teens. However, it would seem from this admittedly small sample that young children, too, would welcome the opportunity to learn to read in the mother-tongue. They can also give fairly clear reasons why they want to, largely related to contacts in the family with parents and grandparents.

I asked my small class of young adults the following questions:

Can you read in your first language?
(If yes) what sort of things do you read in your first language?
(If no) Do you want to learn to read in your first language?
Why?

Why not?
Why do you want to learn to read in English?
What sort of things do you want to read in English?

All these adults could read in their first language, well enough to read novels and newspapers except for one Portuguese student, José, who was near-illiterate in his first language and, having lived and worked in Britain for 12 years, saw English as fulfilling the whole range of his reading needs. For most of the others, reading for pleasure would continue to be predominantly in their first language. Sheela and Rashmika said simply that being able to read Hindi or Gujerati was important because it was 'my national language' or 'my mother-tongue'.

When asked about English, not surprisingly, the examples of things they wanted to be able to read were related to public rather than private roles. These comments were typical: 'I want to be an electrician—book will telling you how you can do'; '—newspapers' . . . (But don't you read Indian newspapers?) 'Yes, but Indian newspapers only giving Indian news.' 'For the driving test—can't read, can't pass.'

Ravinder, quoted here, is fairly typical of a learner already literate in his mother-tongue—Punjabi—but with a clear sense of the range of needs to read in English, related to roles he aspires to in his immediate community, and in society at large. The profile emerging from Ravinder's description of his own literacy needs is shown in Table 1.

TABLE 1 *Literacy needs (Ravinder)*

Literacy need	Role of reader	Example of reading material	Likely language
For:			
survival (basic day-to-day uses)	e.g. motorist/pedestrian e.g. consumer	Highway Code road signs instructions on equipment	English English
learning (especially skills)	student	textbooks, manuals	English
citizenship (knowing about and acting on rights and duties)	e.g. supplementary benefit claimant	forms	English
	e.g. well-informed member of the immediate community	local newspapers	Punjabi and English
	e.g. well-informed member of the wider community	national newspapers	English
maintaining personal relationships	e.g. friend e.g. grandson	letters	Punjabi
personal pleasure	reader in purely personal capacity	comics, novels, magazines	Punjabi and some English

Yasmeen, from Pakistan, after 2 years in Britain, was more interested in reading for personal reasons. She mentioned reading for pleasure in both English and Urdu: 'I like to read novels in English. (Do you go to the library?). I've got some library books. They are both about ghosts. Scary ones you know. I like Dracula. (Do you read books about Dracula in Urdu as well?) Yes, I read one. I couldn't sleep until two nights—it was so scary you see. My father bought it for me. It was in Urdu. (Is Dracula a popular story in Pakistan?) I never read these stories in Pakistan, only here.' Yasmeen also mentioned children's books. Reading to her young sister in English is one of Yasmeen's roles, as her mother is illiterate in both Urdu and English.

Rama, from India, is shortly expecting her first baby. She has also been in Britain for just over 2 years. For her, the most important reading material at the moment is the 'baby book'. This is her life-line, giving her confidence in her future role as a mother. 'I'm interested in reading and writing. So they gave me one book for babies. So I'm reading, this is helpful to go to hospital. It's called "From pregnancy to fourth year old child". (Can you understand it all right?) Sometime I see dictionary, sometime help my husband . . . that's (the book) very important to know how we will cope in future with baby. If I got some general knowledge that will be helpful. I want to read about hospitals. (When you go to the clinic is it difficult to understand?) Actually sometime I feel difficult but I read at home this book, so it helps with the clinic.'

Learner-readers may identify with a wide range of roles varying according to age, sex and circumstances. The important point is what it means to be a law-abiding and well-informed citizen, a good mother and an acceptable employee in any given society, and what reading needs these roles demand. They are obviously culturally determined, as suggested earlier. You may need to do different sorts of things to be counted as a good wife/mother/workmate in different cultures, and reading behaviour must count as part of general social behaviour, as witness the case of Pat, quoted in *Working with Words* by Jane Mace (1979).

> A thing I used to go hot and cold about, quite a lot, is if I'd go to lunch with a group of girls and we'd be looking at a paper and they'd say, 'Pat, what's our stars, what's the stars say?' I used to go hot and cold about it because I knew that there were words I was going to stumble at.

For Pat, being able to read the stars was part of being a sociable workmate; Rama felt that being able to read the 'baby book' written in English helped her to be a responsible mother; for some of the younger bilingual children, reading in their mother-tongue (whether they could currently do so or not) meant that they could fulfil their roles in the family as son or daughter and grandchildren. For Sheela and Rashmika, literacy in their mother-tongue was simply part of their national and cultural identity. Literacy in one or more languages helps us not just to **do** certain things but to **be** certain things, such as a good son or mother or friend or a good Hindu or Muslim. Both the acquisition and maintenance of literacy in one or more languages are dependent on what social roles we aspire to in any particular social context. While literacy in the mother-tongue helps to ensure participation in the contexts of home and family, literacy in the standard language is one necessary condition for access to the institutions of power in the wider society.

In the next section I shall consider how, as teachers, we might help learners to see reading in a social context from the beginning of learning to read.

Some Implications for Teaching Reading in a Social Context

A framework for literacy awareness

I have suggested so far that reading behaviour is part of social behaviour seen to be appropriate to particular situations. Biliterate individuals or groups will make use of different languages in day-to-day reading and writing tasks, as they do of their spoken languages.

How might we draw learner-readers' attention to the range of reading behaviour which surrounds them, including—for bilingual learners—attention to the choice of one or another language to be spoken or read in a particular situation?

Many linguists have in recent years wished to consider language not merely as an abstract system, which has little to do with real people in real situations, but as it actually occurs in use. Fishman (1965), for instance, offered a way of looking at the language use of bilinguals in certain communities by asking us to consider **who** speaks **what language, to whom** and **when**. As our concern is here with a particular kind of language behaviour, that is reading behaviour, we might modify this to consider rather who reads what kind of things in what language to whom, on what occasion and in what general context—for instance home, school, street or temple.

The simple framework which emerges gives us a way of helping to make learners literacy aware. It can be used both to catalogue the reading experiences of children or adults and to heighten the awareness of reading behaviour, particularly for those learners who may not have previously considered the nature or purpose of print.

One might, with children, begin with the context of home and family. It is true that, as we saw, home and family reading experiences are richer for some children than for others. However, even if homes do not have books, there is other reading material, such as print on labels, household equipment and on television. In a 'reading awareness' discussion a multilingual group of 8-year-old children showed that they were very much aware of the range of things to read at home. These were some of their comments when asked what sort of things they saw to read: On the cooker—'off' and 'on'—'New World'; 'On BBC1 you see Ceefax', 'advertising' and (also on television) 'Thames'; 'when the programme's finished you see where the programmes were made—'Vision mixer'.

Bilingual children are likely to have a particularly rich and diverse experience to draw on; for even if they cannot read in their mother-tongue, they may have noted that letters written to or by their parents and possibly local newspapers are in a script different from that of the words on the cornflakes packet, for instance. A typical response from a 5-year-old Japanese girl, Hiroko, is shown in Table 2.

TABLE 2 *Uses of languages at home (Hiroko)*

Home and family	Language	Who?	To whom?
Newspapers	English and Japanese	Daddy and Mummy	Self
Labels on tins	English and Japanese	Mummy	Self
Letters	Japanese	Daddy and Mummy	Parts out loud to family
Television	English	Whole family	Self
Books	English and Japanese	Mummy and Daddy	Self

From the familiar environment of home one might, for children new to school, move to the context of school itself and direct attention to all the different printed artefacts on display and the different events which involve reading seen to go on in school. In this way children can be socialized as readers in the new environment. In a multilingual school, which has tried to reflect the multilingualism of the surrounding community, one might have the kind of framework shown in Table 3.

TABLE 3   *Uses of languages at school*

School	*Language*	*Who?*	*To whom?*
Posters	English	Teachers and children	Self
Notices on doors	English	Teachers and children	Self
Books	English and other	Older children	Self
	languages	Younger children	Out loud to teacher
		Teachers	Out loud to chidlren
Things written by	English and other	Teachers, children	Self
children (on walls)	languages	and parents	

In this way children see how reading is part of day-to-day life and that the organization of communities depends partly on the printed word. Being able to read allows us to be active members of these communities.

Introducing the functions of reading

After discussing the range of printed realia and sharing observations of different reading behaviour, one can move on to consider more particularly the uses or functions of written language. In what way does it communicate different things in different situations? A printed notice at Ealing College reads: 'ALL ACCESSORIES MUST BE REMOVED FROM BICYCLES.' In order to make sense of this—that is, to understand its function—we need to make a number of assumptions. Firstly, this message, one assumes, originates from an authority rather than, say, students or the bicycle-owners themselves. Secondly, who is the notice aimed at? Are, for instance, potential thieves to interpret this as an invitation (indeed, instruction!) to 'remove all bicycle accessories?' Aware, perhaps, of this ambiguity the producers of this particular message, the College authories, have as an afterthought labelled it 'WARNING'. This functional label directs the message clearly at the owners of the bicycles.

The above example shows us that much of the print we see around us is directed not at the public in general but at particular groups—bicycle-owners, the motorist, the dog-owner, the shopper or the shoplifter. Most of these groups are likely to consist of adults rather than children. Michael Stubbs (1980) makes the point that many of the functions of literacy are not accessible to young children in the way they are to adults. For this reason it is much easier to take a functional approach to early literacy in teaching adults. Nonetheless, while children do not take on such a wide range of social and therefore reader roles, they too need some awareness of the diverse uses of print in order to cope adequately with many situations and to judge what affects their own interests. This means being aware of what different messages mean in different contexts; while they may ignore newspaper headlines, they may not ignore DANGER or POISON and will very quickly pick up ICE CREAM and COCA COLA. Frank Smith (1983) quotes the research done with 3-year-old children, in the United States who were asked to read the word *MacDonalds*. Not one of them failed to do so.

While children will learn to read messages whose content is close to their hearts, it is clearly not true that all children, or indeed adults, left to themselves will take an interest in the full range of printed messages around them. How can children's attention be drawn to the functions of print? Halliday (1973) maintains that children even as young as 5 are aware that spoken language is used in different ways for different purposes. They know what language is because they know what language does. How then can we encourage children to see what reading does?

Halliday offers an account of what he calls 'models' of child language use; these models represent the various ways children are aware of uses or functions of language; ways, that is, in which they themselves use language to effect change, assert themselves and relate to others, and also ways in which others use language to them. The reader is referred to Halliday (1973) for a fuller account of these uses of language. Here I have selected some salient uses of language in the child's spoken language—uses which are also, in the medium of print, relevant to the child's experience as a reader. Moreover, the functions of language that Halliday describes are not language-specific. Linguistic minority children will therefore be aware of a similar range of functions in their first language and, as a second language is acquired, will become aware that their two languages and/or literacies serve slightly different functions in everyday life.

The earliest functions of language that the child is aware of are the instrumental and regulatory functions. Children see language as instrumental in achieving wants and needs; they also see language as regulatory when it is used to control their own behaviour. Other important models of language are the personal, through which the child expresses a growing personal identity, and the imaginative model, where language is seen not as necessarily about anything but an object of fun and amusement in its own right, as with plays on words and jokes. Another model of language, important in the adult world but less important for the child, is what Halliday calls the representational model, where emphasis is on the exchange of information, where language is primarily telling us something.

One can adapt Halliday's models to give a functional framework to early literacy, taking—as instances of print to introduce to the learner—messages in English and other community languages which show a diversity of functions. Children are surrounded by examples of regulatory language in their everyday lives, such as posters, signs and labels giving instructions. The regulatory function in print is so powerful and prevalent in a child's environment that one might well take this as a starting point from which to introduce other functions of print.

With some slight modification of Halliday's hierarchy of language functions, a simple framework for early functional literacy emerges. If Halliday is right, children will have no difficulty in responding to what these messages mean—far less than with some of the written language met in typical early readers for children. Halliday himself quotes the functionally empty *See Spot Run* kind of style which even quite recently-produced reading schemes occasionally employ, e.g. 'Look we can run. We can run like this' (Ginn Reading 360, Level 2, Book 1, *Ben and Lad*).

Some of the functions of print are reader-centred rather than writer-centred. In reader-centred language the writer is concerned primarily with creating an effect on the reader. In what I have called writer-centred language the writer is concerned to express a personal opinion or point of view. One might introduce reader-centred language first, where the reader merely receives the message, as in the case of regulatory language, moving on to consider kinds of message which learners might also feel motivated to write themselves, such as simple expressions of likes, dislikes or opinions to display on badges or tee-shirts.

We can then take reader-centred and writer-centred messages in turn in order to highlight for early readers some of the key functions of print—adapted as appropriate to either adult or younger learners (Table 4).

TABLE 4

Functions		Examples	Sample context
READER-CENTRED MESSAGES *(learners will not want to write these).*			
Regulatory:			
Language which is telling us what to do	instructions warnings directions prohibitions	DANGER STOP EXIT	STREET
Representational:			
Language which tells us what things are (i.e. identifying)	signs notices labels	TOILETS STAFF ROOM MRS ANDERSON (teacher's room)	SCHOOL
WRITER-CENTRED MESSAGES *(learners may also want to write these).*			
Personal:			
Language which tells us what people think or feel	expressions of likes, dislikes and opinions	NO NUKES WE WANT JOBS JOBS NOT BOMBS COAL NOT DOLE	PUBLIC DEMONSTRATION
Imaginative:			
Funny language, playing with language for its own sake	jokes, puns and rhymes	BEANZ MEANZ HEINZ	TELEVISION ADVERTISING

Choosing a content for literacy

Written texts must not just have a general function—to warn, inform, persuade or entertain; they must be *about* something, they must have a content. This is particularly true of pieces of writing longer than simple signs, directions or notices. It should be possible to identify what the content of a piece of writing is; whether it is telling us how to make a kite, how to complain if we buy faulty goods, telling a story about ghosts or describing a visit to the zoo.

This may seem uncontentious—obvious, even; but it is frequently difficult to say what much of the material given to children, especially in certain reading schemes, is really about. There is no coherent content and no continuity of text. An example may illustrate this point. This is a fairly typical page from a reading scheme:

Can you draw
a coat and hat
for mummy
write
this is a coat and hat
for mummy

(Through the Rainbow Reading Scheme)

Such texts (misguidedly, I believe, involving the early learner reader in reading and writing at the same time) have neither a function nor a content. They are not *doing* anything nor are they *about* anything.

In adult literacy the need to look for a relevant content has predominated. I quote the case cited by Mace (1979).

In 1977, a certain MP complained that the material used to teach adults to read and write at the Friends' Centre, Brighton, was left-wing in bias. Among the offending articles were: a comprehension exercise on an article about Mao Tse Tung's death; extracts from the *Sunday Times* and *Write First Time* (an adult literacy publication) as discussion material on the role of the Health Service; a topic sheet on the 'nuclear gamble' at Windscale. Presumably the MP meant that the content was political, and provocatively so. But what is the content of adult literacy materials to be if it is not to relate to some kind of social and political reality? As Roger, a student at the Centre, said: 'We've got to read something and I'm bloody sure I'm not reading Andy Pandy.'

Literacy is political. It is no accident that literacy schemes have been associated around the world with movements for greater public awareness of political issues. In 1964, Paulo Freire was imprisoned and later exiled because the literacy programme he had established in the north-east of Brazil—described in Freire (1972)—was placed clearly in a political context. Freire felt that introducing people to literacy necessarily involved the discussion of the political, social and economic phenomena which affected their lives.

When the time comes for readers to try their hand at writing, they are likely to want to assert, through their writing, a newly discovered sense of themselves and the world they live in. No doubt this was the incentive of the Bradford man who wrote in *Write First Time* a poem which criticized the economic policies of Prime Minister Margaret Thatcher. The poem began:

Come, Mrs Thatcher,
Let me lead you through this desolate land.

William Shelton, the education minister responsible for adult education, threatened (as reported in the *Sunday Times*, March 1983) withdrawal of government financial support of *Write First Time* if its producers did not in future 'exercise greater editorial control over material'. The threat itself proves how powerful the written or printed word is when a group with relatively little influence in our society, the newly literate, are feared for what they might write about public and powerful figures.

The content of early literacy must come from learners themselves. Once they become aware of the power of print to regulate and guide their lives, they are likely to want to see in print words, phrases and longer texts that represent important things in their experience. Children as well as adults can be guided into literacy in this way. Soderbergh (1981) notes how even very young, deaf children can begin to acquire a sight vocabulary by the simple strategy of pointing to things they are interested in and indicating that they want to see the name of the toy or person written down. For adults, thinking and talking about words which express central preoccupations—even fears—in their lives helps them to clarify their own position on certain issues. We might call these 'high content' words—words which convey a powerful meaning to the individual learner. Using these words in the context of early reading and writing can help to give people some feeling of control over areas of their lives; so even students with rudimentary English language and literacy skills will offer words such as RIOTS and DISCRIMINATION and will identify with simple local newspaper headlines such as 'HOOVER CLOSES: loss of 2000 jobs.' Words like JOBS, RIOTS, UNEMPLOYMENT, IMMIGRATION and RACISM are high in content value for certain groups.

A Case Study of Literacy in Context

Teachers and students at the Friends' Centre in Brighton were recently given the opportunity to see the acquisition of literacy in a wider context; an invitation from The Gambia in West Africa prompted them to consider literacy needs and experiences in a more global way. The Gambia, while it aims eventually to use a native African language for literacy, continues to use English for official purposes. The Gambia Literacy Service asked the Centre if respective literacy teachers and students might exchange information about each other and their lives and the towns in which they lived. This would mean, for the Brighton group, collecting and collating simple information about Brighton and also writing to their Gambian friends something about themselves. They would be writing to people who knew nothing about them, what they looked like, how many children they had, or the events of their day-to-day life. There was a real audience and real information to be communicated. In other words, reading and writing would have a context and a function.

The Gambian invitation also provided the content for the literacy classes over the next few weeks. Literacy tutors selected, adapted and simplified as appropriate, information about The Gambia sent by The Gambian Literacy Scheme and from other sources. Maps were brought out, languages, dress and customs discussed and a small previously unheard-of African country became real for the Brighton students.

In this chapter I have suggested that reading is a natural activity for those who are brought up in literate and literacy-aware families. Not all homes, however, help children to become fully aware of how powerful and pervasive the printed word is in our society. Responsibility to offer a rich literacy environment then falls on the school itself, which needs to provide children with a full array of literacy experiences. This means not merely providing reading kits and reading schemes, but a range of different books, story-telling and the opportunity to talk about reading. Reading does not just happen; neither is it 'taught'. The development of reading needs careful nurturing, and reading behaviour is most likely to flourish in those environments which are rich in literacy-related experiences. We need to consider the whole context in which early reading takes place so that at home, in school or in the literacy class learners can feel part of the reading behaviour around them.

Secondly we need to show learner-readers that print has a wide range of functions; we need to be aware of what it is communicating to us in any particular situation. For written, like spoken, language arises out of a need or a desire to communicate. Reading material should always be presented to learners in a clear context with a clear communicative aim.

Finally, reading material from simple one-word messages to fairly long texts should have a content which is meaningful to the individual learner; and getting meaning from reading involves bringing meaning to reading. In the next two chapters we shall look at what happens when reader meets text. How do readers get meaning from what they read? What kinds of understanding—of the nature of print and the nature of the worlds described in print—does our reader require?

Note

1. The Mother-tongue and English Teaching Project (1978–80) was a 2-year research project monitoring a 1-year Punjabi–English bilingual education programme. The research was conducted by Olav Rees and Barrie Fitzpatrick at Bradford University.

2

The Reading Text

Chapter 1 looked at reading in a social context. We looked at the range of social situations in which reading takes place and at the functions of print in different contexts. We are still left with the question as to what reading is. In this chapter I shall look at reading as the data which the reader works with. What are the distinctive features of structure and meaning in written English texts? And what likely difficulties may they present to E2L learners?

Let us first consider the structure of written language, moving on to focus more closely on features of meaning, at the level of words, sentences and whole texts.

Structure in Texts

Letters and other marks on the page

One view of the nature of print, implicit in many approaches to the teaching of reading, is that letters or combinations of letters—sometimes known as **graphemes** —represent sounds. This view is largely true. The difficulty is that it is also partly false. For instance, the so-called magic E rule, where the final -e lengthens the preceding vowel, is observable in *bone, tone* and *cone*; however, we see that the rule breaks down in the case of the common word *one*.

How are learner-readers to account for exceptions to the rules? They realize early on that attempts at phonic decoding only occasionally lead to a successful understanding of the word. As John Holt (1969) asks, 'Why do we tell children things that about one minute's thought would tell us are not true?' One answer might be that, in the case of the English writing system at least, the truth is too complex. Why should we imagine, however, that children cannot cope with complexity? They do so in many areas of their daily lives, especially if they are bilingual or multilingual. Donaldson (1978) suggests that in learning to read children can be helped by seeing from the beginning that several different kinds of rules are operating. As Donaldson says, 'There is no reason to suppose that children of 5 cannot understand a system that contains options'.

How might we, as teachers, deal with the options? The reason why clear graphophonic rules operate only some of the time is that there are other rules about the English writing system which over-ride the rule concerning letter/sound correspondence. There are clear, though complex, rules about the English writing system which have been fully discussed by Albrow (1972) and Stubbs (1980) but which nonetheless have tended to be neglected in discussions on reading. I shall, therefore, give them some attention here.

While it is true that letters can be sounded out either individually or blended in various ways to produce recognizable English sounds, there is not, as often claimed or implied by teachers of reading, a one-to-one correspondence between letters and sounds. Even Southgate *et al.*, in their generally excellent book *Extending*

Beginning Reading (1981), seem to suggest there is such a correspondence when they say 'approximately 35% of first years and 45% of second years [in the junior schools they surveyed] knew the sounds of all 26 letters of the alphabet'. This statement at least implies that there are 26 sounds to match 26 letters: in fact there are 44 distinctive sounds—or **phonemes**—in English. Individual letters may have a number of different sound realizations or they may not be sounded at all. Learners encouraged to think there is a consistent match between sounds and letters will quickly become frustrated. It is, for instance, not particularly helpful for the reader to consider what 'the sound of -i- is' when one takes contexts such as *height, weight, question* or *iron.*

In fact, it is the letters themselves, rather than the sounds they represent, that give the reader more consistent information in English. Firstly, they provide more reliable information than sounds do about grammatical parts of speech, signalling, for instance, whether a word is a noun or verb, or more particularly a singular or plural noun, or a past or present tense verb. For instance, it is the final letter -s at the end of nouns rather than the sound [s] that signals plurality in English; the words *niece* and *grapes*, which end with the same sound but not the same letters, have nothing in common, whereas *grapes* and *knees*, which end with different sounds but the same letter -s, are both nouns with a plural form.

A helpful thing, then, for the learner-reader to know is not what sound final letter -s on nouns gives, which will in fact depend on the preceding sound and will therefore vary, as in *buses, drinks* and *cars*, but that the final letter -s on nouns consistently signals plurality in English. The presence or absence of -s- therefore marks a crucial grammatical distinction. As long as the reader recognizes that a word is a noun (and an awareness of word classes is important in reading, as I discuss later) he is enabled to generalize that a single final -s signals plurality. (Exceptions are few, e.g. bus, circus, chorus, gas, where the -s always follows a vowel.) The reader can then anticipate a plural form of the following verb, for example:

> The girls . . .   are
> *or* were

While there is not a one-to-one match between the letter -s and the sound [s] there is a clear consistency between final letter -s on nouns and grammatical marking for plurality.

The syllable -ing, as an inflected ending on verbs, tends to be very distinctive for learners. Teachers often note how it will 'leap from the page' so learner-readers may, as my learner Joyce (introduced in Chapter 5) did, on coming across the word *laughing*, read it as *-ing + laugh › laughing*. However, it is not the -ing cluster in itself which is so distinctive but its signalling of a progressive verb form, e.g. 'He is laughing', or a participle, e.g. 'Laughing and cheering, they watched the parade'. The -ing does not have this kind of recognizability where it exists in words like *finger* or *ring*, but only when it tells us something helpful about the grammar of the sentence.

A further example of how the English writing system gives consistent grammatical information is in the case of final -ed on verbs. The important thing to know about the -ed suffix is not how it should be pronounced, which will vary and, indeed, in fast reading out loud may barely be pronounced at all, but its consistent signalling of past time in simple written sentences. Rather than sound a word out, the reader may need merely to **look** at the word. The reader can, by simply looking at the word, identify the verb stem, for example *plant*, and the marking for past tense, -ed (= planted). That it is the letters -ed and not the sound [ɪd] that are important is shown by pairs of words such as plant*ed*/fet*id*, where the ending is identically pronounced. This is not significant, however, as the two words have nothing in common, in terms of either grammar or meaning. Such examples show us that it is not **phonetic** similarities which are important but **visual** ones, as we see in the case of *brushed, painted, joined.*

To show further the importance of visual information alone, (a) and (b) here are identically pronounced:

(a) the girls
(b) the girl's

Phonetic information does not here help the reader to make a crucial distinction between plurality in (a), on the one hand, and the notion of possession in (b), on the other.

Once again, a proper understanding of what the marks on the page signal is needed for the learner-reader to predict what follows. In other words, the presence or absence of the simple mark ' (not representable at all by sound) tells us whether a verb or noun is likely to follow; e.g.

The girls want . . .
The girl's book.

With the example of ' we see that important information is conveyed not only by the letters on the page—regardless of the nature of their representation in sound—but by other sorts of marks. There is no doubt that these present difficulty for the learner-reader. Teachers and writers of reading books for early learner-readers need to be aware of potential confusion. Eight-year-old Mark, coming across a dash, asked (cf. Case Studies 1), 'What's that line mean?' He thought, understandably, that the dash might be giving crucial grammatical information, like a full stop, or that it was some kind of attitudinal marker, like an exclamation mark. As it happens, the dash in this instance was not telling us anything important and could easily have been omitted.

It is also the look rather than the sound of words which helps us to generalize, not just about their **grammar** but about their **meaning**. Lexically related words, that is, words belonging to the same word family or lexical field, tend to be spelt similarly, as with *site, situation* and *sited.* Conversely, homophones, that is identically sounding words, tend to look very different and to be semantically distinctive, as for example *sight/site, right/write/rite/wright* (as in 'wheelwright' or 'playwright'), and *prophet/profit.* The reader will be helped to relate known words to new words in a text by looking for visual similarities, not phonetic ones, e.g. *write–writer–writing* versus *right* and *rightly.* The learner-reader needs, for example, to relate the word *knew* to *know* and *known*, because the initial -k is maintained across all forms of the verb and all other derivations from it, such as *knowledge* and *unknowingly*.

Many second language learners, especially if familiar with a phonetic writing system, get very confused about this feature of English. They tend to associate sound, spelling and meaning. Yasmeen, for instance, on hearing these lines of a story read aloud to her:

'She knew money didn't grow on trees'
'She knew there were Tom and Steve and Sarah'

(Peter Abbs, Linda's Journey)

asked with some consternation 'Is that new N-E-W?' She was aware that *new* as the opposite of *old* makes little sense in this context. At the same time she was misled through her assumption that there is a consistent sound/meaning relationship in English.

There is little doubt that for the learner, in particular the L2 learner, the English writing system presents particular difficulties, as compared with other writing systems. This is because the regularities offered by the English writing system, as Stubbs (1980) points out, tend to help those who are already reading fairly fluently far more than those who are beginning to learn to read. An understanding of many of these regularities is indeed available only to readers of relatively difficult material. Nonetheless, teachers of reading need to be aware of the sorts of regularities displayed by written English to which learner-readers' attention can usefully be drawn during early reading instruction and in general class language work. One implication is that discussion of the structure of words, and work with derivations—building up new words from known ones, might play a more important part in pre-reading and early reading than work with phonics. In Chapter 6 we give closer attention to the implications of this discussion for introducing second language learners to print in English.

Sentence structure

We have seen that learner-readers are helped by an awareness of the internal structure of words and by a knowledge of which features of words carry important grammatical information. But it is not just an awareness of the structure of words which helps the reader of English. Learner-readers need a knowledge of English **syntax**; at the simplest level, for instance, they need to know that English is a subject/verb/object (or SVO) language. Word order is part of English grammar; we cannot readily reverse subject and object, as in some other languages. In the sentence 'The dog bit the man', subject and object are clearly not interchangeable without a radical change of meaning.

The reader in English is also helped by the knowledge that the verb takes agreement with the subject; e.g.:

The girl loves John.
The girls love John.

The native-speaking reader will here anticipate a form of the verb which agrees with either a singular or plural subject. Native speakers have an intuitive under-standing of these and other key features of English syntax. Without this knowledge, or linguistic competence, as it is described by linguists, the reader is unable to make informed predictions about how the text will progress.

The view that reading behaviour, like listening, is largely based on predicting is now a familiar one, following on the work of Smith (1971) and Goodman (1967). We are continually assessing the probability of one chunk of language following another, whether it be at the level of word, sentence or much longer stretches of text. If for instance we take the opening words of this text:

'The girls w . . .', it is more likely that a verb such as *wanted* or *waited* or *wallowed* will follow 'the girls' than a preposition such as *with* or an adjective such as *wild*. This is not to say of course, that any of the latter are impossible, e.g.:

The girls with blonde hair . . .
The girls who saw . . .
The girls wild with desire . . .

These are, however, not the first options that come to mind, as can be quickly shown by simply asking, as I did, a sample group of native speakers to complete the sentence. All twenty native speakers whom I asked continued with a verb of some kind, usually a neutral, rather bland choice, such as *walked, wanted* or *waited*.

Native-speaking readers, as discussed more fully in Chapter 5, proceed on the basis of likelihood, unconsciously rejecting options which go against their knowledge of English sentence structure; and as soon as they are reading with any fluency, learner-readers also predict beyond the sentence. In doing so they are dependent on knowing how sentences may connect. Even very young native-speaking children will recognize the role of items of language such as *and* and *but*, which co-ordinate simple sentences. Some connectors, however, such as *whereas* and *although*, are less familiar to early learner-readers simply because they are more characteristic of written language than of the everyday, spoken language they are familiar with. This brings us to consider how far spoken and written language share the same syntactic features.

Written and spoken language

Though reading, as the sequence of letters and words on the page, and speaking, as the sequence of sounds we make, are both language, writing is not dependent on speaking. Reading is not 'speaking written down'. The medium of print is distinctive from the medium of spoken language. We mislead learner-readers, therefore, if we suggest that what they might expect to read is identically structured to what we say and hear. Speaking, much more than writing, is context-bound, that is, related to the immediate situation. More, therefore, can be taken for granted between speaker and hearer than between writer and reader. Clearly this depends on different kinds of speaker/hearer and reader/writer role relationships, and it is important to stress that 'taken-for-grantedness' is also a part of writer/reader communication, as I discuss in Chapter 3.

Nonetheless, most speaking is very differently structured from most writing, as perhaps this extract from a conversation between myself and Peter, a student of mine, shows:

> P. 'You went to that lady's place . . . that lady or something?'
> C. 'Mrs. MacKay . . . yeah . . . I went'
> P. 'I saw you goin' there . . .'
> I was goin' to go to Kirkcaldy to stay an' my landlady say, if you want, I can get you fixed up at Kirkcaldy an' to get a good job in a hospital there 'cos you like your hospital job, no? I say, Oh no, what about my learnin' and she say, Oh yeah . . . say you can get learnin' there. I say, Oh no I got used to you now.
> C. 'Well, I think actually, well how far away is Kirkcaldy?'
> P. 'Kirkcaldy is about two . . . a mile n'a half, not far from there to Edinburgh at all.'
> C. ''Cos actually you'd probably have to come here if you went to Kirkcaldy.'

Of course, this is an example of very informal conversation; the language of, say, a political speech would be much more formal and much closer in structure to writing. Nevertheless, all spoken language is much more loosely structured than typical writing. Because it is usually less planned, it is full of false starts, for example, 'Well I think actually . . . well how far away . . .', and incomplete or apparently ungrammatical sentences, for example 'You went to that lady's place . . . that lady . . . or something.' Because the surrounding context and certain kinds of background knowledge supply much of the information about who or what is referred to, it is less explicit, e.g., 'I say, Oh no I got used to you (i.e. C) now.' There are also more cases of **ellipsis**, that is cases where certain items of language are omitted—often in response to a question from another speaker, as in 'Mrs. MacKay . . . yeah . . ., I went (i.e., I went to that ladies' place).

In the absence of the kind of contextual information that is available in face-to-face conversation, writing needs to be more fully structured and more explicit. Writers of early reading material sometimes aim to make early reading books more accessible by making them supposedly close to the typical speech of the reader (cf. Chapter 8 for examples of such materials).

There are several related problems in this approach. Firstly, real-life spoken language, written down, is in fact very difficult to read, as we have seen; secondly, one of the most important things for beginner-readers to realize is that written language is different from speech. Goodman and Greene (1977) observe that children tend to learn very early to expect what they find in print to differ from their own language. Smith (1977) mentions this awareness as one of the two fundamental insights which children require before they can learn to read at all.

The second basic insight, claims Smith (1977), is that print is meaningful. As discussed in Chapter 1, the **context** in which reading occurs provides much of the meaning. Many learners can make a fair guess, for instance, that a word pointing to what they know is a car park is likely to say just that. Here we will look at meaning in a slightly different way; we will consider the kinds of meaning we can draw from the text itself.

Meaning in Texts

Experienced readers expect texts not just to be structured in certain ways but, above all, to make sense. It is frequently observed that much as we hear what we expect to hear, we read what we expect to read. Errors of structure in texts, due to typesetting errors, for instance, are frequently overlooked in the reader's pursuit of meaning. Teachers of reading now generally agree that children should 'read for meaning' from the beginning. But what do we mean by 'reading for meaning'? Which parts of the texts provide us with meaning? Does meaning reside in the words on the page, in sentences or in larger chunks of text? In the rest of this chapter I shall consider some of the kinds of meaning we can look for in words, sentences and whole texts.

The meaning of words

One way we might try to predict a learner-reader's success in getting meaning from a particular text is to consider the number of words which are new to him. On the face of it, reading as 'knowing the words' is a commonsense view. Indeed some writers equate so-called 'whole-word' techniques with meaning-emphasis approaches, and most *Look and Say* approaches make a similar assumption. Words are introduced on flash cards prior to reading, on the assumption that the learner then 'knows' the words contained in the reading primers and is therefore equipped to embark on 'reading for meaning'.

However, most teachers are aware that learners may 'know' a word in one context but not in another. Learners may stop dead at a familiar word which, phonically, is readily decodable. Joyce, for instance, had no difficulty with the word *hand* in 'She put her hand on Harry's arm.' She 'knew' the word, one might therefore say; but later in the same text she had difficulty with:

Harry felt for the clock
and looked hard at it.
The hands shone up at him.

(Kathleen Wood, *All the Long Night*)

This kind of phenomenon is familiar to teachers and researchers on reading. Jessie Reid, in her study of 5-year-olds (1966), showed that children had more success with the word *darkness* in context (a) than in (b):

(a) I can see his face in the darkness.
(b) Darkness was upon the face of the deep.

In sentence (a) the word *darkness* is much more clearly cued-in by the context. The figurative language in (b) creates greater difficulty.

Polysemy and homonymy

The term used for cases like *hand* above, where one word carries several different but related meanings, is **polysemy**. **Homonymy** is the term used where we have a single word with several unrelated meanings, e.g. *bank* in (1) 'I went to the bank to get some money', and (2) 'We walked along the bank of the river.' Whether polysemy or homonymy is involved, one frequently observes that it is not the words on the page that cause difficulty for the reader, but an unknown or unanticipated association of the word with a particular **meaning**.

Moreover, the more frequent the occurrence of a word, the greater the variety of meanings it can have. Many of these words—because they have high frequency as **words** and are supposedly easy to read in terms of length and are easily decodable—are commonly selected in children's readers. However, what is often neglected, and is crucial in the case of children as learners, is that children may not associate the word with the appropriate meaning. For example while *mouth* in 'Open your mouth' will present no problems for young readers, 'They arrive at the mouth of the river' may well cause difficulty. Young children know the word but they may not yet have acquired the meaning. This kind of difficulty is highlighted in the case of learner-readers for whom English is a second language and who may not have a great range of meanings at their disposal to assign to the words they come across.

There is, in fact, a case to be made for introducing the less common words in early reading. Simply because they are less common, they carry more distinctive meaning. For a start, they are more likely to have just a single meaning assigned to them and to be more visually distinctive. Teachers frequently comment on the fact that children read words like *aeroplane, buttercup* and *elephant* with greater ease than *animal* or *flower*. This is not really surprising, for apart from its visual distinctiveness the word *elephant* has more **content** (cf. Chapter 1) for most people than the word *animal*; it more readily conjures up a particular scenario (such as jungle, zoo or Africa) than does *animal* or even *dog*. The reader is helped by specific rather than general content. A further point is that the shorter, more common words are also more likely to have **homophones**, that sound the same, e.g.—*pair/pear, whole/hole, flour/flower*—another source of confusion. Difficult words in the sense of long or hard to decode phonically cannot then be necessarily equated with difficult meanings—rather the reverse, in fact.

Content and structure words

The words we have been discussing above are commonly known as **content** words. They denote objects, events or states which we can readily talk about; we can say what they look like, how they feel, what sort of action they describe, and so on. We can say what distinguishing features an elephant has, for example, or even draw a picture of it. There are other sorts of word to which we cannot assign meaning in the same way—words such as *but*, and *the*. We cannot draw a picture of *but* or say what it is like. Peter, the learner quoted on page 22, was an Anglo-Indian and a total beginner to reading at the age of 40. He observed, 'It's the little words I can't get. I can get all the long ones.' The 'little words' were those words like *so* and *and* and *that*, which form the grammatical skeleton of a language and are commonly known as **function** or **structure** words. I shall refer to them as structure words. Peter found the structure words difficult because he continued to see reading as built up of discrete words, each with some kind of describable meaning, and he could not assign a meaning to these 'little words'. While they are the hardest to learn out of context (for example with *Look and Say* flash cards) in context they are usually highly predictable. This is because the range of choices is restricted, as can be observed if they are omitted in a simple text:

'Sita looked . . . . . . window . . . . . . children playing . . . . . . street'.
(Sparks Readers, *The Wishing Bottle*)

There was a further reason why Peter had difficulty with the little words, a difficulty to do with his own use of spoken English. While he was fluent enough in English, he tended to omit many of these structure words, such as *at*, auxiliary *do* and *have*, and the verb *to be* in certain contexts, e.g. 'He say you (are) the best . . . you (are) never off at all.' For learners like Peter, in the very early stages of reading, before they have realized that writing is more fully structured than most speaking, these little words can create a difficulty which other learners are unlikely to have.

There is another potential source of difficulty with the structure words for all learner-readers. If we take a sentence such as:

(a) 'After one year the student knew 5000 words and could read the *Sun*'

the simplest structure word in one sense, is, in another, the most difficult. All learner readers quickly learn to recognize the word *and* and to recognize its role as a conjunction. However, the meaning of *and* here is not the same as in:

(b) I got up and had a bath.

The causal meaning of *and* in sentence (a) is central to the whole sentence meaning. Learner-readers need to see that linking words, such as *and* and *but*, may have meanings over and above their role as sentence coordinators, and that some words familiar as words may encode concepts more commonly expressed by other structure words. For example Hiroko, an 8-year-old Japanese girl, had difficulty with the following lines, in her reading book:

She could not climb the ladder
For her legs were too small.

Hiroko could read this but she failed to answer my question 'Why could she not climb the ladder?' The difficulty was the apparently 'simple' word *for*. It is rarely used in spoken English to signal cause and effect. *Because* would have offered no such difficulty; it is a far more likely choice of conjunction and it also introduces the answers to 'why' questions:

Q. 'Why could she not . . .
A. 'Because her legs were too small'
 not
A. 'For her legs were too small'

Reading for meaning, then, involves an awareness of how structure words such as *so, for* and *though* typically express concepts such as consequence, cause and effect, concession, and so on. While we are familiar with the difficulties of multiple meaning in the case of the content words, less attention has been paid to the range of meanings which structure words may take on, and how these meanings are assignable only in context.

Following the discussion in McNally and Murray (1962) on key words, most of which, as among the most commonly used words of the language, are structure words, Southgate *et al.* (1981) advise: 'Teachers should check which of the [200 key] words each child does and does not recognize.' However, recognizing or not recognizing words is not the best way to describe what is going on when learners read or fail to read the structure words. Peter had no difficulty with sentence (a) below, but did not 'recognize' the same word *that* in (b):

    (a) Give me that book.
    (b) You can see that he is in danger.

                                                         (Ladybird, *Danger Men*)

John, a 5-year-old, failed to read *one* in this context, though the same word raised no difficulty elsewhere in the text:

    (c) Here is an apple for you
          And one for Daddy

                                    (Ladybird, *Little Red Riding Hood*)

The reason that structure words may be read without difficulty in one context but fail even to be attempted in another is not only that the same words may express different concepts, but they may encode varying grammatical functions: *that* in sentence (a) is a demonstrative adjective, of high frequency in both speaking and writing; but as a conjunction in (b), *that* has relatively low frequency.

One, in sentence (c), refers back to something already mentioned in the text. Words which refer backwards or forwards in the text to other words or parts of the text (sometimes called **reference items**) cause particular difficulty for learner-readers. Another example from Peter's reading of *Danger Men* may make the point:

    (1) In one film a man jumps from a horse.
    (2) In another film one falls from a car.
    (3) In another, one falls from the top of a mountain.

                                                        (Ladybird, *Danger Men*)

Peter read *in one film* in line (1) with little difficulty. In the following lines, however, *one* refers back not to *film* but to *man*. It is hardly surprising that by line (3) Peter, now quite confused, reads *one film* for *one falls*; and complexity is compounded even further by the word *another*, which refers back to *film*.

Reference items such as *one* and *another*, which refer to other parts of the text, and those structure words which occur rarely in spoken English but are frequent in writing, should be introduced cautiously. Writers of children's books need also to respect the order in which children acquire the more difficult connecting words, such as *unless* and *however*, sometimes known as **logical connectors**. Many native-speaking children do not understand the concepts expressed by these words before the age of 7 or 8. It has, for instance, been observed (Clark and Clark, 1977) that words with a negative factor are acquired later than their positive counterparts.

This means, for instance, that *if* sentences are conceptually simpler than *unless* ones. The difficulty of items such as *unless* is likely to be even greater for second language learners without full competence in English than for young native-speakers.

What is a word?

We have continued to use the term **word**, but readers, including learner-readers, process chunks of language rather than words. These chunks or **items** of language, as they are sometimes known, may not coincide with words in the sense of the marks on the page surrounded by space on either side. For example, in *on top of*, it is the meaning of the three words taken together which is important; they form a single item, so that we have several words for a single meaning. This may be the case with content words, too, as for example in 'The book *belongs to* me'. Here the word *to* necessarily is part of *belongs*. We cannot omit it. The more items of this kind in early reading the better, as long as they share a high frequency in typical spoken and written contexts. Learners can then see more of the text as whole meanings and process more of the text at a time.

Collocations—putting words together

In deciding how to select a vocabulary for early reading material, word counts are often mentioned. It may, however, be more to the point to consider not word frequency as such but the frequency with which certain words are associated with others in texts, how words **collocate**. The more early reading consists of collocations familiar to the learner, e.g. *brothers and sisters, fish and chips*, the easier it is to take in more of the text at a time. Which items collocate is largely culturally determined; items that may be readily associated by one cultural group may not be so associated by another, and we need to take account of possible culture bias of this kind in texts selected for second language learners.

Do we need all the words?

I have discussed what words are and which kinds of words or items matter most; but is reading to do with reading words anyway—in the sense of processing the meaning of strings of word sequences?

We do not, in fact, read words. We do not first assign a meaning to all the words in a text and then arrive at a global meaning, which is the sum of the parts, though learner-readers often assume that this is what happens. Experienced readers are aware of what are the important words or items, which carry the action forward in a narrative or which express the main or key ideas in a discussion. They are aware that we do not need all the words. If challenged to do so, most of us could not offer a clear, dictionary definition for each content word in any text. In the text extracted below few people will know the meaning of the word *odalisque*. They will probably, however, deduce that it is something exotic or daring—a drawing or picture—which can be pinned up on a wall. In this instance, such a general or class meaning is sufficient for overall understanding of the text:

. . . Paint what wall remains red or orange and pin up pictures of nudes or even odalisques'
(Susan Mayfield, *One Room Living*)

Sentence meaning

If we can agree that reading for meaning is not reading words in the sense of putting supposedly known words together to arrive at meaning, is it **sentence** meaning that we should be talking about? Goodman and Green (1977) introduce the learner Tim, who reads the sentence, 'I looked him over and found he was ripped down both sides and one ear was chewed almost off' as 'I looked all over him and found a rip . . . and one ear chewed almost off.' *Was* in *was chewed* is optional; *rip* as a noun can sensibly replace the verb here. Tim, as a native speaker of English, knows this. He is 'unpacking the structure', as Goodman and Green describe it, in an alternative way. He is aware of what items of structure may be omitted and where nouns may replace verbs. Florence, aged 5, reading a Dr. Seuss book, similarly restructures the text, e.g.:

Text: Will is
            up the hill still.
Florence: Will is still up the hill.

and

Text: My brothers read a little bit.
Florence: My brothers can read a little bit.

(Dr. Seuss Books, *Hop on Pop*)

The restructured versions of the text produced by Tim and Florence retain the meaning of the original. This kind of restructuring is what skilled adult readers tend to do on the rare occasions they are required to read out loud. They see the underlying meaning of a sentence, or indeed strings of sentences, and are likely to produce some restructuring in an oral rendering with no significant loss of meaning. The kind of restructuring that Tim and Florence show in their reading reveals an understanding of the underlying meaning. Where learners simply give the surface structure, that is, the actual words on the page, this evidence is not available to us.

Text meaning

Perhaps we should look beyond word or sentence level at the meaning of **texts**? (I am using this term to apply to anything from a one word message, such as DANGER, to a whole book. What both *Danger!* and the lengthy novel *War and Peace* have in common is that they are complete texts. We can give them a label which suggests this, such as 'notice' or 'novel'.) We need to consider not just what words or sentences mean, but what whole texts mean.

As we progress through a text, we build up meanings. For this reason reading actually gets easier towards the end of any extended text; the options as to what might happen next or what views the writer will express are reduced as we progress. Any one sentence needs to be interpreted in the light of the previous sentence or sentences, at the same time as it anticipates what is to come next in the text. Indeed, we cannot easily pluck sentences out of a text. They can only be interpreted in their context. Random examples from two very different texts may make the point:

(1) My advice briefly was to find new friends

(Colin Spencer, *The Guardian*, 14 October 1983)

and

(2) He'd point out to all those who came to watch that he was smaller than Namjit but he wasn't afraid of him.

(Farukh Dhondy, *East End at Your Feet*)

In (1) it is understood from the rest of the text to whom the advice was given and about what; in (2) the reader is assumed to know who would point out and what it was they came to watch. We need to refer forwards or backwards in the text to complete the sense. It is for this reason that beginner-readers, still reading at word and sentence level, have greater difficulty than more advanced readers, who are able to process more of the text at a time.

We see, then, that we are not simply predicting as we read. That would indicate a wholly linear procedure. Certain items in the text direct our attention backwards or forwards in the text; examples are the references items such as *one* (cf. page 26) and *this* and *he*, as in 'He'd point out . . .'. In fact we frequently do a 'double take', going back to check our interpretation of something read earlier, when we find it does not fit. We may have misread either the structure or the content. We are continually searching a text, moving both forwards and backwards. To arrive at an understanding of a whole text we do not merely add the bits and pieces together in linear fashion; we need to make connections across the text, linking up the relevant ones.

Genre

One way of considering what whole texts mean is to consider the genre they belong to. Experienced readers are aware that there are different types of written texts, or **genres**. Genres are often taken to refer to literary writing, but one might extend the concept to include recipe, menu or newspaper editorial. A particular genre has both a distinctive content and a characteristic structure. As soon as we embark on the reading of any extended text, we need to be aware not just of the general content but of how it is organized, if we are to be able, for instance, to find our way through the *Yellow Pages* or a daily newspaper. We have expectations about both the structure and the content of texts. These expectations allow us to anticipate how texts may develop. So we predict what comes next in reading, not just on the basis of what we know of the grammar of English and of how meanings collocate, but on the basis of our familiarity with the genre.

There are different kinds of textual organization within genres; for instance, menus may list dishes in order of eating or classify them under vegetables, soups, salads and so on. There may or may not be a separate wine list. Knowing about the range of possibilities relates to everyday, real-life experiences. If you go to expensive restaurants, for instance, you will have different kinds of 'menu expectations' than if you eat at the café down the road.

For E2L learners certain genres, for instance certain kinds of story, are likely to be more accessible than others. There are a whole range of different story genres: fable, fairy story, detective, horror, thriller, ghost story, and so on. We have expectations about how the content of such stories will develop, to do with typical characters, their roles and likely outcomes. There seems to be a consensus both within and across cultures about the conventional roles of characters in stories, particularly in fairy stories and folk tales. Applebee (1977) notes that characters restricted to fantasy help children to build up clear expectations of the outcome of stories. Children are very clear about the role of witches and fairies, for instance; giants and dwarfs may, understandably, create greater difficulties. Adults, too, from widely differing class and cultural backgrounds show a clear agreement about roles, plot and outcomes in stories and fables. I gave the title of the story *The Tiger and the Woodpecker*, (retold by Anna Ajitsaria in a series of bilingual reading books, 1984) to a group of young Indian students recently arrived in Britain and a group of very sophisticated Soviet teachers respectively. I asked them to predict the story. In each case the consensus was clear. Though slightly differently expressed by the two groups, it was 'The weaker but the cleverer wins.' Character, roles, the involvement of some kind of conflict, and the outcome were all readily predicted from knowledge of the genre.

It would seem, too, that folk stories have some universal features, not just of content but of structure. At least so Mandler *et al.* (1980) suggest when they say 'similar types of organization are found in folk tales from around the world'. Arising as they do from an oral tradition, it may be that the structure of folk tales is a cultural universal, reflecting the way all of us best remember stories. Certainly in the Mandler study, which looked at how stories were recalled by groups of Liberians—both children and adults, literates and illiterates—it was found that non-schooled children and adults from a generally non-literate society such as Liberia recalled stories in a fashion very similar to schooled children and adults from a literate industrial society (the United States). Certain stories, it seems, are recalled by people of different ages and different backgrounds in highly similar ways.

The implications of such findings are that the classic folk tales offer the most predictable genre for linguistic and cultural minority readers, whether children or adults, in moving into L2 literacy; and because they are originally based on an oral tradition, children and adults who are illiterate in their first language, but come from an oral culture, are also likely to recognize the genre. From hearing similar stories read aloud they will, for example, anticipate a typical repetition of similar events, often three or four times. So the Little Red Hen is four times rejected by her three friends when she asks for help, and in a Punjabi folk tale, *The Two Sisters*, each sister has to face four challenges or tests of her goodness. While more sophisticated stories adopt conventions such as the flashback or story within a story format, another advantage of folk tales for early readers is that they have a clear linear structure, describing a sequence of events, which are highly predictable in their ordering and content.

In this chapter I have considered reading 'on the page', moving from a description of the smallest items of written language to whole texts. I have looked at how written language is structured in certain ways, but more particularly at meaning—the meaning of words, sentences and whole texts. However, to look at reading merely from the standpoint of what is on the page is to consider only part of the whole. We need to consider how meaning is created, not just by writers in the first place but by readers in the process of reading. In the next chapter we shall look at the reading process from the point of view of both readers and writers.

3

Readers, Writers and the Reading Event

In the previous chapter we looked at some characteristics of form and meaning in written texts. We began to see that simply knowing the structures and vocabulary contained in the text was not enough. There were different kinds of knowledge, to be drawn from sources other than the text itself, which readers might make use of. Knowing about genres, for instance, is as much to do with real-life experiences of story-telling, cooking or restaurant visiting as with knowledge of the particular linguistic features of written English. In this chapter I shall consider more closely this other kind of knowledge, which readers bring with them to any particular reading experience. We might call this 'knowledge of the world'.

As well as world knowledge of various kinds, readers bring a whole range of experiences and attitudes to any real-life reading situation. Most importantly, they bring a purpose which determines how carefully, reflectively or sketchily they read. It is what readers bring with them to reading that enables them to make use of certain resources and strategies while reading.

A difficulty may arise where there is a mismatch between the sorts of knowledge, expectations and purpose which the *reader* brings to the text and the kind of knowledge, expectations and purpose assumed by the *writer*. This is likely to be the case where reader and writer come together from different cultural or sub-cultural groups. In this chapter I shall take the perspective of reader and writer in turn, concluding with a discussion of the kinds of interplay of knowledge involved in interpreting a particular written text on a particular occasion.

Constructing a Meaning

Meaning does not reside solely in words, sentences or even longer texts. Readers bring meaning with them to texts. As Carrell (1983) says, 'The text itself does not carry meaning. A text only provides guidance for listeners and readers as to how they should construct the intended meaning from their own previously acquired knowledge.' In the absence of the relevant background knowledge we may fail to construct any meaning at all. An example of a simple text may illustrate this point:

> The Great Britain pack has performed without distinction in the two tests so far. Their lack of pace has been starkly exposed by the mobility and speed of such players as Broadhurst, a magnificent open-side prop.

Though most of us could give a dictionary definition of each of the words here and find no difficulty with the sentence structure, many of us, coming cold to this short text, cannot make sense of it. We can understand it on one level but we cannot interpret it, for a very simple reason: we do not know what it is about. Surely, it will be argued, we read in order to find out what something is about? In fact, we are rarely—in real life at least, as opposed to some educational contexts—in the situation of not having some idea what a particular written text is about: first we have chosen the book or newspaper it comes from—we know the **source** of the text; secondly we know what **genre** it is—folk story, article, advertisement or report; and finally we know what the subject matter or **topic** is. Indeed, it is usually because we are interested in the subject-matter that we have chosen to read the text. Here, as soon as we say 'sports page' or 'rugby', meanings are related across the text. We need, in other words, certain kinds of prior knowledge in order for the text to make sense—knowledge about the topic, source and text type. What we get out of a text depends partly on what we bring to it.

There is a real difficulty for some adult illiterates because they simply do not have enough knowledge of the world to bring to certain kinds of text. There is a mismatch between the reader's current knowledge and that assumed by the writer. Writers of newspapers understandably assume that no elaboration is needed to identify President Reagan, for instance. They do not expect to have to identify him as 'The President of the United States'. Hillyard, an adult student from Dominica (cf. Chapter 5), was an almost total non-reader at the start of reading instruction and, though quick and intelligent, he was not able to fill in from his background knowledge in the way that writers take for granted. Many of the references in the popular daily newspapers we looked at eluded him. The television, which was always switched on, did not seem to offer Hillyard the same opportunity to reflect on a particular topic or issue. The reason, I believe, is that television, unlike print, is not a participatory medium. Hillyard's situation is similar to that of many cultural minorities whose illiteracy in English has continued to exclude them from mainstream discussion of the political and social issues of the day. It is a *Catch 22* situation; because they are illiterate, they have been denied access to certain kinds of knowledge of the world. Because they lack this knowledge, largely taken for granted by writers of even simple adult material, they may remain illiterate.

Linguistic and cultural minority groups often have a further difficulty in drawing on their stock of knowledge as they try to make sense of the content of texts in the second language. This is a difficulty stemming from the kinds of cultural assumptions made by writers who assume that readers share with them a knowledge about certain norms of behaviour and attitudes which tend to be so much a part of everyday life that they are largely taken for granted. Indigenous readers not only have a linguistic competence to predict the linguistic features of texts; they also bring to reading what we might call a **cultural competence**. Our cultural competence is a very complex package of beliefs, knowledge, feelings, attitudes and behaviour, as Skutnabb-Kangas and Phillipson (1983) have pointed out. In terms of reading, the term might be used to refer to the ability to recognize, interpret and predict certain kinds of phenomena or behaviour described in texts.

There may be a mismatch between the reader's actual and supposed cultural competence on a number of levels. Firstly, L2 readers may not know about certain kinds of culture-specific behaviour. This was the case with the following part of a story written for teenagers with some reading difficulty. In the story, Linda is determined to go on holiday, but Dad refuses to give her any money:

'In that case,' said Linda, 'I'll hitchhike.'
'Hitchhike?' said her Mum.
'You're not hitchhiking', said her Dad.

(Peter Abbs, *Linda's Journey*)

Hitchhiking is what we might call a culture-specific phenomenon. In reading the story to my class of teenage Asian learners, a lengthy explanation was required. Knowing about hitchhiking is a culture-specific piece of knowledge.

Often prior knowledge is assumed not of phenomena, such as hitchhiking, squatting or flat-sharing but of particular persons, events or institutions which writers assume are part of their readers' general stock of knowledge, almost by virtue of "being British". This is the case with the references made in this adventure story for older remedial readers:

> Gran can remember the war (*What war?—The Falklands? The invasion of Grenada?*) and the power cuts (*taken for granted feature of 'the war'*) so she makes sure that Hitler (*Who?*) will never put her in the dark again.
>
> (Ann Oates, *The Running Man*, Part 2)

Eleven-year-old Sarla (cf. Case Studies 6) cannot draw on enough prior knowledge to get her through this part of the text. Indeed, the indigenous children of Sarla's age—11–12—were not very clear either about these references. They simply had a general idea that Hitler was someone bad—and foreign!

In other kinds of text, particularly newspapers, references may be made to ephemeral phenomena. Writers, especially in the popular press, make reference, often elliptically, to what they assume is known at the time of writing by the broad readership. Often this is not 'news' in the normally understood sense. An example might be: ELSIE QUITS THE STREET (*Sun*, September 1983). This is not, as the naive or uninitiated reader might suppose, a politically famous street such as Downing Street but *Coronation Street*, a TV soap opera popular with white working-class people in particular. E2L readers may understand well enough what is said, but not what is referred to. They may be unable to arrive at an appropriate interpretation.

Understanding not What, but Why. The Pragmatics of Texts

A rather different kind of potential difficulty arises in considering not **what** is said, but **why**. Why do writers follow one statement with another which is (apparently) quite unconnected? Why do they describe people doing or saying certain things in response to other things which, on the face of it, bear no relation to what has gone before? In reading texts, as in real life, we expect people's responses or reactions to be relevant to what has gone before, that is, appropriate to the situation. If we look at the following extract taken from the first page of a novel whose setting is Asian communities in the West Indies, we can see that the basic situation is familiar, indeed universal—childbirth. Bipti has gone back to the home of her mother Bissoondaye for the birth of her child:

> 'What is it?' the old man asked, 'Boy or girl?' 'Boy, boy,' the midwife cried. But what sort of boy? six-fingered and born the wrong way.
>
> The old man groaned and Bissoondaye said, 'I knew it. There is no luck for me'.
>
> At once, though it was night and the way was lonely, she left the hut and walked to the next village, where there was a hedge of cactus. She brought back leaves of cactus, cut them into strips . . .
>
> (V. S. Naipaul, *A House for Mr Biswas*)

A Western reader is likely to understand what is said—there are no obscure references—but probably not why the second part of this text follows the first—why, that is, that Bissoondaye suddenly decides to go off to the next village to fetch some cactus leaves. What has that got to do with the birth of the baby? Is it anything to do with the baby's deformity? We need to turn the page to find out that it is apparently something to do with warding off evil spirits. (Even then my own assumption was not quite right: according to my class of Indian students, leaves are always put round the door to announce the birth of a child—in Indian villages, at least.)

To make sense of texts we need to bring to reading a knowledge not just of what things are but of why people behave in certain ways or respond in certain ways to the behaviour of others. More particularly, we need to be able to interpret how language is used in everyday situations. As Griffin (1977) puts it, 'A knowledge of facts about language use in the real world is needed for good reading.' This sort of knowledge of verbal and non-verbal behaviour has been called a knowledge of pragmatics or facts about real life. Many of these so-called facts about everyday life are once again culture-specific. They are to do with social norms—what roles people may assume in certain situations, what they may say in such roles and what interpretation is made of what is said. Access to this last kind of culturally determined meaning is perhaps the most difficult for a learner from another culture. What is thought worthy of comment or elaboration by a writer is related to these norms. Likewise the reason why certain answers follow certain questions, or why questions are asked at all, for example:

'Please,' said Ginger, 'Have you a light'
'Pardon' said the man.
'A light' she said.
The man looked at her.
'How old are you', he said.

(Peter Abbs, *Ginger and Sharon*)

In what way is the man's question a relevant or appropriate response to Ginger's request for a light? Why does the man have the right to ask what in other circumstances might be an impertinent question? We need to know what the conventional views about smoking are, which, like other behaviour and views about behaviour, are culture-dependent.

In connection with culture-specific behaviour, I recall this conversation between myself, Yasmeen and Rama. I am commenting on a drawing they have done of a bride, who is crying. This is so far from the conventionalized image of a bride in most Western cultures that I express surprise:

C. But I don't understand why. When you get married you should be happy, shouldn't you?
Y. Not Indian woman—Indian/Pakistani woman.
C. Why?
Y. Because brother, sister, mother, father leaving.
C. They must leave their brother and sister . . .?
Y. Brother, sister, house, mother, father. She's going new house, new mother, father, mother-in-law.
R. All people cry.
C. (to Rama) So when you got married your brother cried?

R. Mother, father, sister—everyone.
C. You cried?
R. Yes.
C. Did your husband cry?
R. No, he happy!

This discussion would seem to confirm the point made in a paper by Steffenson, Joag-Dev and Anderson (1979) that in Indian marriages the groom's family is dominant, and that a marriage is 'traumatic for the bride's family, unlike the American (or British) case, where the occasion is generally a happy one'. In fact, Indian friends and students have told me that the tears are partly a convention. Brides have to be seen to cry!

The fact that different cultural groups have different expectations about both behaviour and events in such situations has implications when it comes to reading. In the study by Steffenson *et al.* (1979) two groups of adult students, white Americans and Indians, were asked to read and recall two letters describing respectively a typical American and a typical Indian wedding. Interesting cross-cultural differences emerged regarding what kind of information was recalled and how the information was interpreted. For example, this was one section of the American passage:

Did you know that Pam was going to wear her grandmother's wedding dress? That gave her something that was old, and borrowed, too. It was made of lace over satin, with very large puff sleeves and looked absolutely charming on her. The front was decorated with seed pearls.

One Indian student had this to say about the American bride's dress:

'She was looking all right except the dress was too old and out of fashion'!

In interpreting what people do or say in texts we need to see their behaviour in the context of what is considered commonplace or unremarkable. We need to know not just what counts as conventional or acceptable behaviour, but what are conventional attitudes to behaviour. The main news story in the *Sun* (14 January 1984) was about *Sun* Page Three girl Pamela, it read:

Sun Page Three girl Pamela agreed to strip for the video film. 'I wouldn't have done it for anyone except Lord Lichfield. After all, he is a member of the Royal Family.'

To make any sense of this short text the reader needs to draw on several of the kinds of culture-specific knowledge I have so far described; he needs for instance to understand

(1) the reference to a cultural phenomenon, *Sun* Page Three girl;
(2) conventional attitudes to stripping in particular circumstances;
(3) conventional attitudes to the Royal Family.

Scripts

In understanding what is going on in a text, as well as having expectations about behaviour and attitudes to behaviour, we need also to know about everyday experiences in the culture shared by writer and reader. These are experiences which are so routine that in recounting them in speaking or writing we allow our reader or listener to fill in most of the detail. These experiences have been called **scripts** by Schank and Abelson (1977). We have, for instance, a script for visiting restaurants, going round the supermarket and getting on a bus. These scripts, or chains of events, are so familiar to the general reader that it would be tedious for writers to recount every stage of the procedure. Scripts are culturally determined: there are different scripts—in different cultural or sub-cultural groups—for having a party, for weddings, even for having a meal. Here is a text which makes reference to a script for Sunday dinner. It is taken from a British daily newspaper, the *Guardian*. The 'roast' will require no further elaboration for the indigenous British reader—though it may mystify certain L2 readers:

> A little while ago I received a letter from a reader saying that she went to stay with different friends at week-ends, and at Sunday dinner, after the roast was placed on the table . . .
> (Colin Spencer, *Guardian*, 14 October 1983)

So far, so good—but then there is a surprising departure from the script:

> . . . they asked her if she would like a boiled egg.

Nothing in the text so far helps us to fit the 'boiled egg' into the Sunday dinner script. The difficulty for the general *Guardian* reader is that the writer is assuming a shared sub-culture with his reader—he is writing as a vegetarian for other vegetarians. Once we realize this, the script begins to make sense.

As well as **scripted situations**, there are what Schank and Abelson have called **instrumental** scripts (showing how to do things such as make a kite or make tea,) and **role** scripts (for example, what is involved in being a son, such as running errands for Mum). Once again, these scripts are culturally determined.

There are scripts, too, for sub-cultural activities—what we might call 'deviant scripts', such as for shoplifting or pick-pocketing. It seems clear enough to most of us what is happening in this text, where I have highlighted the key parts of the script:

> I want that record . . . I'm going to take it . . .
> Come on . . . you get the record . . .
> I'll talk to the man at the counter
> Then you put it under your coat and walk out.
>
> (Peter Abbs, *Ginger and Sharon*)

Ravinder, from India, who had at the time been in Britain for about 2 years, simply failed to realize what was going on, although in a general way his knowledge of English was up to the linguistic demands of the text. The difficulty was that he had not anticipated Ginger's and Sharon's behaviour here. This was, I suggest, for two reasons:

(1) It was very alien to him; he would have no script for this behaviour.
(2) Ravinder was unfamiliar with the genre of delinquent teenager stories: he

had not fully understood the role of Ginger, established early in the story as a bad lot and likely therefore to behave in certain ways.

In short, a knowledge of scripts enables us firstly to predict what is coming next in written narratives. For example, if we agree that there is a script for 'visiting someone in hospital', then most indigenous children reading this simple text from a children's reader will anticipate correctly here:

> Sally's daddy said: we are going to see Auntie Pat in hospital. Sally and her daddy went to a shop to get some . . .
>
> (Link Up, *Auntie Pat in Hospital*)

The item in the text, *flowers*, is not so readily predictable by Asian children, for instance, because flower buying is not part of their script for 'visiting people in hospital'.

Secondly, if we are familiar with the script we are able to fill in what is missing: the major part of a script will not usually feature in a text, simply because it is familiar to the reader who will be expected to 'read in' that knowledge.

Thirdly, if readers do not know the basic script they cannot appreciate departures from the script. And as Schank and Abelson (1977) point out, these are what give us the story, which they define as 'a script with one or more interesting deviations'. We need to know what is ordinary and taken for granted in order to appreciate what is highlighted as exceptional. In the novel from which this short extract is taken, Brenda and Freda are two hard-up working-class women:

> 'You shouldn't have spent your money on that', said Brenda desperately, glancing at the table laid for two with the bunch of dried leaves removed from the mantelpiece and set in the middle of the cloth.
>
> There were wine glasses too and a bowl of real butter, and stuffed olives on a saucer. God knows where they had come from, but two napkins, starched and folded, lay beside the blue-rimmed plates.
>
> (Beryl Bainbridge, *The Bottle Factory Outing*)

Native-speakers who know about the 'table setting' script for British working-class families will note the deviations from the script, among which would be wine glasses, real butter, olives and most importantly real (starched)—not paper—napkins. These are the bits which tell us the story. This is not going to be an everyday meal.

It is not being suggested that a text lends itself only to a single interpretation. Differences of individual experiences and general world view will mean that any interpretation of a text is personal to some degree. However, experienced native-speaking readers are likely to have greater resources to draw on, from their background knowledge of the world as well as a full knowledge of the English language, in order to arrive at a credible interpretation of a text.

It is not being suggested, either, that being a good reader in a second language involves being culturally assimilated. It is not that one has to share the life-style and ideology of the writer and the majority readership; one has to *know* about them. As it happens, I do not share *Sun* Page Three Pamela's views about the Royal Family. Knowing about them, however, is part of my cultural competence.

The Role of the Writer

I have so far taken the reader's perspective in looking at the reading process. We might shift at this point to consider the writer, and ask whether writers might not resolve difficulties of interpretation simply by being clearer. The difficulty, of course, is that what to one reader is greater clarity, to another involves stating the obvious. The linguist Grice (1975) observes that there is one rule of conversation, which he names the 'quantity' rule, by which we do not say more than is necessary. The same applies in writing; the writer does not say more than is necessary. She expects the reader to fill in, drawing on the various kinds of knowledge of the world described in the previous section of this chapter. Day-to-day interaction in both the spoken and written medium would be impossibly burdensome if we did not, by and large, avoid stating the obvious.

It is writers' judgements of the reader's knowledge which determine how explicit they are. Some kinds of knowledge must be taken for granted, otherwise texts would be full of what would be, for most readers, redundant information. Imagine the following introduction to the story of *Toussaint l'Ouverture*:

Toussaint was born in the island of Haiti. An island is a piece of land surrounded by water . . .

This is an unlikely opening to the story simply because most writers would take it for granted that the general reader knows what an island is. The statement 'An island is a piece of land surrounded by water' is therefore over-informative. The writer is more likely to fill in information about Haiti, and indeed this is what she opted to do:

Toussaint was born in the island of Haiti in the West Indies in 1743.
(J. D. Bentley, *Toussaint l'Ouverture of the West Indies*)

Writers are continually anticipating how much knowledge can be assumed on the part of the reader, and what needs elaborating.

The reader/writer relationship through print has been characterized as a dialogue (cf. Widdowson, 1979) much like the speaker/listener one, though clearly not aided by the possibility of the receiver checking back with a 'What exactly do you mean by . . .'. In the absence of this verbal come-back, writers are continually filling in the reader's response, that is 'anticipating what lack of clarity might arise from lack of shared knowledge' (Widdowson, 1979) or anticipating agreement or objection. The writer of text (a), as the reader will know, having seen the book from which it comes, is a sociolinguist. The reader might therefore register some surprise, even objection at the point where the writer states, apparently somewhat ethnocentrically, that 'Britain is monolingual'.

(a) There is certainly no real need for anyone visiting or living in this country to know any language other than English. For many purposes, Britain is monolingual.
(Peter Trudgill, *Accent, Dialect and the School*)

At this point a likely reader reaction would be something like:

But I thought contemporary Britain was multilingual!

Perhaps anticipating some such response, the writer continues:

> However this does not in fact mean that this country is a linguistically homogeneous or uniform place.

The writer is here conducting a dialogue with his reader; he offers a controversial opinion in order to go on to qualify it. The implications for this kind of interaction between reader and writer in a teaching context are discussed in Chapter 7.

However, writers do not merely anticipate the nature of the reader's response, whether it be objection, request for clarification or concurrence; they give their readers an identity. They make assumptions about the kind of reader they are addressing. It was mentioned in Chapter 1 how writers, publishers and newspaper editors classify readers—often quite explicitly—in terms of class, occupation and sex. Writers also make judgements, far less consciously, about the readers they are addressing. For example, most professionals write as members of a dominant social group; this means they are likely to be middle-class, male and white; and on the whole they assume a reader who comes from the same social groups, as revealed perhaps by this extract:

> There is a time and a place for 'talking shop' and wives tend to object when husbands do it at a dinner party.
>
> (Criper and Widdowson, *Sociolinguistics and Language Teaching*)

In most writing, even where it is ostensibly directed to the general public, women are likely to be talked about rather than talked to; and much the same is the case with linguistic and ethnic minority groups, who also tend to be marginal to the interaction between reader and writer.

For linguistic minorities a clear exception would be in those cases where writers are quite explicitly addressing second language learners in texts which have the expressed aim of helping them to improve their English. Such texts, however, written primarily to exemplify areas of English grammar and vocabulary, may distort the usual reader/writer dialogue. For writers are then focusing on the language system itself rather than communicating through the language; and in the real world—or worlds—beyond the didactic setting of the classroom, writing has an identifiable function, whether it be to amuse, inform or persuade. On the reader's part, in turn, there is a reason for reading—to share feelings or experiences, learn facts, be helped to reach a particular decision, and so on. Any reading experience makes little sense in the absence of any of these factors. Moreover, the surrounding circumstances of what we might call a 'reading event', such as place, time of day—even time of year—as well as the kinds of knowledge assumed as shared between reader and writer, all help to place reading in a context. Let us conclude this chapter, therefore, by considering some of these contextual constraints in the case of a particular, real-life reading event.

A Particular Reading Event

I have so far omitted to mention one of the most important things that experienced readers know about reading, namely, that a failure to understand need not matter.

Once again, an example of a real text—this time a complete fully contextualized one—may make the point.

DAN-AIR

This is not the luggage ticket (baggage check) described in Article 4 of the Warsaw Convention or the Warsaw Convention as amended by the Hague Protocol, 1955. Baggage checked subject to tariffs, including limitations of liability, therein contained. Carrier will not be liable for baggage not claimed immediately upon arrival.

DA 9 9 5 5 4 7   **LONDON/GATWICK**

This text, handed out to Dan-Air passengers at Majorca Airport in January 1984, was—and still is—to me quite uninterpretable. I understand all the words but not the message. More to the point is the fact that it did not matter. It did not matter because I did not feel that failure to understand was likely to affect my interests or well-being in any way. In real-life reading situations there must be a purpose in reading the text at hand: we need to feel that the advantages to be gained outweigh the interpretive effort. In short, we need to be motivated.

The degree and kind of motivation will also determine **how** we read a particular text. We can choose the extent to which we wish to engage with the text; we read different things in different ways for different reasons. We may skim a newspaper, book or magazine, making a very rapid overview of the contents before deciding whether to commit ourselves to a more careful reading. When we want to find the answers to particular questions, such as the time of the next train, we will scan the text until we locate the part relevant to our needs and interests and then read that with some care.

By way of summing up, therefore, we shall consider what motivates us to read a particular text in the first place; what our reading purpose is. Secondly, we might consider how we read, related to what we want to get out of the experience. At the same time we may observe what kinds of knowledge are brought into play during the reading event.

Reading purpose

It is the time of a General Election in Britain and a certain leaflet has been put through everyone's door in a particular neighbourhood. We might consider both what the sender's purpose is and what the receiver's purpose in reading it might be. It reads:

(a)
STRONG ALLIANCE Policies for a STRONG BRITAIN.

If we turn over, we read:

(b)
Who says the SDP/LIBERAL ALLIANCE has no Policies?   Well they are wrong!

What will motivate us to open up the leaflet and read further? It largely depends whether we form part of the group to whom the text is directed—the electorate. Some committed supporters of other rival political parties will not be interested. Others, however, will have a very clear purpose in reading on, namely to reach a decision about what action to take in the polling booth in a few weeks time. Indeed, the reader is likely to have an even more specific purpose, that is, to find out the party's views on a particular issue. He may scan the whole to find a section on unemployment, for instance. Once he has located this part of the text, he will read it carefully, as it describes the issue which will probably most affect his voting behaviour (cf. (c)).

(c)

UNEMPLOYMENT

(i)

1.   The Conservatives say that unemployment is
2.   worldwide and we have to grin and bear it. What
3.   they don't say is that unemployment is worse in
4.   Britain than in any other major country. Since they
5.   have been in power, unemployment has grown from
6.   5.4% to 13.2%. Two million extra people out of a job.
7.   Unemployment is wasteful. It leads to despair
8.   family breakdown and increased crime. Anyone
9.   who shrugs their shoulders at unemployment, as
10. this government does, is heartless and unsuitable to
11. remain in power.
12.   There is no reason to accept 3½ million
13. unemployed.
14.   Our plan to get Britain back to work is as
15. follows.

(ii)

16. * We will cut VAT, to expand the economy and
17.   reduce prices immediately.
18. * We will launch an emergency programme to
19.   create jobs in construction, new housing, home
20.   modernisation, and sewer maintenance. And we
21.   will provide extra help in hospitals and the social
22.   services.
23. * We will pay firms a job subsidy to take people off
24.   the dole.
25. * We will abolish the jobs tax.
26.   This programme will create 1 million new jobs
27.   over 2 years. It will cost £3 billion, but it is carefully
29.   costed to ensure that inflation is kept under control

Mature readers, then, not only have an appropriate view of the general purposes of print in a literate society, they have a specific purpose in reading the particular text on a particular occasion. They read flexibly and selectively in line with this.

Knowledge of the language system

As well as purpose, the reader brings to his particular reading task a knowledge of the conventions of the English writing system, as described in Chapter 2. If he is an L2 reader, these may be different from those of the L1 writing system. The exclamation mark here may serve as an example:

Well, they are wrong!   (in (b)).

More particularly, readers need to know about English sentence structure in order to predict word classes, such as nouns or verbs or adjectives. As discussed in Chapter 2, native-speakers of a language know intuitively what kinds of words can follow others. Here, for instance, we will predict a particular word class to follow (b) 'Well they are . . .'—*wrong/right/fools*, rather than—*but/him/have*. We also, of course, predict for **sense** at the same time. Once we have identified the purpose and source of the text, i.e. as coming from the SDP/Liberal Alliance, we would hardly expect:

Well, they are right!

Then we need to be able to make connections across the text, identifying what reference items such as *this* (line 26) refer to, and understanding the functions of connectors such as *since* (line 4) and *to* (line 23).

Knowledge of the world

We make use firstly of our knowledge of the **genre** to predict the general organization of this text, in which a current problem is stated (column i of (c)) with a view to outlining a solution to that problem (column ii (c)). This kind of knowledge is partly to do with knowing about the typical structures of texts, and partly to do with knowledge of the world.

Another kind of world-knowledge brought into play here is knowledge of the **topic**. In other words we connect words across the text to build up a sense of what the text is about. In this text, topic knowledge will relate the items 'the economy—programme—inflation' to the field of 'party politics' rather than to 'linguistics' or 'television'.

Most crucially, the reader comes to the text with an ability to interpret the **function** of party political broadsheets of this kind, which is at least partly associated with a knowledge of cultural norms. Literate adults in our society are immediately aware that this leaflet aims to persuade us to behave in a certain way, more particularly, to vote for the Liberal/SDP Alliance in a few weeks time. In other words its function, in Halliday's terms, is 'regulatory' (cf. Chapter 1).

An even more particular kind of world knowledge is required to make sense of:

(b) **Who says the SDP/LIBERAL ALLIANCE has no Policies?** **Well they are wrong!**

The reader knowledge assumed here is that the Alliance has been generally criticized during the election campaign as lacking clearly defined policies. The reader needs access to this knowledge to understand the function of the rhetorical question and answer as a refutation of criticism.

Opinions

Finally, the reader brings to reading not just various kinds of world-knowledge, some of which is culture-specific, but also **opinions** about the world in general and the world of the text in particular. This allows him to evaluate the content and views expressed in the text in the light of his own views of the world.

It would seem, then, that what readers bring with them to a text enables them simultaneously to do a number of things. An attempt is made to represent an admittedly very complex process in Table 1.

To sum up, making sense of a particular text on a particular occasion is, firstly, to do with the reader's familiarity with the conventions of written language in general

TABLE 1 *A model of the reading process*

Readers BRING TO THE TEXT . . .	Which enables them WHILE READING TO . . .	*Example from accompanying text, as extracted in (a), (b) and (c)*
1. **A purpose**	Read flexibly and selectively.	Reader scans text for part relevant to personal interest, UNEMPLOYMENT (c); (once located this is read carefully).
2. **A knowledge of the language system** including:		
the writing system	Interpret the conventions of the writing system.	Exclamation mark in 'Well they are wrong!' (b).
sentence structure	Predict word classes.	'We will pay firms a job subsidy' (c), line 23: (sub + verb + Ind. O. + Dir. O.).
connection in texts	Make relevant connections across texts, e.g: reference logical connectors.	'This programme . . .' (c) 26, where 'this' refers back to whole of previous text (16–25). 'Since they have been in power . . .' (c) 4, where 'since' + perfect tense signals a clause describing period of time.
3. **A knowledge of the world** including:		
knowledge of genre	Anticipate organization and content of text.	UNEMPLOYMENT (c) (i) states problem; (ii) proposes solutions.
knowledge of topic	Relate content words to overall topic.	Unemployment: jobs—job subsidy—the dole (c).
culture-specific knowledge, e.g. of text function	Interpret the whole function of text and parts of the text.	'Who says the SDP/Liberal Alliance has no policies' (b) (i.e. we know that people do say it). Rhetorical question signals a refutation.
4. **Opinions**	Evaluate the content of the text in the light of existing knowledge and views of the world.	3½ million unemployed (c) (line 12). Is this something to worry about?

and written English in particular. Secondly, it is to do with the kinds of meaning readers are able to draw from a text—how fully they can interpret the text in the light of their past experiences of the English language and of the world. Readers attempting to make sense of written language need to interpret the text, using different sorts of clue to fit the parts together. The difficulty, as we have seen, is that not all the parts are on the page. The missing bits must be found in the readers' existing stock of knowledge. When we talk of getting meaning from texts we are talking also of what we bring to the text.

In this chapter we have looked at some of the factors which affect our ability to interpret written texts, including the ease with which we are able to interact with the writer. In the next chapter we will consider the case of very early learner-readers, involved in an interaction not just with the text, but also with the teacher. How might the teacher mediate most helpfully in the process of learning to read, guiding the learner towards the use of strategies which will help him to begin to read for meaning?

4

Learning to Read—Learner, Teacher and Text

In Chapter 3 it was suggested that reading starts before we ever look at the page; that the kinds of knowledge, experience and opinion that the reader brings to reading determine his interpretation of the text. As we saw, success is dependent not just on linguistic and world-knowledge but also on motivation and attitude. In the next two chapters we will look more particularly at the context of learning to read, considering not just the learner himself, but the role of teacher and text in the early stages of learning.

In this chapter I shall suggest firstly, that reading aloud is best seen as an interaction which involves teacher and learner in an exploration of the meaning of text; secondly, that in evaluating the errors early learners make, we might consider not quantity so much as quality, and look not just at the kind of error but at likely reasons for the occurrence of error. Throughout this chapter I shall refer to the two studies of learner-readers mentioned in the chapter and also to the case studies included at the end of the book (Chapter 9).

Reading as a Shared Experience

How does any reader in a learning context perceive the immediate activity of reading? How, for instance, do early readers, reading aloud to teachers or their peers, see their respective roles? Even the physical proximity of teacher to learner, whether side by side or face to face, will influence the nature of the reading event. Similarly with the nature of the interaction: does the learner read aloud to the teacher, with the teacher only interrupting when the text fails to make sense, or does the teacher also have access to the text and intervene when the learner reads something other than what is on the paper? Do they take it in turns to read?

Reflecting on our own teaching style can be instructive. I was uncomfortably reminded of my behaviour as a teacher on hearing how Judith Graham, as described in Meek *et al.* (1983), observed herself in a video play-back of a lesson with her student, Jamie. She was turning the pages of the book for him! Instances of teacher control of this kind show how reluctant we often are to offer our learners autonomy as readers.

For many children, reading aloud to teacher consists of coming up to the front of the class to read. As Southgate *et al.* (1981) point out, teachers in a busy class may be simultaneously hearing a child read while attending to other children's spelling queries. In such cases, children may be encouraged in the view that reading aloud is to be done as quickly as possible, without pause for comment, query or reflection. It may be, as Southgate *et al.* (1981) suggest, that it would be better to give individual children more time less frequently. For without more than the perfunctory few minutes of a harassed teacher's time (and Southgate *et al.* observed that the average time with a teacher was only 50 seconds), it is difficult to ensure that the experience of reading aloud to the teacher is one from which children may learn—learn, that is, about the nature of texts and the range of strategies available for getting meaning from them, including, of course, the importance of drawing on one's own knowledge of the world.

Given time, the experience can be one which is shared and enjoyed by both teacher and learner. There needs to be time to talk about books or other reading realia in a general way, and time to discuss why a particular book has been selected and to conjecture on the events and outcome of the story. Learners with little experience of books need guidance in handling and responding to them. Many learners start on the book, even one they have picked up themselves, without looking at the title. Even the notion of authorship may not be clear to a not-so-good reader. My learner José, mentioned in Chapter 1, for example, thought that the author's name on the front of the book referred to the two characters in the picture.

In exploring the text together with a learner, the teacher might choose to ask questions which do not test how many words are known, but which encourage learners to reflect on what they are reading. This will involve 'What do you think' or 'Why?' questions, designed to encourage the exploration of the text for implications, rather than the customary 'What does X mean' type of question or 'What's this word', a question I put, quite unhelpfully, to Nadeem (cf. Case Studies 2). Southgate *et al.* (1981) note how rarely it was that they observed a teacher ask any question at all—whether a yes/no question or an open-ended one—on the content of a child's reading. One of our roles as teachers is to consider which kinds of question can encourage greater engagement of the learner with the text.

More important, perhaps, than teachers asking questions, is learners asking questions. For without the ability and willingness to ask questions—of teachers and of texts—learners cannot take charge of their own learning. Teachers may need to ensure that E2L learners have an appropriate language for learning, an important part of which is the language of enquiry. Examples of language which they might need in order to enquire about the reading process and the reading text are: 'What's that X for?', 'Why is he running away?' or 'What's the difference between Y and Z?'

The 'teacher' may be a fellow pupil, of course. Many teachers favour the idea of peer-group reading. Its effectiveness, however, would seem to depend on how well-equipped learners are to help each other. Kellie (1982), in a study of peer-group reading, wished to find out how children helped each other at points of reading breakdown. In most cases the children simply provided the unknown word, because, so Kellie conjectured, that was what their own teachers did when they themselves read aloud. What was missing was the joint exploration of the text which he had hoped to observe.

We should, I believe, aim for shared reading which, whether pupil to pupil or teacher to pupil, involves interaction, and which is an experience valued and enjoyed, as Bennett (1979) describes it, by all those involved; one where perceptions are shared, where real questions are asked and where the 'right' answers are not necessarily knowable. This means accepting that texts may be open to several interpretations; even that texts or parts of texts are not readily interpretable at all (cf. Chapter 3, page 41) and that it need not matter. Effective reading is not to do with knowing everything on the page, nor is it to do with 'not making mistakes'.

In the rest of this chapter we will consider how the early learner's reading performance can be evaluated, not in terms of the number of errors made but in terms of his ability and willingness to make sense of the interaction, both with the teacher and with the text.

What is Error?

Fluent readers reading aloud will rarely reproduce exactly what is on the page. Misprints will be ignored and there will usually be some restructuring or omission of the text (cf. Chapter 2, p. 28). Are we to characterize these as instances of error? We need perhaps to distinguish these phenomena from the sorts of replacement or omission which signal a clear loss or change of textual meaning. Moreover, even quite good readers occasionally make lapses in reading aloud, due to momentary inattention. Corder (1973), talking not of reading but of second language learners' speech, calls these lapses 'slips of the tongue'—an expression which can also describe reader behaviour in reading aloud.

One important characteristic of 'true' error as opposed to slips of the tongue is that there is a system. There is a reason why error occurs; and if we can, by looking at the learner's reading data, find some pattern of error occurrence, we are perhaps on the way to being able to offer help.

Error—Good or Bad?

For the moment we will take error to mean any departure from the text in a reader's oral rendering of it. When readers 'get it right', i.e. reproduce the text as it stands, how they do this is not easily apparent. It is when they depart from the text that learner-reader strategies are most readily observed. In this sense, at least, error is helpful.

No so long ago error was 'a bad thing'—both in the teaching of languages and in the teaching of reading. Prevalent methodology, either explicitly or by implication, left one in little doubt that the teacher's job was to prevent the occurrence of error altogether through carefully guided and controlled teaching and access to materials. 'It is easier to prevent a wrong response than to correct an error', rather surprisingly occurs in the BBC *Adult Literacy Handbook* (1975), not on the whole given to such prescriptions.

An alternative, and now more generally accepted view is to see error as a part of learning. 'The more often you want to be right the more you must risk being wrong', says Frank Smith (1971). Good learners, so it has been observed by language teaching methodologists, are prepared to take risks—to try out hypotheses. This applies not just in learning a second language, but in learning to read in either a first or second language and, indeed, in learning anything. Learners need the opportunity to err. Far from denying them that opportunity, teachers should encourage risk-taking. Both learners and teachers can then get feedback through the errors. The development and change in the student's reading strategies will be apparent to the teacher largely through the changing nature of his errors. In other words, the kinds of error made will reveal the system being operated by the student; what hypotheses he is forming about the reading process. Diagnosis and appropriate help is then possible; and of course the student, on his part, gets feedback as to ways in which his 'bid' was or was not along the right lines.

Learner Miscues

Because of the difficulty of the term 'error', with the perhaps inevitable connotations of failure, the term **miscue**, introduced by Goodman in 1964, is now preferred in discussions of the reading process. A miscue refers to any replacement, omission or addition the reader makes to the text. An analysis of reader miscues shows that they can be described in terms of what features of the text the learner reader is attending to, related to three **levels** of language, which I discuss more fully in Chapter 5. The three levels, following Goodman (1973), are:

(1) **Graphophonic:** graphophonic miscues show a replacement by the reader of a word similar in sound or appearance to the word in the text, often with a sacrifice of meaning, e.g. 'He got earth in his cars (ears)' Manjit (cf. Chapter 5). This miscue is—as is often the case—more graphic than phonic; a single mark on the page makes a minimal visual difference between *ears* and *cars*.

(2) **Syntactic:** syntactic miscues show a replacement by the reader of comparable or identical parts of speech, or a reordering of sentence structure. Syntactic miscues may be of several kinds: first are those cases where the miscue fits the whole syntax, even if the sense of the text is not maintained, e.g. 'But Mother answered that the most elegant (important) . . . thing was to be well'—where the miscue by Mark (cf. Case Studies 1) fits the overall syntax. Then there are miscues which involve syntactic replacements or reorderings, with little if any change in meaning. Kate, aged 5, for example restructures:
    (a) 'She put in bacon and egg' as
    (b) 'She put bacon and egg in'.
Finally, one might include here those miscues made by non-standard or non-native speakers which are attributable to the way they *speak* English. In principle these can be treated in the same way as Kate's rendering of text (a) above. The (b) version is, as with most native-speakers, more natural to her—more typical of what she would say. In the same way, for Vijay (cf. page 54) 'Karen like the soon park' is syntactically equivalent to the text's version 'Karen liked the zoo park'. In other words, the omission of the -ed suffix on the verb and a pronunciation of *zoo* as *soon* are both general features of Vijay's system of English at the time of reading. The relationship between a learner's spoken language and the language of the text is discussed more fully in the next chapter. Suffice it to say here that where miscues appear to be a reflection of the learner's own grammar of English (including pronunciation), we will classify them as syntactic miscues.
    It should be noted, incidentally, that all but the very earliest or weakest readers tend to miscue with a part of speech that at least fits the preceding syntax. This is so even if the miscue is a nonsense word, e.g., 'There was this pigeon sitting *climbly* (calmly) on the roof of the shed' (Nadeem, Case Studies 2), where Nadeem retains the adverbial -ly suffix.

(3) **Semantic:** semantic miscues show a replacement of a content item in the text with another one closely related in meaning, e.g. 'He cut them up into little pieces (bits)', (Pauline, aged 7). Replacements may also be due to the learner's own typical vocabulary. For this reason many children can be observed to replace a word such as *Mother* in the text with *Mum* or *Mummy*.

In practice it is not always easy to distinguish these levels; often the miscue will be semantically and syntactically possible in the light of the previous part of the text and also graphophonically similar, e.g. 'Father gave them a great special (surprise)' (Mark, aged 8; Case Studies 1).

However, miscues which may semantically and syntactically fit the preceding context may not fit the following one—as is the case here. If Mark had read ahead he would have seen that we cannot say 'Father gave them a great special. One minute he was . . .'. It is the better readers who scan ahead, often in fact correcting the miscue when they find it does not fit the subsequent context, e.g. 'The golden sapiel wagged his tail . . . spaniel wagged his tail' (Kate, aged 5).

Self-correction is a particularly useful window on the reading process. In general, the better learners—because they are reading for meaning—will, if they make a graphophonic miscue which does not fit the context, immediately self-correct. Self-corrections should be viewed positively in those cases which show the learner rejecting what is unacceptable to the overall sense of the text.

We see, then, that getting things 'wrong', in the sense of not reading what is on the page, does not necessarily mean ineffective reading. As we saw in Chapter 2 and on page 48 in this chapter, native-speaking readers—including good young learners—tend anyway to restructure the text slightly when reading with fluency. In other words, syntactic miscues of this kind show a native-speaker-like competence in the language and in the case of E2L learners can be viewed positively, particularly if the miscue results in only a slight change of meaning.

When it comes to semantic miscues, the learner gets the rendering of the surface text 'wrong' only because he has been able to get directly at the underlying meaning. As with syntactic miscues, the occurrence of semantic miscues can signal an advance in reader strategy, as with Hillyard's semantic miscue here: 'when Toussaint was a little (small) child'. Hillyard has taken an immediate route to the meaning, not needing the intervention of the surface form. This was the first time Hillyard had made this kind of miscue and, as his teacher, I saw the instance as something of a breakthrough in his development as a reader.

So learner-readers can get the words wrong and yet be effective readers; the nature of the errors tells us that they could only have made such an addition, omission or replacement because they had understood. Conversely, learners can get all the words right and yet not be making sense of the text. There are learners who exactly reproduce the text and yet have, we suspect, a very imperfect idea of what is going on. There are also learners who correct unnecessarily, or hyper-correct, as Sarla does here: 'No, said Mike—No, Mike said' (Sarla, Case Studies 6).

Many second language learners are in the group of low-error or hyper-correcting readers. Di Mellish (1982) comments on the group of children she studied as follows:

> Some of the children I observed were quite capable of identifying words and reciting what was printed on the page, some even with acceptable intonation patterns. Yet these children were often gaining very little meaning from the text.

As evidence of this she describes those children who 'read a page of print and then stop in mid-sentence at the end of a page, having, they think, performed the task expected of them'.

The Place of Stress and Intonation

Mellish talks of the children she studied reading with 'acceptable intonation'. What is the place of stress and intonation in evaluating a learner-reader's rendering of the text? In miscue analysis more attention has been paid to the reader's syntactic, semantic and graphophonic miscues respectively than to the overall style of delivery. Teachers tend to talk of 'reading with expression'. What do they mean? Is the learner's stress and intonation as helpful a window on the learning to read process as an analysis of miscues in terms of the three levels of language just described?

In general, one would expect that stress and intonation were indeed indicative of how much and what sort of meaning was gained from a text. Sylvia Warham (1981) writes of ways that readers, in rendering a text aloud, distinguish through intonation between what is assumed as 'known' between reader and listener and what is new information and therefore to be highlighted in an oral rendering. She describes how examination of tone choices made in reading aloud showed that a reader used a falling tone to mark new information and a rising tone to mark shared information, e.g.,

Father bear looked after the flowers in the garden.
Mother bear kept the rooms neat and tidy.

Father and mother bear have already been mentioned in the text; *flowers*, *garden*, *rooms*, *neat* and *tidy* are treated as new information.

Readers also use contrasting stress to highlight parts of the text, e.g. 'But that's *my* name!' (Sarla—Case Studies 6). Sarla here reads not only the stress but also the exclamation mark, so to speak. Elsewhere, however, she fails to read the exclamation mark, giving *surprised* a rising tone and thereby indicating a misunderstanding of the function of 'Will my mother be surprised!' Sarla reads this as a 'real' question, i.e. 'Will my mother be surprised?' rather than 'Will my mother be surprised!'

However, a difficulty with learners reading aloud in a second language is that they may not use the same stress and intonation system as native-speakers—not in their spoken language, generally, and hence not in reading aloud. Therefore stress and intonation will not reliably indicate a second language learner's interpretation of the text. Many E2L learners, for instance, read on a monotone yet reveal, on questioning, that they have a fair grasp of the text.

Nonetheless, oddness of stress and intonation in reading aloud can point to learner/text difficulties in the case of both L1 and L2 readers. Consider how one would read aloud this text:

The king was a good king
In fact everyone agreed
They had never seen a better king
He was fair and just and
very kind to the people
He never sent anyone
to the dungeon without feeling
a little sorry that he had to.

(Ginn 360, *The King, the Dragon and the Witch*)

Experienced readers with an intuitive understanding of features of texts will quite naturally stress *had* and drop their pitch on *to*. They are aware of the omission, through ellipsis, of he 'had to' (put people in the dungeon). All the learners in Di Mellish's group (E2L learners but quite good speakers of English) read . . . sorry that he $\overrightarrow{had\ t\grave{o}}$, ignoring the invitation to drop their voices provided not only by the complete sense but graphically by the full stop. In no case was this inappropriate intonation corrected. Questioning revealed that it was indeed the case that the children had not understood. They missed the underlying proposition that the king did put people into the dungeon. They picked up the meaning contained in 'He never sent anyone to the dungeon' but did not understand the subordinate clause 'without feeling a little sorry that he had to'.

While one must be cautious about so-called pronunciation errors (cf. Chapter 5)—errors of stress and intonation inconsistent with the learner's typical use of these features in his own speech should be taken note of. How, for instance, does one evaluate Nadeem's rendering 'rubbēd'? (Case Studies 2). We need to consider that he does not normally give full stress to the -ed as a past tense marker.

Monitoring the Learning Process

An analysis of miscues offers a tool for describing different kinds of learner error. The kinds of miscue, including the use of certain kinds of stress and intonation, made by learners are a helpful guide to what parts of the text are being used by the reader in processing print. Miscue analysis can show up (as conventional tests do not) important qualitative differences in error. Southgate *et al.* (1981) describe how two learners with the same reading ages on conventional tests showed markedly different strategies on a miscue analysis assessment.

So miscue analysis can be a valuable descriptive tool. Goodman and Burke (1973) and Weaver (1980) give complete and rigorous models for analysis, which teachers can adopt and modify in ways that suit them best. Whether one chooses to do a full analysis or a transcription of learner/teacher interaction of the kind given on page 54 and in the Case Studies, the opportunity is offered to monitor a learner's changing or developing reading strategies over time.

The emphasis is not on testing but on a continuous assessment of the quality of error and general reading approach. Where, for instance, a learner-reader's profile shows a high proportion of graphophonic miscues, a low number of self-correction of such miscues, non-use of preceding or succeeding context and no restructuring or semantic replacement, he can be more carefully monitored over time.

Sources of Miscues

As claimed earlier in this chapter, there is always a reason why errors occur. Where it is a case of momentary inattention, I have preferred to adopt Corder's term and to talk of a 'slip'. It is useful to attempt to establish not just the level of miscue but its likely source, in order to guide learners towards the use of more productive strategies. What, in other words, are the miscue-causing factors? Any attempted explanation for the occurrence of miscues is bound to be speculative. Nonetheless, I shall here suggest a simple classification.

In the case of E2L learners, error may be connected firstly with the learner's own language system, that is, the linguistic resources he brings to the text. There are specifically non-native-speaker errors, for example: 'I must signing' . . . (I missed signing on) (Yasmeen, Case Studies 5). Native speakers would be likely to quickly reject the -ing suffix to *sign* after *must* because it would not accord with what they know of English. Also, there are other miscues characteristic of E2L learners which are attributable to the learner's current pronunciation or syntactic usage in English at the time of reading (cf. page 48). Miscues connected with the learner's own use of or competence in English are here called language-provoked or **L** miscues.

Secondly, miscues may be provoked not so much by the learner's inability to predict the structure or meaning of the text as by an unpredictability of both content and structure in the text itself, creating difficulty for native- and non-native-speakers alike. Examples from two learners in the Case Studies are:

(1) 'Lindy and Billy soon found themselves laughing' (Mark, Case Studies 1)

and

(2) 'Linda is 16 and works in a toy shop. Kid's stuff, thinks Harry' (Maqsood, Case Studies 3).

The first is possibly a rather adult expression; a reflexive pronoun + participle has low predictability after the verb 'found'. The second creates difficulty because the writing has been made to represent colloquial speech (cf. Chapter 2).

Then there are miscues provoked simply by unknown words, in particular items such as proper names which, if unfamiliar, regularly create difficulty. Miscues caused primarily by the text itself, I have labelled 'text-provoked' or **T** miscues. More particularly: **Tco** where the expression is colloquial; **Tcu** where there is a likely cultural difficulty for an L2 reader in particular; **Tlit** where literary style involving the use of expressions or vocabulary rarely used in other language contexts, spoken or written, appears to have provoked some difficulty, and **Tsp** for specialist terms, with which, for instance, Yasmeen's text abounds (cf. Yasmeen, Case Studies 5).

Last are those miscues provoked by the learner's failure to make use of the resources available to him. These we might call strategy-provoked or **S** miscues. And an example might be:

'The train was dr . . . druve (due) to leave' (Nadeem, Case Studies 2).

It is unlikely that Nadeem was unfamiliar with the common expression 'due to', particularly when collocated with trains and departures. If he had read ahead and then back-tracked, it is likely that he could have repaired this error. However, to talk of negative learner strategies is not necessarily to blame the learner, for we may have to consider how the learner acquired those strategies in the first place—possibly from teachers who encourage a limited view of what reading is all about. We might more properly use here the term, familiar in second language learning, of 'teacher-induced' error, to describe those cases where certain teaching approaches appear to have encouraged negative or at least limited learning strategies. Many **S** miscues therefore will be teacher-induced.

In talking of **S** or strategy miscues, however, we must remember that some miscues show the learner using positive strategies; that is, they show the learner-reader drawing on all the resources available to him, both from the text itself and from his own background knowledge.

Examples are:

(1) cases where the learner, on reading ahead, is observed to back-track, when by processing more of the text he accumulates enough information to self-correct, as in the example of Kate, already quoted: 'The golden sapiel wagged his tail . . . spaniel wagged his tail'.

(2) Cases where the miscue is a synonym, as was the case of Hillyard's substitution of *little* for *small*, cf. page 49: 'When Toussaint was a little (small) child'.

(3) Cases where the miscue is semantically appropriate, if not synonymous, and graphonically very similar, as well as fitting the syntax, e.g., 'The woman next door planning the day as quickly (quietly) as possible' (Ravinder, Case Studies 4).

We might call these positive strategy or S+ miscues, on the basis that in each of these cases learners are displaying reading behaviour which is characteristic of effective, mature readers and shows the reading for meaning process at work.

It is also revealing to observe how learner-readers themselves monitor the whole situation, how they bring themselves not just to the text but to the task of reading aloud to the teacher, and in what ways they comment on what is going on in terms of the content and any textual difficulties. It is not just positive strategies but positive attitudes which set some learners on the road to effective reading. It is these positive strategies and attitudes that we can try and encourage in the less confident learner readers.

Reading as an Interaction: the Case of Vijay

(The reader is referred to Chapter 9, Case Studies, for a discussion and evaluation of the reading miscues of other learner-readers.)

Vijay

Vijay is 6-years-old and still speaks very little English; he came from India 2 years ago, but has been troubled with an ear infection which has hindered his progress in English. This has now cleared up and he is beginning to make good progress. He is withdrawn from his regular class for language and reading work. Dorothy, working with him here, is the teacher to whom he goes for language classes. He is reading the book 'Karen at the Zoo' from the reading scheme *Link Up* (Jessie Reid and Joan Low).

Notes on the reading

(1) Miscues are given superscript numerals and printed in bold type.
(2) Sounds are given in brackets, thus [   ].
(3) When the unknown word or words are given by the teacher, they are capitalized.
(4) A learner's ultimate success in repairing a miscue or in picking up the teacher prompts is indicated with an asterisk*.
(5) The learner's spontaneous comments or responses to the teacher are italicized.

Notes on the analysis

The analysis refers both to the interaction between Dorothy and Vijay and to those described in the Case Studies (Chapter 9). The five columns in the analysis may need some clarification.

(1) The **miscue** is any omission, replacement or addition by the reader to the text (hesitations are not included).

(2) The **level** of miscue describes the kind of miscue made by the reader, depending on whether attention has been paid primarily to graphophonic features of the word, the syntax of the text, or the semantic (or meaning) level of the text. Often a miscue will suggest a combination of two or even three levels.

(3) The **source** of miscue attempts to attribute a likely cause for the occurrence of the miscue, whether primarily

> language or **L**-provoked;
> Text or **T**-provoked;
> strategy or **S**-provoked.

A **slip** is seen as not necessarily provoked by either the learner's language or strategy or text difficulty; merely the result of temporary loss of concentration.

(4) **Learner response** notes the behaviour which accompanies the miscue and the way the learner attempts to resolve the difficulty presented by the text, for example by sounding out or spelling the word which is creating difficulty, by reading ahead or by back-tracking. The learner may be prepared to tolerate a miscue which does not maintain meaning in the text and simply read on. This in itself is suggestive of a certain learning style. Important, too, is the way in which the learner uses the teacher as a resource during the interaction. Does he merely wait till she resolves the difficulty for him? Does he ask for the meanings of new words? Does he engage in any debate or comment about the text?

(5) **Teacher prompt** notes the teacher's preferred strategies in offering help, whether by simply providing the unknown word or by guiding the learner's attention to any of the three levels, i.e. the graphophonic features of words themselves, or to the overall syntax and meaning of the text. Moreover, choosing not to correct is also an option, and teachers' reasons for exercising this option can reveal much about their view of the learning to read process.

The interaction

Vijay	Dorothy
T. Karen was in Hill street	
V. Karen was in **leel**[1] street	HILL
T. One day	
V. One day	
T. She was going to school	Good
V. See was going to school	
Then we read all of . . .?	Yes, then you'll be able to hear it on the tape.
T. Karen came to the bus stop	
V. Karen **[k] [p] [k]**[2] came to the bus stop	CAME
T. A big bus was	
V. A big bus was	
T. at the bus stop	
V. at the bus stop	
T. The driver was going	
V. The driver was going	
T. into the bus	
V. into the bus	
T. Karen was reading	
V. Karen was reading	
T. the name on the bus	
V. the name on the bus	
T. It was Zoo Park	
V. It was **soon**[3] Park	
T. The bus was going to the Zoo	
V. The bus was going to the soon	Can you see the name 'Zoo Park' on the bus?
Soon Park	That's right it was going to the Zoo.
T. Karen liked the Zoo Park	
V. Karen **like**[4] the soon Park	
T. and she liked the big bus	
V. and she **like**[4] the big bus	
T. Karen went into the bus	
V. Karen went **to the**[5]—*into the bus	

Vijay   **Dorothy**

T. The bus went to Park Street
V. The bus went to Park Street
T. It went along Park Street
V. It went a . . . along Park Street   Good boy.
T. And it came to the bus stop
V. And it **comera**[6] . . . it came to the bus stop   Nearly right—it's CAME.
T. At the Zoo Park
V. At the soon park   Let's look at the sign.
                                              What does this sign say?
Soon Park. Close—open.   It doesn't say . . . The door's open isn't it, so
                                              that she can go in.
                                              How much is it for adults?

Adult 30, children 15
T. Karen went into the Park
V. Karen went into the Park
T. The Zoo Park was a big Park
V. The soon park was a big park
T. It had lions and polar bears
V. It **lia**[7]   No.
   had lion and (whispers 'teddy bear')
   teddy bear[8]   They're not Teddy bears, they're called polar
                                              bears.
T. And giraffes
V. **polar bear and giraffe**[9]   What colour are the polar bears?
   white
T. It had sea lions and fish
V. It had sea lion and fish
T. And a crocodile
V. And a . . .[10] cocolile   CROCODILE
   Cocolile (V. attempts to pronounce this with
   some enjoyment)
T. Karen went to the polar bears
V. Karen went to the **Cola bed**[11]   POLAR BEARS
T. She liked the little bears
V. She like the little bēd.—*This?*   That's right, the little baby bears.
   (referring to the picture)
T. Karen went to the lions
V. Karen went to the lion
T. And she went to the giraffes
V. And she went to the giraffe
T. She liked the big giraffes
V. She like the big giraffe   Can you see a big giraffe?
                                              What's this giraffe doing in this picture?
little   Yes, it's a little giraffe.
                                              What's it doing?
eating
T. Karen met the penguins
V. Karen **le . . . le . . . bed**[12]   MET
   the **[t] . . . [p] . . .**[13] penguins   That's called . . . remember? PENGUINS
T. And she liked them too
V. And see like the **the**[14] . . . them too   No, it's not 'the'. THEM
   What's that, miss?   PENGUINS
T. She went to the crocodile
V. She went to the . . . cocolile   You know that word, don't you?
T. and the big fish
V. and the big fish   What do you think the keeper was going to do
                                              with the fish?
eat it   He was going to eat it? It was the crocodile
                                              that was going to eat it. He was going to throw
                                              it to the crocodile.
eating this fish?   Yes, the crocodile was eating the fish and these
                                              animals, what were they called?

Vijay	Dorothy
penguin	What colour are the penguins?
black and white	What is your favourite, Vijay—the lions, the penguins, the polar bears or the giraffes?
black and white	Oh, you like those two colours, but which is your favourite animal?
lion	Why do you like the lion?
lion sing	Sing? They roar.
singing	They roar, like this.
	Can you make a lion roar?
I make it like this. Look!	
(Vijay makes a face)	Oh, you're making a face, a fierce face. Shall we listen to the tape?

The comment

The text: The text is part of a popular reading scheme, *Link Up*. It is well structured, particularly for a second language learner, in the sense that it takes the simplest sentence patterns in English, e.g. subject–verb–object (*Karen liked the Zoo*), subject–verb–adverbial (*Karen was in Hill Street*), subject–verb–complement (*The Zoo Park was a big park*). The language of the text is reinforced by the social sight vocabulary in the pictures, that is, vocabulary which is clearly contextualized, such as OPEN and ZOO PARK. This prompts some of the talk between Vijay and Dorothy about whether the zoo is closed, how much Karen will pay, and so on. The only place where the structuring of the text trips Vijay up is when the pronoun *them* is introduced referring back to *penguins*.

Vijay: Vijay's preferred strategy is to sound out unknown words. His attempts at phonic decoding, however—as with most of the other learners in the Case Studies—tend not to pay off. Vijay's English is still fairly restricted, both productively and receptively, and many of the miscues can be attributed to his as yet limited knowledge of English. He systematically omits the -ed suffix on past tense verb forms and he has an idiosyncratic pronunciation of some items such as *zoo* and *she*, which he sometimes though not always pronounces 'see'. He does not understand questions very readily (for example, *What's that giraffe doing?* is not at first understood).

However, Vijay is beginning—as a learner—to draw on certain resources. Several of his miscues suggest positive strategies such as looking ahead in the text, bringing his own knowledge of the world to bear on the text (even if not quite appropriately, as with 'Teddy Bear') and 'practising' new words such as *crocodile*. We see him effectively using what little English he has in order to learn; he uses very simple verbal strategies, e.g. 'This?' and 'What's that, miss?' to confirm what is being talked about, showing that he is engaged with the text.

When the tape was played back Vijay monitored his own performance very carefully, intervening in exasperation as he followed the text through a second time.

Dorothy: Dorothy's preferred strategy observed here is to simply give Vijay the word that creates difficulty. It is likely that she did not wish to interrupt the flow of Vijay's reading. She does not 'correct' Vijay's pronunciation or syntax when it diverges from the text (cf. Chapter 5). Most noticeable is the way she effectively draws Vijay's attention to the social sight print in the pictures which clearly and

The analysis

No.	Miscue	Level of miscue	Source of miscue	Learner response	Teacher prompt
1.	leel (Hill)	graphophonic (non-word)	T: unknown place name	—	gives
2.	[k] [p] [k] (came)	—	L: remote from own language (V. not yet using many irregular past tenses)	attempts to sound	gives
3.	Soon Park (Zoo Park)	syntactic	L: V. systematically pronounces *zoo* as *soon* in this rendering	leaves	leaves
4.	Karen like the soon park and see like the big bus. (K. liked the . . . and she . . . etc.)	syntactic	L: V. not yet using -ed forms consistently; *liked* is systematically read as *like* on this occasion (also *see*/*she* sometimes pronounced as homophones)	leaves	leaves
5.	Karen wert to the (Karen went into the)*	syntactic	S+ V. is predicting well here, making use of the simple English he knows	self-corrects immediately when he sees that 'to' does not quite fit the sense	—
6.	comera (came)	graphophonic (non-word)	L: difficulty with some past tense forms (cf. 2)	—	gives
7.	lia (had lions)*	omission of structure word 'had'	S+ V. appears to have miscued because he was looking ahead in the text (generally a positive strategy)	immediately gets it, with teacher prompt	comment 'no'
8.	teddy bear (polar bears)	semantic? + syntactic	S+ V. substitutes known collocation for unknown one & L: omits plural ending	whispers, trying out his guess first	gives
9.	polar bear and giraffe (polar bears and giraffes)	syntactic	L: V. systematically omits plural -s in own speech and throughout this rendering	leaves	leaves
10.	— (crocodile)	—	T: new word	V. tries out a pronunciation of this new word with apparent enjoyment	gives
11.	cola bed (polar bears)	graphic	T: V. still thinking of *crocodile* & L: some difficulty with pronunciation	—	gives
12.	le . . . le . . . bed (met)	graphic	L: difficulty with some irregular past tense forms	attempts sounding	gives
13.	[t] [p] (penguins)	—	T: new word	attempts sounding	gives
14.	the (them)	graphic (also fits preceding text syntactically/semantically)	T: V. anticipates the + noun as in preceding part of text	—	gives

appropriately reinforces some of the language of the text. She involves him too in consideration of likely outcomes (e.g. 'What do you think the keeper was going to do with the fish?'); she invites him to think about his own favourite animals. She is, even at this early stage, encouraging reflective reading.

The range of available strategies

By way of summing up our experience so far, we can look at the overall strategies which were most popular with Vijay and the six learners described in the Case Studies. That is, we can consider both what resources they draw on when faced with difficulty in the text and how they attempt to repair the difficulty. For it is useful to consider not just the nature of learner error and the likely reasons for its occurrence, but how effectively difficulties are resolved by the learner during the interaction with the teacher. The final column in Table 1 therefore shows the 'pay-off'.

TABLE 1 *Frequency with which particular strategies were used by learners during the reading interactions*

	Phonic sounding	Fill in with word that fits previous context	Fill in with word that does not fit context	Non-sense word	Read ahead	Back-track	Ask T. for word	Ask T. for meaning	Do nothing	The pay off
Mark	—	7	—	—	—	2	2	1	3	8
Vijay	3	5	—	2	—	—	1	—	—	2
Nadeem	—	—	6	8	—	—	—	—	—	2
Maqsood	2	2	3	1	—	—	3	—	—	5
Ravinder	1	4	2	4	—	—	—	—	—	4
Yasmeen	4	—	2	1	—	—	—	3	—	1
Sarla 1	6	6	7	1	—	—	—	—	—	3
Sarla 2	3	3	2	—	—	2	—	—	—	4

Clearly these strategies are not mutually exclusive. A learner may use several strategies on any one occasion—indeed, this is what good learners are likely to do.

What strikes one from such a comparison is the wide range of individuals' preferred ways of coping with difficulty in texts when reading with or to the teacher. Mark and Yasmeen are the only learners who ask for clarification of the text. Yasmeen, in particular, uses the time with the teacher to discover the meaning of new words. Both Yasmeen and Mark are prepared to take charge of their own learning. At the same time, Mark could be said to be unadventurous in one respect; he is prepared to wait for the word to be provided by the teacher, to do nothing. He knows he does not know it. Nadeem, on the other hand, is very reluctant to pause or reflect on the text; he fills in with a similar-looking or sounding word, regardless of whether it fits the context, or whether it is a real word in English. But he does not give up. Mark has the greatest success rate in picking up the cues offered by the teacher.

None of the readers here had difficulties attributable to decoding the text, with the possible exception of Vijay. If anything, there is an over-use of decoding tactics. Nadeem, for instance, is able to sound out unknown words with remarkable facility, or even to read them unhesitatingly, but he tends not to assign an appropriate meaning to the words. There is often the near-miss effect, leading to the production of nonsense words. The problem is that new words remain unknown unless the learner works out a plausible meaning from context, as Sarla apparently does in the case of *burn* (Case Studies 6), or adopts the sensible strategy of asking the teacher not what the word is but what it means. Only Yasmeen does this.

For all of them, the difficulty is not with reading words; what they tend not to do is move away from a problem word to search the surrounding text. Sarla, for instance, is initially perplexed when I suggest that looking at the rest of the text will help, rather than continuing to worry away at the unknown word. In fact, none of the readers are observed reading ahead in the text, and there is very little evidence of back-tracking. In spite of considerable individual differences, the learners are not making use of the full range of potential strategies.

We see, then, that readers have a range of strategies at their disposal to help them cope with points of breakdown in reading aloud, whether caused by cultural difficulty, mismatch of learner and text language, completely new words or words in unfamiliar contexts. Good learners of reading—or, indeed, of anything else—have worked out that if you cannot do it one way, you should try another; there are different routes, represented in the case of reading by a range of textual cues (and extra-textual knowledge) to success. Poorer learners need to be encouraged to acquire a similar flexibility of strategy.

At the same time, teachers have a range of strategies they can recommend to their learners. Too often the teacher's advice to poor readers might be summed up as 'If you can't do it this way, (and this is the only way), just keep trying'. Thus poor learner-readers can be observed making persistent but vain attempts to sound out words, for instance, rather than trying an alternative strategy. Helping learners to be independent readers involves showing them how to get at text meaning for themselves in the most effective way. It may, on occasion, be appropriate simply to give the learner the unknown word, when he is reading with some confidence and fluency and is clearly engaged with the text, as Vijay appeared to be during his reading with Dorothy. On the other hand, to use this as a sole strategy would be to neglect the considerable resources which the learner himself can draw on from the whole text and from his own knowledge of the language and of the world.

Misunderstanding not What, but Why: the Case of Balvinder

One learner is not included with the other Case Studies because she seemed to make remarkably few miscues. When she did miscue, her strategies for repair were effective. Balvinder's difficulty was of a different order: she understood the text on a literal level. However, she could not, apparently, interpret what had happened.

Learners like Balvinder may make few, if any, miscues and read apparently with meaning, understanding questions at word or sentence level put to them by the teacher. They understand the meaning of individual parts of the text but miss the point of the whole.

Balvinder is aged 8, at school in a largely Asian school in West London. Her first language is Punjabi but her teachers consider that she is to all intents and purposes a native speaker of English. She is not considered to be in need of extra language tuition, therefore, but there has been some concern about her level of understanding in reading.

TEXT 1 *The Lion and his friends*

1. Old Lion sat warming himself in the sun.
2. He was too old to hunt, but he wasn't too old
3. to be hungry. From the mouth of his cave
4. he watched the path that led to town.
5. "There are many good dinners travelling
6. along this path." He sighed. "But *now*/how can I
7. get those dinners from the path to me? I'm
8. so weak that my paws tremble, but *terrible* if/I'm *am*
9. clever I can still (eat) well." He scratched *and*
10. himself and swished his tail while he made
11. his plans.
12. When Rooster came along the path, Old
13. Lion's mouth curled in a smile as/*the* he called,
14. "Friend Rooster, come (over) and talk for a
15. while. I'm old and tired and can't get about *am*
16. much/*of* these days. Won't you stop for tea with
17. me?"

18. *The* Rooster answered, "Old Lion, your eyes
19. have a hungry look. I (think) I'll keep on
20. going."
21. "The sun is warm and the path is long," *The*
22. Old Lion said. "Just stop for a little while.
23. I have everything ready."
24. "Well, just for a minute,/ Friend Lion. I
25. don't want to be here too long."
26. "Oh, this won't take long," /Old Lion Said *said Lion, said Old Lion*
27. as he led Rooster into his cave.
28. Later, Old Lion nodded sleepily in the sun.
29. He wiped a feather from his chin and said, *cheek*
30. "I'll miss Friend Rooster. But it was nice to
31. have him for tea." *tea with him*

(Ginn 360, *The Lion and his friends*)

Balvinder reads Text 1 without any intervention from her teacher, Di Mellish. In the text as presented, hesitations are underlined, omissions encircled, additions signalled ⋀, and replacements to the text noted above the word. There are not many replacements to the text and most maintain the sense of the text fairly well. One could describe the replacement in line 31 as a restructuring: to 'have someone for tea' may equal to 'have tea with someone'. This is presumably a deliberate ambiguity in the text.

The following conversation between Di and Balvinder follows:

Di What's happened?
B. Miss, he had some tea with the rooster, miss and . . . (unclear)
  He have it for just a minute and . . .
Di What's he done here? (referring to line 28)
B. He nodded . . . went to sleep . . .
Di and he had a feather on his chin—where's that come from?
B. From the Rooster, Miss
Di How did it get there?
B. (pause)
Di Can you read this bit again?
B. 'He wiped a feather from his chin and said I'll miss friend Rooster but it was nice to have tea' . . . he gave him a feather from his body, Miss.
Di Mmm. What does it mean when it says, 'I'll miss him'.
B. He'll miss his friend.
Di Why, where's he gone?
B. He's gone . . . Miss, the lion?

Di No, the rooster.
B. Miss, he's gone somewhere else.
Di It says here: 'But it was nice to have him for tea'.
B. He's gone to have tea somewhere else.
Di Do you think so?
B. Yes Miss.
Di Right, you read the next bit and we'll see.

(B. reads the next section of the story, which describes a similar encounter, this time between Friend Goat and Old Lion. The outcome is the same as that between Lion and Rooster.) Di stops B. at this point: 'he led Goat into his cave'

Di What's he doing here, then?
B. Miss he, the lion led the goat to his cave.
Di What did he do there?
B. Miss he gave some tea to the goat.
Di Do you remember at the very beginning it said he didn't want to go out and get his food. He didn't want to go out hunting. Why was that?
B. Because he was too old.
Di So where's he getting all his tea from?
B. From his friends' houses Miss.
Di Is he? Where does it say that?
B. From his friends' *caves.*
Di But he hasn't been anywhere has he? Read the next bit very carefully and see if you can see what's happening.
B. 'Later Old Lion was warming himself in the sun. I miss friend goat he said as he plucked a tuft of black hair from his mane. But it was nice to have tea . . . for . . . for tea . . . (does not complete) (continues): Much . . .
Di Could you read that bit again?
B. But it was nice to have tea . . . it was nice to have him for tea'—he had him for tea Miss.
Di Mmm. So what did he do?
B. He gave him some tea.
Di (repeating very slowly) He-had-him-for-tea . . .
B. Oh—he ate him up!
Di And what happened to rooster?
B. He ate him up as well!

The text: Although part of a reading scheme, the text avoids being 'reading book language'. A real story is told in simple language. One cannot fairly attribute Balvinder's difficulty here to cultural bias. Animal fables are well known in Punjabi and Hindi story-telling. The predictability of events is dependent on the universality of the animal fable genre, with its characteristic roles and goals. The genre is well chosen, too, for learner readers, as it naturally lends itself to repetition.

Balvinder: Here we see that it is not Balvinder's reading strategies as such which let her down, but her lack of experience of how this kind of story can be expected to develop. She understands what is said, but not why. She cannot make the appropriate inferences. She is either unfamiliar with the genre or not approaching the text with the right set of expectations.

Di: Di skilfully guides Balvinder's attention to the crucial parts of the story, trying to encourage her to relate meanings across the text—to pick up the clues. This encouragement to explore the text, relating relevant parts of the story to each other, clearly takes time but is ultimately as important—if not more so—than discussion about meaning at word or sentence level. Balvinder's response to the text shows that learners may read a text almost perfectly but miss the point entirely. Asking questions about what words mean will not reveal this. One needs rather to ask the one key question which pulls the meaning of the whole text together. This is just what Di does here with her question 'What's happened?'

What Can we Learn from the Learner/Teacher Interaction?

To sum up, taping and transcribing learner/teacher interactions of the kind described in this chapter and in the Case Studies can help to show us:

(1) *The kind of language work needed to be undertaken* with E2L learners in particular, as well as with multilingual classes which include indigenous learners. Examples which emerge from the transcripts considered in this chapter and the Case Studies might be the function of connectors, such as *in fact*, and *of course*, with which Sarla (Case Studies 6) had some difficulty, or work with simple collocations such as *bread and butter, cup and saucer* (cf. Ravinder, Case Studies 4) or lexical groups such as *Zoo animals–domestic animals–toy animals* (like teddy bears) (cf. Vijay).

(2) *The kinds of text to beware of*, for the moment at least, with a particular learner or learners. Examples from the Case Studies might be the over-colloquial, elliptical text which Maqsood (Case Studies 3) reads. A more fully structured text would have given his reading better support at this stage. Similarly, Yasmeen (Case Studies 5) is rather frustrated with the reported speech in the text she has chosen. Conventionalized ways of representing speech, such as contracted forms, give particular difficulty. She might have got on better with a text with a clear narrative line rather than one which moves confusingly from reporting style in the past tense to description in the present tense.

(3) *The kinds of features of texts to discuss and explore* in general language classes. While in the analysis I have described certain miscues as 'text-provoked' this is not necessarily to condemn the text. Learners need to be helped to cope with the distinctive language of, for example, literary texts such as the one Nadeem was reading (Case Studies 2) and distinctive genres such as the fable. It may be, for instance, that learners like Balvinder could be helped to approach texts with more appropriate and helpful expectations.

(4) *How a particular learner is developing reading strategies* over time. Progress may appear to be very slow, and not show up on conventional tests. But a concern with quality rather than quantity of miscues can help us to see how effectively the learner is making use of a whole range of textual cues and acquiring a more appropriate view of the reading process at the same time. The second transcription of Sarla's reading, for instance, (cf. Case Studies 6) suggests development in terms of an unwillingness to tolerate nonsense miscues; appropriate use of stress and intonation to mark new and contrasting information; an awareness of strategies not employed before, such as back-tracking in the text, and generally greater willingness to engage with the teacher and the text.

(5) *Where an analysis includes a record of teacher intervention, we may have*

access to our own behaviour as teachers. We can then have some record of how far our prompts or recommended strategies actually resulted in success for the learner. Moreover, as Arnold (1982) points out, 'Until the teacher listens to herself she may not realize that she has become predominantly a prompter or a sound-it-outer or an over-zealous corrector.'

(6) Finally, *learners may wish to replay tapes of themselves* reading aloud. They too can then have access to their own strategies. We saw how Vijay monitored his own performance as the tape was played back to him.

In conclusion, reading aloud to the teacher involves a complex interaction of text, reader and teacher. Throughout this interaction, both learner and teacher need to keep in mind the purpose of reading in general, the purpose of reading the particular text and the purpose of the interaction between them. What should the learner expect to get out of the one-to-one reading situation? What kind of help does the teacher feel she can give? It is likely, I have suggested, to be not so much the teaching of particular skills as the highlighting of purpose and the encouragement of a wider range of reading strategies.

It is important also to discuss with learner-readers what they think works, getting them to reflect not just on the text but on their own reading strategies. The opportunity can be used, too, to talk about the way the English language works, particularly in writing, and to discuss kinds of texts and kinds of stories. Above all, the teacher's role is to promote a positive attitude to reading. In a sense, this means showing learners that reading is easier than they thought; they have more resources to draw on than they had perhaps realized—both from within the text and from their own existing knowledge of the world.

Clearly, if learners are to be positive about reading, they must feel positive about the situation of reading to the teacher. As Meek *et al.* (1983) say, 'in one-to-one situations, rather than learners feeling they are on trial—in yet another test—we can aim for a lesson which is relaxed, collaborative and reflective'.

At the same time, the teacher may need, with E2L learners, to make some assessment of the learner-reader's language resources—the structures and vocabulary he has mastered and the linguistic and cultural demands of the text. In the next chapter we shall look more closely at the nature of E2L learners' language and at some of the issues which are raised in the case of non-standard or non-native speakers learning to read in English.

5

The Language of the Learner and the Language of the Text

In Chapter 4 (also cf. the Case Studies) we looked at learning to read as an interaction between the reader and the text, with the teacher's role one of monitoring and facilitating the process in the earlier stages of learning. It could be observed that where learners are not yet fully competent users of English there appears to be some difficulty in anticipating certain structures in written texts.

In this chapter I shall examine more closely the relationship between reading and language, in particular when the learner is not a native speaker of the language of reading. I shall begin by discussing rather more fully than hitherto how native-speakers make use of various types of linguistic resources in coming to reading. I shall move on to consider the sorts of language resources that non-standard and non-native speakers may draw on, and the implications for listening to non-standard or non-native speakers' oral reading in English.

The Linguistic Resources of Native Speakers

In describing the resources which native speakers bring to learning to read, Goodman (1973) says: 'The learner of reading has a highly developed language, which is his greatest resource in learning to read.' In other words, the most important thing for learner-readers to realize is that what they already know of language, as users of language in their day-to-day lives, is the best launching pad into reading. Reading is not an alien code to be unlocked by special means.

That native speakers have certain kinds of intuitive knowledge about their own language is evident in a number of ways. When I asked 5-year-old Kate, a native speaker of English, the question: 'What can you say about the word "book"?' she replied first by slotting the word into a simple SVO sentence pattern: 'I read a book; I saw a book in the library.' The item of language most readily came to mind in a linguistic and 'real-world' context—books are 'read' and may be found in libraries. Pressed for more, she continued 'a book is hard and has pages and has print and has words on it'. And then, still playing round with the word, she said, 'I saw 200 books', showing her awareness that even with the form of the word 'book' changed to mark plurality, we are still dealing with the same item of language. Even though she had begun to learn to read what she did *not* say was that book is pronounced 'buh-u-kuh' or spelt B-O-O-K. These are probably the least likely responses, because they depend on the possession of specific skills, namely, of being able to sound out phonically or to spell, and do not reflect, as do features of syntax and meaning, what we intuitively know about our own language.

Native-speaking readers can look at words and larger chunks of text in all these ways:

(1) They can concern themselves with the **look** or **sound** of words, perhaps breaking them up into individual letters and sounds.

64

(2) They can focus on the **syntax**, looking at the structure of the words themselves, noting the parts of words that have a grammatical function, e.g. -ing to signal progressive aspect or -s to signal plurality. They can also note what kinds of item precede or follow the word, that is, where it fits into overall sentence structure.

(3) They can focus on the **meaning** that the word takes on in the context.

In Chapter 4 we saw how these three levels of language represented three levels of cuing system available to the learner reader, described by Goodman (1973) as graphophonic, syntactic and semantic. The learner-readers we looked at showed through their miscues which level of language they were most dependent on. We can use these same three levels to talk about the language on the page and the reader's linguistic resources. The three levels are, whether one is describing the written language of the text or the reader's spoken language:

substance: medium in which the message is encoded;

syntax: a grammar which constrains that certain parts of speech follow others, for instance that 'the' is likely to be followed by a noun;

meaning: a semantic content, carried largely by the content words (cf. Chapter 2, p. 24).

One might show how these three levels of language relate to both the reader's spoken language and the written language of the text thus:

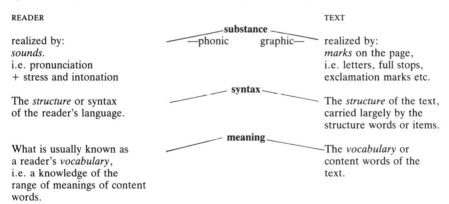

In other words, both readers and texts operate on three levels of language. Although the substance of written language is not a direct representation of sound in English, readers—in reading aloud—are necessarily translating the written language into spoken language. At the same time they are matching up the structures and vocabulary of their own language with those of the text.

With the heavy emphasis on phonics in reading instruction, learners' attention has been centred on language as substance and they have been encouraged to match up, or attempt to match up, letters or groups of letters and sounds. A far more powerful resource, and one already available to native-speaking children, with no knowledge of phonics, is the ability to match up structures and meanings, that is, to predict what sorts of structure follow others, and to match the content words of the text not necessarily with a sound realization but with an appropriate *meaning*. (We saw in Chapter 1 that the 3-year-old children in the American study could all read the word *MacDonalds*; in fact some of them read the word as *hamburgers*.)

Even very young children show early on that they know what kinds of structure and meaning can follow others, Wilkinson (1971) demonstrates this very plausibly. He quotes an extract from a recording of a conversation with a boy of 4½. He cannot read at all but is following the story the adult is reading to him. The extract begins thus: "Let's try this one"—

A little yellow bird flew high in the . . .   SKY.
Looking for a place to build . . .   A NEST.
Can I build my nest in your . . .   BASKET, and so on.

At each point the boy is drawing on his knowledge of the language and the world to complete the sense.

Here is my own example of an even younger child—this time a 2-year-old—predicting spontaneously, though admittedly with the help of pictures, as a story is read aloud to her:

Poppy piled them into her . . .   WHEELBARROW
and carried them . . .   AWAY
Next, Poppy filled her . . .   WATERING CAN
and watered the . . .   PLANTS

(Dick Bruna, *Poppy Pig*)

It should be noticed, however, that the child can predict not so much on the basis of what she typically says as on what she already knows about English. Comprehension precedes production in children's acquisition of language (cf. Clark and Clark, 1977). Children often seem able to understand more than they can actually say. In other words, their linguistic resources—what they know about English—exceed their everyday spoken language.

The Linguistic Resources of Non-standard and Non-native Speakers

On what sorts of linguistic resources do non-native speakers draw in learning to read in a second language? We need to consider firstly how they make use of what they know of English to predict the structure and vocabulary of written English; secondly, we might observe how they match up the written language of the text with their own spoken language when reading aloud.

First let us look at non-standard as opposed to non-native speakers, as it is sometimes suggested or implied that they, too, might have language related difficulties in learning to read.

Non-standard speakers

Teachers are sometimes heard to make the comment about young learners of 5 or 6, 'The problem is, they haven't got the language.' This is said of both native and non-native speakers. Indeed teachers will sometimes say that the non-indigenous children have 'more' or 'better' language than indigenous children. They tend to mean by this one of two things; either 'the children do not say very much in class', or 'the children speak non-standard English', saying for instance *aint* for *is not*, or *done it* for *did it*.

In the first instance, children may not be 'verbal' at school because they do not relate to what is going on in class. Labov (1969) quotes a famous study in which two supposedly 'non-verbal' black American children responded in fully structured and expressive language once engaged in talk with a sympathetic black adult, who was prepared to talk about what they wanted to talk about.

In the second instance, there are no grounds for claiming that non-standard English is 'bad' or 'wrong' English. The non-standard speaker of English uses items of structure and vocabulary which diverge from standard English and which are dependent on both regional and social class origin. Such speakers are sometimes said to speak with a **dialect**. We all speak with a dialect, however, including speakers of so-called standard English. Standard English is one dialect among others, no better or worse linguistically but, as the language of the media, the language used on most public occasions and the language of education, having greater social prestige. Because standard English is often the password to higher education and jobs, both native speakers and E2L learners are likely to want to acquire this variety of English. This does not mean, however, that non-standard speakers do not speak 'proper English'.

While the English writing system does not directly represent speech. it is nevertheless the case that the **grammar** of most varieties of written English is more closely related to standard English than to non-standard varieties of spoken English. How far might this create difficulties in reading for a speaker of non-standard dialect? For example, the text may give: 'He does not know what she is like', where a Cockney would say: 'He don't know what she is like', or a Glaswegian would say: 'He dinna ken what like she is.'

This kind of dialectal mismatch does not appear to be, in itself, a major problem where the standard forms are of high frequency in both speaking and writing. Non-standard speaking children soon become aware of available choices. They realize, for example, that 'He did it' is a variant for 'He done it', that 'know' is a variant of 'ken', and so on. Because comprehending and producing language are not symmetrical processes (Clark and Clark, 1977), people understand many words they never use themselves, and they also understand people who speak quite different dialects of their language. Eventually, non-standard speaking children may extend their language production, becoming bidialectal; that is, they may reserve their mother-tongue dialect for use with family and friends, adding the more standard, 'school' dialect to their linguistic repertoire, to be used on more public and formal occasions, much as bilingual children may specialize the uses of their languages.

While not all of us have distinctively different regional or class dialects reserved for different occasions, we all change the way we speak, depending on the situation; we adapt our **style**, depending on who we are talking to, about what, and on what occasion. This shifting of style may involve a change of either grammar, vocabulary, pronunciation or all three. So, for example, I might say 'Cuppa tea?' to a close friend but 'Would you like a cup of tea?' to a stranger on a formal occasion.

Children, in acquiring their mother-tongue dialect, whether standard or non-standard, learn to recognize and use not just the forms of their language but also different styles. They become aware that on any particular occasion one way of talking is more appropriate than another. Gradually, they build up a repertory of styles. Even very young children are aware that we talk to different people in different ways. Kate, at the age of three, was vastly amused by the adult (female) baby talk she had observed. Roaring with laughter, she repeatedly mimicked the exaggerated intonation of 'Hello Abigail' on one occasion. This was the characteristic grown-up greeting to the new baby sister of Kate's friend, quite different in style, as Kate had observed, from the greeting received by the older children. Most children are aware of the principle of stylistic alternates and are themselves flexible users of language, able to adjust what they say to the situation. Because of this awareness that we use language in different ways in different situations, to different people, children—whether typically standard or non-standard speakers—are ready to accept the written medium as a manifestation of language with its own distinctive features.

Learners of West Indian origin

There is evidence that some learners of West Indian origin under-achieve in reading (Edwards, 1979). This has led to discussion as to whether the language spoken by such learners disadvantages them in learning to read standard English.

Debate has centred on how far non-standard West Indian English, sometimes called Creole, differs in structure from standard British English. Some claim that Creole is so distinctively different that it is better seen as a separate language rather than a dialect of English, and that some West Indians may therefore have a foreign language problem in learning to read in standard English. Sutcliffe (1982) argues that the underlying grammar of Jamaican Creole, for instance, marks it out as fundamentally different from all non-Creole dialects of English and that this makes it arguably more of a foreign language than a dialect of English. However, as Edwards (1979) points out, the decision as to whether a variety should count as a dialect or as a language in its own right is largely a political rather than a linguistic matter. It has been noted, for instance (Trudgill, 1974), that the variety of language spoken by a German living close to the Dutch frontier may be linguistically closer to the variety spoken by the Dutch across the border than to certain other varieties of German. However, one variety is called German, the other Dutch, because the speakers of each identify themselves, respectively, as German or Dutch. In other words, in establishing what is a language in its own right or a variety of a particular language, one needs to consider how the speakers of the language perceive their own choice of language and with which group of users they identify.

Moreover, the language spoken by West Indians living in the West Indies is best seen perhaps as a continuum of varieties, at one end of which standard West Indian English is very close to standard British English, while at the other end we have a variety, or rather a number of varieties varying from island to island, which are barely intelligible to standard British English speakers. Some West Indians, moreover, will have French Creole as their mother-tongue, English Creole being acquired later—as for example in Dominica, where English becomes dominant once children go to school, and where English is the medium of instruction. Still others, especially if brought up in Britain, will speak standard or near standard British English as well, perhaps, as Creole.

The situation linguistically is, therefore, heterogeneous. What concerns us here is whether there is a mismatch between the language typically used by many learners of West Indian origin and the standard English of reading texts, great enough to cause specific difficulty. *Reading through Understanding*, a project developed at the Centre for Urban Educational Studies in London (1978), concluded that there was no such specific difficulty. The project team designed reading materials to help reading in urban, multi-ethnic schools with particular reference to West Indian children. In their discussion of dialect, the excellent teachers' introduction to one part of the materials, *Make-a-Story* (Wight *et al.*, 1978a) states:

> In preparing these materials we also carried out some investigations into dialect in the infant classroom. We wanted to know whether there were important dialect differences in the classroom English of black and white five-year-olds in order to examine the theory that such differences might interfere with the process of learning to read. We found fewer differences than anticipated. The majority (four-fifths) of the West Indian children displayed the same sort of grammatical usage as their white peers. And the speech of the remaining fifth was not dramatically different.

While the research of the *Reading through Understanding* project was not exhaustive and Edwards (1979) suggests that dialect-related difficulty may emerge at a later stage in learning to read, this need not surprise us too much. West Indians, like most language users, are multi-style speakers—indeed they are likely to have a greater repertory of styles than standard English speakers. If they are Creole speakers they will operate along a span of the Creole continuum; or as is the case with the majority of people of West Indian origin born in Britain, they may 'slide' along a language continuum, showing, in varying degrees, Creole features of structure and vocabulary in a largely native-speaking variety such as Cockney. Many young Afro-Caribbeans have adopted anglicized versions of Creole. One such has been termed by Rosen and Burgess (1980) 'London/Jamaican'. London/ Jamaican functions, for teenagers particularly, as a powerful peer-group dialect. The speakers of this dialect, however, generally code-slide (the term used by Rosen and Burgess) adeptly towards standard Cockney, as occasion demands. Indeed, because many young black Britons switch dialects or 'slide' so skilfully in response to the situation and the person addressed (cf. Hillyard, in this chapter) it has been suggested by Sutcliffe (1982) that they have a heightened awareness of their own use of language. This kind of awareness (namely that styles, dialects and languages change from situation to situation) should be an advantage in getting to grips with written language.

One must be cautious, therefore, in drawing conclusions as to a specific dialect- or language-related difficulty for learners of West Indian origin. Standard English texts may offer difficulty for a minority of learners for whom Creole is dominant. Rosen and Burgess (1980) noted only 1 per cent of such learners in their sample of London secondary school children. Other learners of West Indian origin are competent to predict standard English forms, even where their own typical usage differs. This is not to say that learners of West Indian origin are not disadvantaged but, as discussed later, disadvantage is likely to be due to factors other than language.

E2L learners

I have suggested that learners of West Indian origin may have extra linguistic resources to draw on when it comes to learning to read. This is also the case with E2L learners whose knowledge of one or more languages other than English allows them additional insights into the nature of language and languages.

If the learner is able to read in his first language, this should be seen as a further asset. It is true that different languages are represented by widely varying systems of writing. The reader of Chinese, for example, uses an ideographic writing system and moves from the top of the page to the bottom; the reader of Urdu or Arabic reads from right to left. However, the learner who is literate in his first language is advantaged through knowing what reading is. Even the notion that a word on the page is something surrounded by space can be hard to grasp for a total non-reader, for the very good reason that the concept is largely acquired through reading itself. As Buck points out (1979), there is considerable evidence to demonstrate that people learn to read only once, whatever the language of their first literacy, and learning to read a second language is an extension of that literacy. So, though specific reading strategies may vary from language to language, the basic process of deriving meaning from systematized graphic shapes seems to be the same process. One might indeed begin with such learners by encouraging them to read aloud in their mother-tongue, providing just a general gloss in English. With students who have even a little literacy in their first language I usually begin by asking them to write something about themselves in the first language.

In making any generalizations, however, we must guard against giving the E2L learner a single identity. The danger of seeing E2L learners as a homogeneous group has already been mentioned (Chapter 1, p. 5). Clearly E2L learner-readers come with many different kinds of resource, linguistic and other, depending on a whole range of factors such as social class, age, the circumstances in which the second language has been acquired and the degree of literacy in the mother-tongue. L2 learners represent a range of abilities and degrees of competence in English. As Wiles (1981) points out 'there will be considerable variation, ranging from very early stage second language learners to advanced bilinguals whose language development needs in English overlap with those of their English mother-tongue peers'. However, for our purposes here we might identify three broad groups of non-native speakers.

The first group consists of those who, though their first acquired language is not English, nevertheless have for a number of years functioned in nearly all the areas of their daily lives primarily in English, which has therefore become dominant. Their English may not be readily distinguishable from that of their native-speaker peers.

Then there are the true second language learners, who are still actively acquiring the second language, as Vijay was (Chapter 4). Their language, which has been called an 'interlanguage', is continually changing and approximating to the target language (the native-speaking variety of English most used in their environment). This interlanguage, because it is continually changing and developing, is hard to observe and record. Nonetheless, the interlanguages of L2 speakers have a system, even a grammar of their own (Corder, 1973). This means there is consistency in their language production almost from the beginning of second language acquisition.

Many features of a learner's interlanguage are idiosyncratic (Corder, 1981). One can, however, observe whole classes of language learners of different language backgrounds using the same features in their interlanguage. Thus in a small group of Asian teenagers (Indians and Pakistanis) who had been in England from 1 year to 18 months, and had different language backgrounds, I observed in general use: 'She's brother' (her brother), and teachers have also reported to me consistent and persisting features used by a whole community of linguistic minority children, otherwise indistinguishable from their native-speaking peers; e.g. 'It be's on the table', 'To do my brush' (brush my teeth)—both observed in a Southall school.

There is yet another group, represented by the person (usually an adult) who has lived in an English-speaking community for many years but has not reached a high level of proficiency in English or has a very limited stylistic repertory. While the language such speakers use may seem to the native speaker barely adequate for many purposes, and even occasionally unintelligible, the speaker has evidently not been motivated to extend his linguistic range. He has always somehow got by, possibly because he has largely lived and worked with other non-native speakers of English. The language system of such second language speakers is often characterized by considerable fluency of delivery, and simplification of structure as in the following example (Mr. M. is talking about arranging a marriage for his daughter):

CW.   You choose a boy?
M.   Yes, I choose . . . this . . . everything . . . I like . . . this you want choose you no come in my home again . . . you go—get out. I stand there. This one they say I want choose I choose. You want choose I no want you choose. You want choose you no come my home. Finish . . . I say I like I choose first one boy. You say I no like this one. All right. I see other one. First my daughter I go—I went India last years. I choose one boy. This one about . . . er 17, understand? I come here, I there arrange there this one for marry. I come here, take picture . . . everything. I say you like this one? You like? You no like, you say I no like. No good. See. This said that's all right. You everything do. I understand now . . . He's a like him nice boy and very good this one. In the college this one . . . in the college.

Mr. M. had lived in Britain for 8 years, and though he had recently begun to attend English classes for language and literacy, his language did not appear to be becoming more standard. It appeared to be fossilized (one term used to describe such language systems—which tend to show similar features whatever the speaker's L1 background—is 'fossilized interlanguage').

The Reader's Language: Sounds, Structure and Vocabulary

What the learners we have just been describing have in common is that their language system may show significant differences from that of their standard or near-standard speaking peers. What implications does this have for early reading instruction? How will these particular learners match the sounds, structure and vocabulary of their own language with the letters (and other graphic information), structure and vocabulary of the text?

Sounds

The first thing I do is give my students ear training exercises.

(Adult Literacy Organiser)

The sounds the reader makes—the way he pronounces individual sounds, and his stress, rhythm and intonation—are clearly only relevant to the reading process in reading aloud. Vocalizing is a necessary stage in the learning to read process, if only because the teacher is then able to use reader miscues to assess progress and, if necessary, offer the learner more productive strategies. Also, vocalizing can help to clarify sense groups in more complex texts, as Marland (1977) points out. One can observe, for instance, how even very experienced readers faced with a complex text such as certain kinds of Civil Service language, tend to subvocalize, 'mouthing' the text.

In reading aloud, the matter of the reader's **accent** may become an issue—the way the reader pronounces words; a Yorkshireman and a Londoner, for example are likely to pronounce the word *bath* differently. The most prestigious accent is Received Pronunciation, commonly known as RP, spoken in its 'pure' form by very few people, though certain BBC newsreaders come closest to it. Leaving aside the uncertainty as to how RP can best be described, does this accent, or some approximation to it, offer the learner-reader any advantage? Does accent—or pronunciation generally—matter in reading? The teacher quoted above clearly felt it did. She felt it was a problem in terms of their learning to read that her Cockney learners could neither pronounce nor apparently hear the difference between *four* and *foal*. A West Indian Creole speaker might similarly pronounce *rat* and *rot* the same—as homophones, that is. The second language learner, when reading aloud, may make no difference—to the ear of the average native speaker of English, at least—between *ship* or *sheep* or, if a Japanese learner for example, between *rest* and *lest*. Alternatively, the learner may have such an unusual pronunciation that the word he vocalizes bears no resemblance to a native-like pronunciation or—to the teacher's ear—to any other word in English.

Does it in fact matter that the learner treats *ship* and *sheep* as homophones? It is not just second language learners who have homophones; all accents of English, including RP, contain numerous homophones. Therefore, if one argues for correcting the learner who reads *foal* and *four* or *ship* and *sheep* as homophones, one has then to consider whether one would correct a southern English speaker for whom *where* and *wear* are pronounced the same. In other words, whether one has a high-prestige southern English accent or low-prestige Cockney accent makes no difference in terms of decoding the text. As there is no clear phoneme/grapheme correspondence in English, all learner-readers are equally disadvantaged, whatever their accent (cf. Trudgill, 1975). Since the teacher quoted above was concerned to 'correct' the Cockney learner, who read *foal* and *four* as homophones, would she therefore encourage certain upper-middle-class children to discriminate between *tar/tower/tyre*, which are homophones for some 'advanced' RP speakers?

It is inappropriate and confusing, in short, to correct the accent of learner-readers who are non-standard English speakers; and the principle is exactly the same with non-native speakers of English. If *rest* and *lest* are homophones for the second language learner at a certain stage in language learning, then our concern should be not to get him to discriminate because RP does, but to be sure that he has not made a meaning confusion. It may be argued that second language learners should be given a native speaking pronunciation variety as their goal. One might then wish to practise discriminating pairs of words such as *ship/sheep* based on distinctions made in RP. While there may be a place for this in general language teaching, though work on stress, rhythm and intonation is likely to be more important, it should not be part of the reading lesson, where priority should be given to building fluency and confidence.

Children and adults must be allowed to read in the accent of their interlanguage at the time. With some learners, this may have fossilized; with others, still in the earlier stages of acquiring the second language, it may be changing, and so harder to observe. However, the principle is the same for all native and non-native speakers; it is damaging and confusing to 'correct' a learner-reader's accent, whether Indian, Glaswegian or West Indian. The learner will anyway be unlikely to hear differences which he does not himself produce.

To conclude, then, there is on the face of it 'no reason why a person cannot learn to read standard English quite well in a non-standard pronunciation' (Labov, 1972).

Structure

Ray is reading quite well but we're trying to get him to sound the -ed on the ends of words.
(Literacy teacher)

Ray was an Afro-Caribbean learner in an adult literacy class who, reading in his West Indian dialect,[1] omitted the -ed in contexts such as *He painted his house*. The first thing to be said is that we all, standard English speakers included, do not 'sound the -ed on the ends of words' in fluent reading aloud, in such contexts as *I used the brush, I fixed the car*. There is a barely perceptible difference in fast reading aloud or speaking between *I fix the car every weekend* and *I fixed the car yesterday*. There was no evidence in Ray's reading that he had not understood the past time reference, for what is crucial in such cases is not whether a grammatical suffix is pronounced, but that the grammatical signalling, in this instance of past tense, is understood. Careful questioning about the meaning of the text can establish whether a reader has grasped the grammatical function of items like the -ed suffix. For just as sounding the -ed on verbs is in itself no evidence that past time is understood by the learner, so its absence in a reader's oral rendering of a text does not indicate necessary lack of understanding. One might in fact say 'Ray is reading well because he is not sounding the "-ed" on the ends of words.' In other words, he was reading fluently in the manner most natural to him which, in his case, meant a tendency to reduce not just the -ed in *fixed* but the -ed in *wanted*.

The learner may, in reading standard English texts, omit word endings as Ray did, or replace the structure words in the text with his own variant (e.g. *was/were; did/done*) or add structure items (cf. Hillyard **goin** for *go*, page 85). There may even be changes of word order with some Creole speakers. Whatever the case, miscues which reflect a non-standard speaker's own language system, whether they show reduction, replacement or expansion of the standard forms of the text, should not be corrected. An analogy might be made with younger learners who may miscue in similar ways, though for different reasons—to do with the rate of acquisition of certain areas of English grammar. Here is an example of a native-speaking 8-year-old reading *Goldilocks and the Three Bears*:

> Goldilocks woke up. When she saw the three bears she (*what do you think she . . . read ahead . . . she something up and escaped . . . means 'jumped'*) springed up and escaped.
>
> (Ladybird, *Goldilocks and The Three Bears*)

The child gets *spring* as a synonym of *jump* with my prompting, and incorporates it quite happily into the system of regular -ed past verbs.

An adult learner, Joyce, reacted as follows to the word *shone* in the text below:

J.   The hands . . .
CW. shone
J.   Shone—I don't know that word
CW. Shone, you know . . . something . . . er . . . shines bright
J.   (with recognition) oh yes . . . shiny . . . shine 'the hands shined up at him'

Joyce is not a native speaker of English, but as we note later (cf. page 80) had lived in an English-speaking community for many years. She did not appear to be extending her competence in English grammar. If we accept that Joyce is not a true second language learner (cf. page 70), it may not be appropriate to correct her English, either in or outside the context of reading aloud. It is a delicate and not readily resolvable situation, for Joyce wants her English to be more acceptable to native speakers (i.e. more standard); yet many language teachers will agree that it is notoriously difficult to change someone's language system significantly if it has served in day-to-day communication for many years, as is the case with both Joyce and Mr M. (page 71).

With learners still developing and changing their English so that it approximates to a desired target, i.e. with 'true' E2L learners, the situation is different. Nonetheless miscues attributable to the learner's interlanguage, like dialect miscues, should not be corrected during the reading lesson. In the case of Vijay (Chapter 4), Dorothy accepted his version of the text while he was reading. However, as his language teacher, she would note that he was still not using the simple past tense, for example, in the way his native-speaking peers were. This would be dealt with on another occasion, rather than interrupting the flow and pace of his reading.

Clearly, explicit teaching of the forms of what is currently accepted as standard English may be necessary for true E2L learners, and oral practice of the forms of English can of course be integrated with reading, as we illustrate in Chapter 6. However, language instruction should not take place while the learner is reading aloud, since it is likely to distract from the real purpose of reading. Teachers' comments on a learner's language rather than on his reading confuse and demoralize him when he is reading aloud. Non-standard speakers in particular will perceive such comments as criticism, not of their reading, but of the way they speak their native language.

Jim Wight, who led the *Reading Through Understanding* project, takes this point further, suggesting (1976) that children of West Indian origin may be disadvantaged if their dialect is rejected by teachers when they are learning to read. As he says, 'rejection of children's dialect when they are learning to read may well be critical, encouraging "barking at print" rather than understanding'. In fact, dialect or interlanguage miscues, far from being a cause for concern, may actually show a development in a reader's strategies. They tend to occur at times of greatest fluency and confidence, when the reader has moved beyond a faltering, word-for-word rendering of what is on the page. In other words, when he is beginning to read for meaning.

Vocabulary

Write down the words they don't know; then they can learn them at home and improve their reading age.

(Teacher to assistant in Adult Literacy class)

Teachers and learners, as we have discussed, tend to see reading difficulties as 'not knowing the words'. This usually refers to the content words, or the part of language intended by the term 'vocabulary' (meaning the nouns, verbs and adjectives). It is clearly true that difficulty may be created for the reader by the genuinely new words, that is, by words not previously met in any spoken or written context; and also that too many such words will cause reading breakdown, because there is not enough of the already known to help the reader make sense of what is new. Nonetheless, instructions such as the above raise several questions:

First of all, what is 'not knowing words?' If readers like Pauline (Chapter 4, p. 48) make semantic replacements of the kind: 'and he cut them up into little pieces' (bits), can we really say that 'bits' is not known to the reader? What has happened is that the reader, simply because she is looking ahead and reading with some fluency, has replaced the item in the text with what is to her a more predictable synonym. Such replacements, as we have seen, like many syntactic replacements, generally suggest a positive reader strategy. Ray could read *excited* but could not get *put* in the sentence: *He put through a call.* Are we going to say that he did not know the word *put*? In fact, it was not the words which created difficulty, but the way of expressing the meaning, which was odd to him.

We must also ask—What is 'learning words?' It is true that *Look and Say* approaches, for instance, seem to assume that we learn words first (for example through repeated viewing on flash cards) so that we can then 'read' them. This puts the cart before the horse: we learn new words best through reading. We do not learn new words in order to read (cf. Chapter 7 for some practical implications). In fact we cannot either 'know' or 'learn' words, only meanings. By this I mean that we have to consider, firstly, the range of meanings a single word may have (cf. Chapter 2, p. 24), and secondly, the context, which makes an item more or less predictable. As we can see in the Case Studies, Maqsood (Case Studies 3) had difficulty with the very simple and 'known' word, *beer*, while Ravinder (Case Study 4) registered instant recognition of the word *tube-well*, both because he knew what was referred to and because it occurred in a familiar setting. In fact, we all have a vocabulary to describe the things we care about or which are important features of our life-style or environment. However, for E2L learners certain words and their associated concepts may be more readily recalled in their mother-tongue.

An immediate task for us as teachers, therefore, is to tap our learners' sources of knowledge and experience, whether these are, for bilingual learners, most readily recalled in the first or second language. Admittedly, these sources are discoverable only through trial and error. I recall a passage about make-up which Hillyard read with great fluency and interest. On enquiry, it emerged that he 'usually put on a bit of make-up when he went out in the evening'. This at least should serve as a moral against a stereotyped choice of material based on sex!

To sum up the argument so far, our role as teachers is to be aware of what the learner brings to the reading task as a user of language; since, firstly, the learner's speech reflects—albeit imperfectly—his underlying competence in the language, which affects the ability to predict the structure and content of the text; and secondly, we need to know what are the typical sounds and structures of his speech, so that we can judge which miscues are errors associated with the reading process, and which are a reflection of the learner's interlanguage or dialect.

In other words, we should be familiar with a learner's **accent**, whether native-speaking or not, fossilized or changing. This can admittedly be difficult when phonological differences from those native-speaking accents known to us are such as to impede meaning. Our learner's stress, rhythm and intonation may also differ from standard English. With E2L learners there may be, for example, some transfer into English of patterns of stress and intonation typical of the first language. Once again, it is important to observe what are the learner's characteristic differences of stress and rhythm and intonation rather than to 'correct' them during reading aloud. Then we need to consider the learner's **syntax**; it may be that his use of tenses is characteristically different from standard English usage; finally, we should consider the learner-reader's **vocabulary** stock, for if we select the right kind of subject-matter, our learners will have a greater potential range of meanings to slot in at various points in the text.

A cassette recorder is therefore helpful, not just for analysing miscues, but for getting samples of the learner's language in free conversation. In taping and transcribing samples of speech, as well as reading miscues, we may be able to see some relationship between the learner-reader's typical spoken language and his reading miscues. Below are three case studies of non-native speakers of English learning to read in the second language.

Three Learners: Speaking and Reading

There is room here only for small samples of speech and reading, so any conclusions drawn about the relationship between learners' language and their reading strategies and miscues can only be tentative.

Manjit

Manjit is 12, comes from India and has been in Britain for 15 months. His first language is Punjabi. He attends a Middle School, following the ordinary Middle School curriculum in the morning. In the afternoon he attends a language class where, in a very small group, he is given extra help with his language and reading. I visited the school over a period of several months to help Manjit with his reading.

Manjit's language

Extract 1: *Pirates* [December 1980]

CW. Tell me, what you're going to do at Christmas, Manjit?
M.   Me. I'm going my sister on Gravesend, Miss.
CW. What are you going to do there?
M.   I like play in the sea Miss.
CW. In the sea? In the sea?
M.   In the river, Miss, by my sister house, Miss, big sister.
CW. How many brothers and sisters have you got?
M.   This one my cousin, my uncle sister, Miss, no . . . uncle girl uncle girl and I got a my one sister and two brother—me and I got two other brothers.

Now turning to the reading book, *The Storm*

M.   (pointing to picture) Black sky and black sea.
CW. Why is there a black sky and black sea?
M.   There coming lot rain or something wind.
CW. What do we call that when there's rain and wind and the sea's very rough?
M.   I don't know.
CW. A storm.
M.   A storm. Oh, yes, I know.
       (turning to another picture)
       Miss, he's no dead, Miss. There Green Pirate. Then coming there Blue Pirate.
CW. How can you tell it's the Blue Pirate?
M.   Miss there's blue ship. Miss, he lucky. He's no broke his ship Miss. Oh there he come.
CW. Who's that?
M.   This . . . er . . . blue pirate, Miss. Their ship not broken Miss it's good ship.
CW. Who's the good pirate?
M.   This one Miss. Blue Pirate.

Extract 2: *The Cake* [March 1981]

CW. What did you do on your birthday?
M.   I hid a party. Miss Brice gave me cake—birthday cake. We make here birthday cake—chocolate. One I take home and one we eat here.
CW. How did you make the cake?
M.   This day I was hurt. Somebody hit me in the head bad and I no see this all how to make—I don't see this cake how to all make it. Miss make it because I'm hurt here in the head, somebody hit me in the . . .
CW. So you didn't help to make the cake?
M.   Only little, we bring flour, then cocoa then get two egg, mex together, put in the flour and the cocoa and mex them all little bit like that mex; then we put in the gas.

Points to note:

Sounds

Manjit shows an idiosyncratic use of certain vowel sounds in his interlanguage, transcribed here according to standard spelling, e.g. 'I hid (had) a party' and 'mex (mix) them all'. The vowels are carefully, even deliberately sounded, as though he is over-correcting following 'special teaching' of the vowel sounds.

Vocabulary

In Extract 1, Manjit initially refers to his cousin as his sister, possibly a reflection of the different kinship terms in his own language and culture.

Structure

—Simple past tense is variably represented either by the standard English form, e.g. 'Miss Brice gave me cake' or by the simple present as in 'One I take home and one we eat here'.

—The negative past tense is also variable, e.g. 'I no see': is corrected to 'I don't see' (I didn't see).

—There is a tendency to omit structure words, such as definite and indefinite articles, e.g. 'Miss it's good ship'.

—Manjit's use of prepositions tends to differ from standard English use; they are either omitted, e.g. 'I'm going my sister' or replaced 'On Gravesend' and 'In the head'.

—There is some apparent difficulty with English word order, e.g. 'I don't see this cake how to all make it.'

—The verb 'to be' is also occasionally omitted in, for example, 'he lucky' and 'Their ship not broken'.

—Possessive 's' is omitted as in 'my sister house' and 'uncle girl'.

It will be observed from the evidence presented here that a number of Manjit's language structures are variable. In the case of negative forms, for instance, Manjit seems to be in the process of working out a rule. This suggests that, as one might expect of a learner in Manjit's circumstances, his English is continually developing and changing. For this reason any generalizations we make must be tentative.

Manjit's reading

Notes:

—As with the case studies, miscues are printed in bold type.

—Learner comments or responses about the text are italicized.

—Where a word is given by the teacher it is capitalized.

The text being read is from 'Gregory the Green', in the *Griffin Pirate Stories* by S. K. McCullough; (this first brief extract is from an earlier *Pirates* book).

Manjit	CW
T. He didn't see the red sky	
M. He didn't see the red sky	
T. he saw only gold	
M. he saw only gold	Tell me about the pirate, then.
M. *He not see the red sky, he see only gold.*	
T. I will see whether I can find	
M. I will see . . . I will see	WHETHER
I **can to** find	
T. the Island of Emeralds, said Greg	
M. the Island of Emeralds, said **Gregory**	
T. So he sailed on and on over the sea.	
M. So **the** sailed on **the . . . on away**	No, read again.
So he sailed on **the** on and on over the sea	
T. He sailed on, till one day he came	
M. He sailed on **T–I double L**–*tall?*	TILL
one day he came	
T. to the Island of Emeralds	

Manjit	CW
M. to the Island of Emeralds . . .	
T. Greg went on to the Island	
M. Gregory went on the—**his** island	
T. to **dig** for emeralds	
M. to **big** for *art*	To dig for what?
(art—M's pronunciation of 'earth')	Ah no, not to dig for earth—to dig for emeralds.
T. and he dug a hole and	
M. and he **dig** a hole and	
T. the hole fell in on top of him	
M. the hole **fall** on top of him	So what did he do?
All stone coming on the head, Miss.	Yes, so what did he do though?
He sit, miss.	Yes, but he?
He's looking down.	No, he dug a hole, didn't he?
T. Just in the same way	
M. **Jig** in the **small away**	JUST—SAME
T. as on the Island of Rubies	
M. as the—on the island of **Emeralds**–Rubies . . .	
T. and went to look for	
M. and went to look for	
T. the Island of Sapphires	
M. the Island of Sapphires	
T. I will see whether	
M. I will see . . .	WHETHER
T. I can find sapphires, he said	
M. I can find sapphires, he said	
T. He sailed away on the sea	
M. He sailed away on the sea	
T. He came to the Island of Sapphires	
M. He came to the Island of Sapphires	
T. and he dug a hole in just the same way	
M. and he **dig** a hole in . . . the **away** same **away**	JUST
T. and in just the same way the hole fell in on him	
M. and in just the same **away** and **all fall** in on him	
T. 'It is very hard', said Greg	
M. It is very hard, said Gregory	
What's a matter here? He dead.	
(M. is looking at the picture)	
T. in just the same way	
M. in just the same **away**	
T. he got earth on his face	
M. he got eart' on his **head**	FACE
T. and earth in his ears	
M. and eart' in his **cars**	
(M. can see I am not happy here—he hesitates then attempts to spell out)	
E–A–R–S—**cars?**	You can't say 'earth in his cars.'
—ears.	
T. and a rock fell on his head, too!	
M. and a rock **fall** on the head . . .	
T. He wanted his gold	
M. He **went** his gold	Read that again.
M. He **went** his gold	So what did he want?
He want gold, but no gold on the island, Miss.	
T. I will see whether I can find	
M. I will see *Miss, what's this?*	WHETHER
whether I can find	
T. My gold, he said	
M. My gold, he said	
T. But Greg was not very good	
M. But Gregory was not very good	
T. at finding the way	

Manjit   C.W.

M. at finding the **away**
T. He sailed about but he didn't
M. I—he sailed about but he didn't
T. —find the way back to the island
M. find a way **black** *no* back to the island
T. And as he sailed, he sang
M. And **is** he sailed he sang
T. This is what the green pirate sang:
M. **His**—this is . . . the green pirate sang   WHAT
T. Just the same, it's hard,
M. Just the same it **hear**   IT'S HARD
T. I find it very hard
M. I find it very **head**   HARD
                                                         What does it mean if you find something hard?

   Hes no find easy, Miss.

Points to note

—Manjit's miscues are mainly graphophonic. He shows little reliance on cues of structure or meaning.
—Structure words which have low frequency in spoken English and which Manjit himself would not use cause difficulty, like the often-repeated *whether* in this text, and *till*, both introducing subordination.
—Nevertheless he is able to predict items of structure which tend to be omitted in his own speech. He has no difficulty with prepositions and articles.
—Though Manjit mostly follows the text, he does occasionally read in his own interlanguage, e.g. 'And he dig a hole and the hole fall on top of him.'
—Occasionally, although he reads the standard version of the text, he switches into his own interlanguage when asked to comment, e.g. following the first extract: 'He not see the red sky. He see only gold.'
—Phonological confusion occurs once, when I do not realise that Manjit is giving his variant of 'earth' which sounds something like 'art'. 'Earth' is an acceptable miscue, in that Manjit is using semantic cues here and associating dig/earth, though he reveals a lack of native-speaker competence in using structure to refine this prediction—we do not dig *for* earth.
—Manjit's idiosyncratic use of vowel sounds also appears to be illustrated here. In his careful 'reading aloud' style he occasionally changes the vowel sound, e.g. 'he went his gold'. However, when asked to comment on what he has read, he says 'he want gold'.

Joyce

Joyce is from Thailand and in her 40s. She is married to a Scotsman and she and her husband usually speak English together. Joyce approached her local literacy scheme a few years ago because, though literate in her mother-tongue, she had not any literacy skills in English.

anguage

wo extracts Joyce is talking to her literacy tutor, Barbara.

Extract 1: *Two Women*

> You know women very difficult t' get 'nother man quickly, you know, man . . . get 'nother one er . . . (easily) yes . . . (Joyce is now talking about an acquaintance, C.M.) very difficult, very funny people, he manager South Africa . . . he name C.M. He marriage long time ago, 22 years marriage. He got two son. Secretary for . . . he like too much, much too much, going out to party. . . . I say that manager C.M. he going party I not going. I say my goodness me, I never see a man like that. Later on, you know, he divorce 'e wife—wife no want 'e divorce. So then he say he no divorce he run away. He lost everything, he lost job, company fired he (fired him?) yes fired him. She got two son. He marriage that one—not her marriage, because a divorce man no can marriage again in the church. So that secretary and he going to . . . what is it called . . . er . . . they going to er . . . Spain. So they got no job, nothing. That secretary got one son, baby son born. Secretary she left her husband. She going back mother father. So he got no job, no wife (so he lost the other woman too!)

Extract 2: *Christmas presents*

> I always use that one . . . somebody say oh no we no use that . . . what I do I don' know. My sister-in-law very difficult. She er . . . birthday 24th December . . . she's . . . Se'tember er this year Se'tember she have 30 years anniversary. I no pay present so I got to pay three present now. My husband very easy. He don' worry too much.

Points to note

Sounds

What the transcript cannot show is that Joyce speaks very rapidly, which with considerable phonological interference from her own language makes her barely intelligible at times. Though not consistently represented here final and some medial consonants tend to be omitted or replaced by a glottal stop, e.g.

[Sou hi go? nou dʒo? nou wai?] So he got no job no wife.

Structure

—There is a general reduction or loss of structure, e.g. 'You know women very difficult t' get 'nother man quickly' (You know it's very difficult for women to get another man quickly).

—The verb 'to be' is systematically omitted as in 'he manager South Africa' (he was a manager in South Africa) and 'My sister-in-law very difficult' (my sister-in-law is very difficult).

—Joyce simplifies her pronoun system so that, he/his/him are all replaced by 'he', e.g. 'He name C.M.' (his name was C.M.), 'Company fired he' (the Company fired him).

—Past tense tends to be replaced by either simple present tense or present continuous, at least as represented by the verb 'go' in extract one: 'They going to Spain' (they went to Spain). However, other irregular past tenses are used as they would be in standard English, e.g. 'She left her husband'.

—Subordination is simplified and not usually indicated by connectors such as *if*, e.g. (1) 'he going party I not going' (if he goes to the party I won't go) and (2) 'he no divorce he run away' (if he didn't get a divorce he would run away). Examples (1) and (2) above also show that concepts such as condition are not marked by *will/would* forms.

—*Do* auxiliary in negative and interrogatives is often omitted, e.g. 'wife no want 'e divorce' (The wife didn't want a divorce). (Though Joyce sometimes uses the 'do' form in the present tense as in, 'I don' know' and 'He don' worry too much.')

Although there is some variation in Joyce's personal grammar, there is on the whole a striking consistency, more so than in the case of Manjit, for instance, who is still in the process of moving towards a standard English target. Joyce's speech suggests that her language has fossilized.

Joyce's reading

Extract 1 (May 1980)

Joyce	Barbara
T. The children were so happy that they	
J. The children **was** so happy that they **must** *no* **but** *no*	P–U–T
T. put the top on the blue bottle and turned it	
j. put the top on the bottle no blue bottle and **top** *no* **turn it**	
T. when they heard	
J. **Wish**—*no* (hesitates . . . when they **have** . . . **H-E he-hear** they **hear**	WHEN
T. the little bell	
J. the little **bot**—little e **bottle** bell	What did they hear? bells, good
T. they wished for their baby back	
J. they **wish** for their baby back . . . again	Another word here?
T. Suddenly he was in the pram	
J. Suddenly he was in the p'am	

(Sparks Bookshelf, *The Wishing Bottle*)

Extract 2 (November 1980)

Joyce	Barbara
T. Just like he's dead Rita thought	
J. Just like he's dead Rita thought	
T. She put out her hand again	
J. She put out **their**—*no* her hand again	
T. and he moved . . .	
J. and he **move**	
T. But he did not want to wake	
J. . . . he did not want to wake (he don' wan'to wake)	BUT
T. She began to listen once more	
J. She began to listen . . . once more (one more, listen one more)	ONCE
T. An aeroplane came out of the dark	
J. An . . . aeroplane came out of the . . . dark	AEROPLANE–DARK
T. and went over the house	
J. and wen' over the house	
T. When it had gone	
J. When it **home-hand** . . . -had **gain** (here again?)	HAD

An aeroplane came out of the dark and went over the house, when it had—

:ard the church clock strike one-two
:ard the church clock sti'ke one-two

(Kathleen Wood, *All the Long Night*)

Points to note

It might be objected that Joyce is getting through the texts only at frustration level and that the material is too difficult. However, the extracts have been selected because the second one shows, I suggest, an advance in strategy over the first.

—Joyce neglects cues of structure and meaning. Her miscues are largely graphophonic, for example 'When it home—hand.'
—Joyce is able to predict items which tend to be omitted in her own speech, such as the verb 'to be'. However, the prompts offered by Barabara tend to be structure words, e.g. WHEN, ONCE, HAD, reflecting some difficulty with these items, as in the case of Manjit.
—She occasionally replaces the item in the text with her own variant, e.g. 'The children was so happy' and 'when they hear (heard)' and there is omission of -ed in 'they wish for their baby back'.
—Consonant clusters cause difficulties for Joyce. This must be taken into account as she decodes the text (and should obviously not be corrected) e.g. 'p'am'; 'st'ike'; 'wan'.
—Joyce finds it hard to predict the past perfect form introduced with subordination in the second extract: 'When it had gone she heard the church clock strike. . . . This would never occur in her own speech, though when Barbara back-tracks for her she is able to predict 'gone' following on from 'had'.
—The development in strategy observable in the second extract is that Joyce is now reading the text more or less in standard but quickly echoing what she has read in her own language system, e.g. 'he–did–not–wan'–to–wake' (he don' wan' to wake). This is Joyce's way of matching up the text with her own language and shows that she is beginning to read for meaning.

Hillyard

Hillyard approached a local literacy scheme asking for one-to-one teaching in his own home. He had come to Britain from Dominica as a young man and had at the time lived in England for 16 years. His mother-tongue was a variety of French Creole, but English had been the medium of instruction at school. He had apparently not attended school regularly and he could read little when lessons were started. I taught Hillyard once a week for about 18 months.

Hillyard's language

Below are several extracts from conversations between Hillyard and myself.

(1) Studying

CW. Did you look at the book at all?
H.   I does take it at work
CW. What?
H.   I does bring it at work with me. When I got the time so I does study . . .

(2) Shopping

CW. Which shop do you go to?

H. Well, Cheach, I haven't got a special shop. I'm goin' all shop you know. Sometimes what I want this shop haven't got it, I have to go . . . I'm goin' Indian shop . . . well, as you know, or as you should know, Southall have got no English shop, only Indian shop . . .

CW. Which shop do you go to?

H. All of them sometime goin . . . according to the thing I want I'm goin' *Safeway*. Accordin' to the thing I want I'm goin' *Tesco*. Accordin' to the thing I want I'm goin'—where's that other one—*Fine Fare*. Today I want a carpet shampoo so I . . . (?) there and get it . . .

(3) Indians in the local Southall community

H. Mark you, I got them for friend, you know, Indian people some of them you know.

CW. What—sorry?

H. I got some Indian for friend.

CW. Where did you meet them—at work?

H. Work.

CW. So some of them you get on all right with . . .

H. Not much . . . just to keep the time goin' you know.

CW. They're different—people from India.

H. Their culture—I can understand their culture at all. Their culture much different than other people . . .

CW. What about English people?

H. English people and West Indian same culture, en' it?

CW. . . . surely there are some things that are different in England from Dominica?

H. . . . because same culture . . . same rule . . . same rule, no different. Food the same, same language, the same dress. English like dance, West Indian like dance, but Indian no like that . . . just goin' in the pub, drink and come back home. Indian no like English picture, only their own picture they like. That's what they like. But English picture and West Indian no difference . . . we can understand Indian language and it's far for us to go to picture. We have to go out from Southall—West Ealing or in the West End of London. . . . But with Indian now they goin' their picture. Indian no dance. No eat food like we . . .

CW. But you've been into Indian houses.

H. Cheach, I've been already when . . . you find they makin' a cup of tea for you. You have to put the tea and the milk together to boil. I find that is fun—it is fun. So when I tell them that's not the way to makin' tea they tellin' me that we and English people we don't know how to make tea!

Points to note

For Hillyard this was the closest his speech came to standard. He clearly adjusted his speech so that it converged towards my own. That this was the case was clear from exchanges with his two young nephews, which though still in a variety of English were not easily comprehensible to me. Then, when older friends from Dominica dropped by, they would occasionally switch completely to a French Creole variety. Hillyard was, therefore, a highly skilled user of language, employing considerable versatility in adapting his language style to the situation.

Vocabulary

'Cheach' is Hillyard's term of address for me = teacher.

uses the Creole negative modal (= cannot) which sounds like the English 'can' but in fact is lengthened (in Jamaican Creole, for instance, ɑn = can/cannot, B.E.). (However, I am told that the distinction the Jamaican Creole pair is just as pronounced as that between spoken 'can' and 'can't'. It may be the case that in Dominica the difference between the affirmative and negative is less pronounced.)

—There is omission of the copula (verb 'to be'), again a classic feature of English-based Creoles, e.g. 'their culture much different', but later 'I find that is fun, it is fun.'

—Habitual action is signalled by progressive forms, e.g. 'I'm goin all shop'. Hillyard also uses 'does' before simple present forms of the verb to signal habitual behaviour ('does' + verb stem shows repeated or customary action in many English-based Caribbean Creoles).

—Though we have only two examples here, past tense is signalled by the base form of the verb: e.g. 'Today I want a carpet shampoo . . . and get it.'

—'No' functions as a marker of negation, for example 'Indian no like that' but the negative with do auxiliary also features in Hillyard's system, e.g. 'we don't know how to'.

—He omits the verb 'have' in some contexts, e.g. 'When I got the time' . . . 'I got them for friend' but not in negatives, e.g. 'I haven't got a special shop'. Also note: 'Southall have got no English shop' (possibly emphatic?)

While one might describe both Joyce's and Manjit's English as in some ways structurally reduced, Hillyard's language is at times stylistically quite elaborate, for example in the repeated 'according to the thing I want . . .' [extract (2) shopping]. He appears to reserve certain forms for emphasis, e.g. 'I find that is fun—it is fun' where the verb 'to be', elsewhere omitted, is given.

Hillyard's reading

Extract 1

Hillyard   **CW**

T. Not many women go out alone in cars at night
H. No many **woman goin'** out **along**-alone in cars at night
T. 'Was it a big car?' He was writing Alex's answer in a book
H. 'Was it a big car?' He **were tryin'**—writing **Alex** answer in a book
T. Roy lived in his father's house. His brother, Oliver was
H. Roy **have**—*no*—**livin'** in his **father** house. His brother Oliver were
T. a mechanic at Lawson's Garage. Roy's father William was
H. a mechanic at **Lawson** Garage. **Roy** father William **were**
T. a painter. He painted houses and sometimes he painted
H. a painter. He **paint** house and **sometime** he **paint**
T. the outside walls
H. the other—outside walls

Extract 2

T. Some of the owners were very cruel. If they thought
H. Some of the owner were very—very cruel. If they—
T. that their
H. if they **does** if they **don'** . . . T H O U-G-H-T—thought that **they**—their
T. slaves were not working hard enough
H. **slave** were not workin' hard (hesitates)

If they thought that their slaves were not workin' hard enough
T. they beat them with big whips. In all the
H. they beat them with big **hips**—big **whip**. In all the

Start again from the
beginning of the senten

Hillyard   CW

T. West Indies
H. West Indies
T. islands whether British or French and also in
H. Islands (hesitates) British or French and also   WHETHER
T. America there were
H. in America there were
T. quite a lot of cruel slave-owners
H. quite a lot . . . a lot of C-R-U—cruel slave-**owner**   So who were cruel?
     The owner of the slave.
T. Sometimes a slave was beaten so terribly that he
H. Sometime a slave **were** beaten so **terrible** that he
T. died
H. **decide** . . . that he **did**—he **die**   So why did he die?
     Because of beatin'
T. Even women-slaves were whipped very harshly
H. **Never**–even **woman-slave** were **whippin'** very . . .   HARSHLY
T. Toussaint's owner was not a cruel man.
H. **Toussaint** owner **were** not a cruel man.
T. He treated his slaves well
H. He **treat** his **slave** well
T. They did not like being slaves but, since
H. They did not like being slaves but **some**—but since
T. they could not get away
H. they could not get away
T. from their slavery, they preferred to belong
H. from their **slaves**—slavery, **they . . . they prefer . . .** they **prefer** to
     belong
T. to a kind owner
H. to a **king**—kind owner
T. Sometimes slaves ran away from the cruel
H. Sometime **slave run** away from the cruel
T. owners and hid
H. **owner** and **had**   HID
T. in the wild forests, and then they often
H. in the wild **forest**, and **they** and they often
T. died of hunger or disease
H. **dead** of hunger or **decided.**   What else can you die of?
                                                                    hunger or . . .? Dis- . . .
     disaster   No, that's a good guess,
                                                                    it's another word for
                                                                    illness.
     Oh, disease!

(J. D. Bentley, *Toussaint L'Ouverture of the West Indies*)

Points to note

—Hillyard is generally using positive strategies in his reading. Like Manjit he
⸺⸺ a number of graphophonic miscues but these are invariably corrected
        ately, e.g. hips–whips; king–kind.
          vare that reading must be meaningful. 'Disaster' to collocate with
          a good guess. Eventually he uses the offered clue of a synonym to
        tly.
            names as a decoding device, with a high degree of success, for
            ⸺-U-G-H-T—thought'.
              lle quite complex structure not shown in his usual speech. He is
                 lict 'enough' for example without hesitation on a second
                advice to back-track).

—He frequently back-tracks spontaneously, if only over a few words, e.g. they prefer . . . they prefer.

—When reading most fluently he substitutes his own dialect for the text with consequent omission of certain word endings, replacements or additions, cf. Extract 1, T: Not many women go; H: Not many woman goin', and the consistent replacement of what sounds like a shortened form of 'were' for was, e.g. His brother Oliver were a mechanic and 'sometime a slave were beaten so terrible.' Where he predicts 'If they does' this is, I suggest a reflection of his own speech in which 'does' may follow any personal pronoun.

Matching the Learner's Language with the Language of the Text

It would seem from the cases mentioned here that the difficulty for non-native-speaking learners reading in English is not that they cannot predict structures largely absent from their own speech. It is true that some learners, such as Peter, who was mentioned in Chapter 2, in the very early stages of reading (where one word is being taken at a time) seem to find it hard to predict items of structure which do not occur at all in their own speech. However, it is also true that all readers have to cope with language which is remote from their own spoken production. It seems to be the degree of difference which is crucial. Complex structure, especially syntax exclusive to very formal styles of writing and therefore relatively unfamiliar, causes difficulties even for skilled readers, the more so when complexity is compounded by ambiguity, unclearness of reference and unexpected word order.

However, the experienced reader, through the mere fact of being exposed to a wide range of written styles, gains greater dexterity in handling complex structure. Gardner (1978) suggests that when Bernstein talks of 'elaborated code', he is describing the 'kind of spoken language which has acquired some of the characteristics of written language'. Experienced readers, familiar with syntactic and stylistic features of the written medium, will tend to incorporate these 'elaborated' features into their own speech, especially in formal situations. This extension to their stylistic repertory in turn enables them to cope better with complex structure, remote from normal spoken English, in a range of reading texts.

Learner-readers tend to have difficulties with texts whose language is particularly remote from what they usually either speak or hear. There are certain items of language of low occurrence in spoken English and non-occurring in many E2L learners' speech which appear to cause particular difficulty. As we have seen, it is not words as such that present difficulty in reading, but the context in which they occur. This applies to both content and structure items. Joyce, for example, has no difficulty with reading 'would' in 'Would you like a cup of tea' even though she herself does not use this form of invitation. 'Would' in the text below, however, created great difficulty:

(Rita is waiting for her teenage son to come home)
The car was coming near

Soon it would stop
She would hear Brian's step on the path
She would hear his key in the lock
Then she would hear him on the stairs
But the car did not stop

(Kathleen Wood, *All the Long Night*)

The final sentence perplexed Joyce. She thought the car *had* stopped, that Brian *was* home. Clearly, this is not to suggest that Joyce cannot understand or express hypothesis in English; merely that in this particular context, this passage, because embedded in straight factual narrative, created difficulty.

Items which indicate hypothesis or introduce certain kinds of subordination, difficult for all learner-readers, are likely to present particular difficulty for E2L readers, at least in the fairly early stages of learning.

However, while complex structure rare in spoken English is best avoided by writers of early reading material, most E2L learners do very soon become able to 'fill out' structure as they become used to the well-formed sentences found in the written medium. They also show an awareness of alternates, for example:

Manjit (reading): He didn't see the red sky.
Manjit (asked to comment on text): He not see the red sky.

Moreover, learners can be observed to match up the text with their own language by echoing what they have just read, converting it into their own system as they do so. This signals reading for meaning and for Joyce (cf. Reading Extract 2) represented I believe an advance in her reading strategies.

A further advance is signalled when the reader converts the text directly into his own dialect or interlanguage—at least in fluent and rapid reading. This shows that the reader is reading directly for meaning rather than word for word decoding. Dialect or interlanguage miscues should therefore never be corrected.

In conclusion, our aim should be in the first instance to observe the salient features of the dialect or interlanguage of non-standard and non-native speakers respectively. At the same time we can encourage E2L learners to make maximum use of their existing competence in English, matching up their own language with that of the written text. The growing gain in reading fluency will in itself reinforce and extend the reader's language competence, in terms of both awareness of possible sentence patterns and a widened vocabulary. An extended competence in turn
?s a firmer foundation for the reader to move on to more complex texts. In
language and reading proficiency develop side by side.
ext chapter I shall consider some ways in which we might simultaneously
?lop the language competence of E2L learners and guide them into a
'anding of the language of written texts.

purposes of this discussion that most Afro-Caribbean learners in Britain can be
kers of English, some of whom will speak a non-standard dialect of English,
'aswegians might.

6

Developing Early Literacy

In this chapter I shall consider the practical implications of our discussion so far for an approach to the development of early literacy in classrooms which include both E2L and indigenous learners. We saw in previous chapters that the L2 reader does not, on the whole, use different strategies in early reading from those used by native-speaking learner-readers. However, from the evidence suggested by learners like Manjit and Nadeem (Case Studies 2) there appears to be a greater tendency to miscue graphophonically and to tolerate substitutions which do not maintain meaning in the text. Not surprisingly, second language learners seem not to use the structures and meaning of texts to predict as effectively as do their native-speaking peers. This perhaps gives us the clue to the best kind of preparation for early reading. We need to show our learners that what they know about language in general, and about English in particular, can support them in their L2 reading. We need to look for an approach which relates literacy to language.

Relating literacy to language has four main implications in terms of a methodology for teaching reading. Firstly, it implies a need to help learner-readers see that the written medium, like any language medium, whether morse code, semaphore or speech, aims above all to communicate. Any approach to classroom reading must be informed by the need to show learners from the beginning that whole texts and part of texts have a communicative function.

At the same time learners need to be aware of what letters and words are, as well as what they do. They need, that is, to develop certain literacy-related concepts.

Seeing reading as language also means developing an understanding of the relationship between the so-called four language skills—speaking, listening, reading and writing. Which skills lend support to each other, and in what ways might we integrate work on language skills in the classroom?

Finally, ways must be found of helping learners to be aware of certain characteristics of written texts, both of their whole organization and of their salient features.

We shall begin with a consideration of several well-established methods of teaching reading, with a view to considering how far they meet our first criterion, namely, that learners should be helped to an understanding both of what written language is and of what it does.

Which Method?

The place of phonics

How far is the early second language reader helped by phonic instruction second language? Where a learner is acquiring a different script along English-language, it is widely believed that he needs to be able to give a sound the letters of the new alphabet, especially when those sounds do first language. Hence, in the teaching of Russian or Arabic, for speaking learners are commonly taught a phonic realization for each letter. The aim is that learners should then be able to break new words down into sound elements. It is true that in the case of 'phonetic' or largely 'phonetic' languages it is possible to give a fairly convincing oral rendering, once the individual sounds are known. Reading aloud—decoding the text—become possible. The difficulties are, however, that it becomes possible to read, in the sense of decoding, without understanding what is read. It may be argued at this point that when learners have to tackle a different script, this first stage—the breaking down of words into constituent sounds—is necessary. But this leads to a second, more serious, objection: the systematic learning of individual sounds, along with the need to build them up, as a second stage, into simple, phonetically regular words, can be so time-consuming that many learners never get to the stage of reading even the simplest authentic texts (texts not specially written for foreigners) in the second language. If they do, they are likely to continue to function at a stage where words are laboriously broken down into sounds and no fluency is developed. They are stuck at the decoding stage, with no strategy to explore the text for the other kinds of syntax and meaning clues we have been describing.

When it comes to English script, a phonics approach is even harder to defend; firstly, because as discussed earlier (Chapter 2) English is not wholly 'phonetic' and many of the most frequent items—the structure words, such as *were, the* and *here*—are not phonically decodable. Learners encouraged to think that English is phonetic, quickly become confused and frustrated. Also, although phonics works some of the time, learners do not know when it will work and when not. Far from being rigorous, as is sometimes claimed, phonics is a hit-and-miss affair for learner-readers, who are not in a position to know with which new words a sounding-out approach will work. And as we see in the case of Sarla's difficulty with 'Hitler' and 'dunno' (Case Studies 6), if the word or reference is not known at all to the learner, even phonetically regular words may not be successfully decoded.

Because it is felt, for the above reasons, that learners will indeed be confused as soon as real texts are introduced, phonic approaches to introducing reading in English as a second or foreign language tend to involve selecting bizarre vocabulary, with very low frequency in most spoken or written contexts, as the first words met in print, merely because they are phonetically regular. An example, ken from a beginners book for Arab Learners of English, is the word *fob*, oduced in Lesson 7 of Book 1, (*New Living English for Jordan*, 1974). It is hard agine a likely, sensible context for this word.

ady literate second language learners of English will tend anyway to apply principles in reading English if their first language script is phonetic. They ry adequate facility to decode, either having been specifically taught or acced phonic principles in their first language literacy. These principles diffe aid them on occasion in the reading of English, as we see with izations se Studies 5). On the whole, however, what helps learners A furthe onetic scripts is not more phonics but an awareness that English is usually based ed to be familiarized with the other, more powerful general- ature of the English writing system, discussed in Chapter 2. ry relevant to L2 readers, is that the teaching of phonics is distinctions made in Received Pronunciation (RP), and a serious objection to phonic approaches or material—for non-native or non-standard speakers of English—is that their own pronunciation may at times diverge quite markedly from RP. For instance, at the time Vijay was reading to Dorothy, his pronunciation of *she* was on some occasions the same as *see*. In terms of his reading, this was in no sense a problem; he had a meaning for 'she'. As a very early language learner he was likely to acquire the sh/s distinction in due course—indeed there was evidence that he was already beginning to do so. In the meantime any phonics work on the difference between *ship* and *sip*, for example, was likely only to be confusing.

This is even more true in the case of the vowel sounds, which are less distinctive, both visually and phonetically, than the consonants. Moreover, the vowels are largely redundant in written language if we compare the two sentences (1) *phncs smtms hlps lrnrs* (phonics sometimes helps learners) and (2) *e coa e oe eu a e oe* (The consonants are more helpful than the vowels).

However, more important than any of these is the fact that it is difficult for all learner readers to understand what is meant by sounds, either conceptually or functionally. George, an adult native-speaking learner, was not at all sure what a sound was, as is apparent here, even though his teacher had done a lot of work with sounds and tended to prompt him in the way she does here:

Daisy: What's that sound? (referring to the letter R)
George: Rock.

Referring to letters as sounds creates some conceptual confusion. Nor is it easy to give sounds any functional reality; we do not in everyday life go around giving the sounds of letters. It is hard, therefore, in a general way for learner-readers to see what sounds mean, to understand what they are and what they do.

Look and Say

Look and Say flash cards with words on them, such as *table* or *chair*, are hardly more meaningful to most early learners than phonics, especially if structure words such as *the* and *but* are also presented. They are not made to relate to anything. Similarly with labelling; teachers sometimes put up labels in the classroom, attaching the words *table, cupboard* and so on to the relevant objects. Again, these labels do not communicate anything to a potential reader; children in the classroom can see that X is a chair, Y is a table. The case is little helped by putting up whole sentences: *This is a table*. They may be whole sentences, but they have no message; they do not tell us anything. They are communicatively empty.

As discussed in Chapter 1, there is a wealth of print in the classroom and schools which is naturally communicative. In talking of labelling of this kind, I am reminded of the over-anxious Mum using a *Teach Your Baby to Read Instruction Kit* who continually walked around with 'Mummy' strapped to her head, occasionally absent-mindedly answering the door to bemused friends or tradespeople. Henry's mother also tried the *Teach Your Baby to Read* materials. The comment of Henry, aged 3, was 'Why do you keep showing me the same words again and again?' Henry already knows one of the important things about reading, which is that words have meaning in contexts, such as on the cornflakes packet or in comics or on buses. Henry did not understand the point of flash cards with words on them, which did not communicate anything. Nor did he understand his mother's behaviour. Why should she keep showing him the cards for no apparent reason?

Reading, like speaking, is best acquired in a meaningful context. Learner-readers need to see from the beginning that print communicates information, ideas and feelings. One way of beginning, as suggested in Chapter 1, is to select printed realia from the environment of the learner. Any items of language, whether spoken or written, are more memorable when they are met in their real context and are high both in content value for the individual learner and in what we might call survival rating. Clear examples of the latter are *Toilets* or *Danger*. Where it is not practicable to take learners out into their familiar environments—the street, supermarket or doctor's surgery—photographs can serve to show the context and function of the message. Learners might use photographs to build up a collage of local environments, each with its characteristic signs.

It is often suggested that one can teach word recognition. However, we do not recognize words, we recognize messages. Rather than talk of a 'whole word' approach it seems more helpful to talk of a 'whole message' approach. The initial words selected to introduce to learners can be chosen because they have a powerful message. *Poison*, for example, on a bottle is not just informing us what is in the bottle; it is saying 'You are warned against drinking this.'

In short, one needs to build up a solid sight vocabulary in context. In real life print is not redundant; it has a function, which is not to teach people to read. Much of the spoken language taught in the early stages to E2L or EFL learners was until recently fairly vacuous. Its aim was to teach people to speak English without considering in what circumstances anyone would ever say 'This is a book' or 'Are you a man or a woman' and so on. I can recall an E2L teacher getting very cross with a small Chinese boy who looked blank when she fired the question at him: *What are you?* The boy was doubtless puzzled because the question was both uninterpretable and communicatively empty. What could she mean, when she knew anyway that he was a boy, Chinese and a student? In order to encourage intelligent responses, both in second language speaking and reading, we need to give the learners something sensible and real to respond to.

Alternative Approaches: Developing an Awareness of Reading-related Concepts and Functions

We should be concerned not so much with the various methods of teaching reading but with ways of making learners more aware of the concepts and functions which relate to reading—what the marks on the page represent at various levels, and what they might communicate in certain contexts.

A case for letter names

I should like here to put in an unfashionable plea for the letter names, on several grounds. Firstly, it is easier for learners to conceptualize what letters stand for than what sounds stand for. We naturally use the letter names to talk about words; they offer learners a language to talk about reading; as for example, 'Is that an L or a T?' rather than 'Is that a "luh" or a "tuh"?' Letters are a way of talking about language in the way that sounds are not, except by phoneticians.

Secondly, letters have the kind of functional importance in real life that sounds do not have. You can, for example, talk about what P.T.O., D.I.Y., G.P.O., and about what people's initials stand for. To explain or attempt to explain to learner-readers how a certain number of sounds stand for or relate to a (usually) different number of letters on the page is much more complex.

The strongest case for using the letter names in preference to sounds is that knowing the alphabet is an important life skill. E2L learners are likely to be asked, 'How do you spell your name?', and if their pronunciation of English is poor they will need alphabet skills to respond to such requests as 'Sorry, how do you spell your street?' and so on. Using dictionaries and indexes of any kind, such as yellow pages or telephone directories, also clearly requires alphabet skills.

In fact, many E2L learners, both children and adults, come to reading in a second language knowing just the letter names. This was Peter's position (cf. Chapter 1). My attempt as a very inexperienced literacy tutor to introduce phonics resulted in confusion and frustration. In retrospect, it seems unfair not to have drawn on the resources he came with. When word analysis skills needed to be called into play—and as suggested in Chapter 4, they are best seen as very much a last resort strategy—Peter was able to employ the letter names as effectively as other learners do phonics. Hillyard, too, would habitually spell out the word, e.g. T-H-O-U-G-H-T—thought (cf. Chapter 5). How do they get there?, teachers wonder. In fact, Dakin (1973) makes the point that 'cat' bears as little relation to kuh-a-tuh as to C-A-T. When either phonic or letter decoding is used it seems likely that, as Frank Smith (1978) suggests, the learner is mentally 'checking out' the word rather than genuinely arriving at the word/meaning through the phonic or letter-decoding strategy alone.

In conclusion, it might be argued that both letters and sounds should be introduced early on. It has been found, however, that small children, at least (Reid, 1958), are often confused by letters versus sounds; that is, they are not sure which is which. Reid found in her study that when children were trying to sound out words they sometimes gave the sound, sometimes the letter name, seemingly at random.

For a number of reasons, then, alphabet skills may claim priority in initial literacy teaching. It should be emphasized, however, that we are not talking of the mechanical skill of being able to recite them, but of understanding both what they represent and how they are used in real-life contexts.

A case for grammar

It is possible to make a case for a return to grammar as a further way of helping learner-readers understand how concepts such as possession and plurality are encoded in writing. For a long time language teachers have been nervous about using terms such as past tense, plural or possessive. In English language teaching there was an understandable reaction against so-called grammatical methods of teaching, which involved the use of a considerable amount of technical terminology and explicit teaching of rules, many of which were simply inaccurate anyway. It was found that learners could talk a lot about the foreign language but not in fact use it adequately in real situations. Resistance to the use of grammatical terms has continued through successive developments in English language teaching, both to native and to non-native speakers.

However, when it comes to helping both first and second language learners to read, a simple metalanguage—a language to talk about language—is helpful for two reasons. Firstly, without this it is hard for learners to ask questions about the text or to talk about reading and language generally. We have already presented a case for the letter names based partly on the fact that it is easier to talk about letters than about sounds. Mackay, Thompson and Schaub (1970) note in a general way the importance of building up 'a language for talking about language'.

Secondly, the Bullock report (1975) points out the importance of labels in aiding children's conceptualizations about language; and if having the labels of 'letters', 'words' and 'sentences' at a learner's disposal (together with appropriate concepts) correlates with reading success, then perhaps it might be helpful to introduce a simple language to talk about the grammar of texts. This is not to suggest that we go back to talking of nouns as 'names of persons, places or things' or verbs as 'doing words', or that we reintroduce clause analysis; but we may be able to help E2L learners particularly by verbalizing what young native speakers know intuitively about their own language. An example might be the plural -s rule which enabled Kate (Chapter 5) to relate *book* to *books*.

Attention to grammatical signals such as apostrophe 's and past tense -ed is best given during reading itself, when learners themselves are beginning to show some curiosity about features of texts (cf. Mark, Case Studies 1). The *Breakthrough to Literacy* word- and sentence-makers (cf. Mackay, Thompson and Schaub, 1970) offer a good opportunity for learner-readers to try out their existing intuitions about the English language and, as they do so, for teachers to introduce a simple meta-language, represented by such terms as present and past tense, nouns and verbs, and subjects and objects. Learners can see, for example, how -ed added to *want* makes it past, and can then generalize that pastness is signalled whenever they meet this segment attached to verbs during reading.

Older E2L learners actually ask, 'Is that the past tense?' It is an important question to be able to ask; they want to check their current knowledge of the grammar of English as related to written texts. Knowing about the language can in fact help learners to conceptualize and generalize about the salient features of written English. If a learner knows, for instance, that -er can make nouns from verbs, because his attention has been drawn to this feature of English, and if he already knows the verb stem, e.g. *play*, and the new noun is associated with some kind of activity, e.g. 'The *player* ran up the field', then he has learnt a new word through reading. He can, that is, work out for himself that *play*+er is 'someone who plays' (contrast *finger*, which does not work in this way).

So learner-readers can be guided towards some awareness of the grammar of written texts, preferably through discussion of texts in one-to-one reading contact or through some of the kinds of class or group language work mentioned later in this chapter.

Language awareness

Most teaching of grammar to date has tended to be accompanied by prescriptive attitudes about language; in other words that there is a 'right' and 'wrong' way of speaking or writing. It is important, therefore, to emphasize that we are not here talking of ways in which to teach 'proper English', but of ways we might make learners 'language aware'—aware, that is, of some of the characteristics and uses of spoken and written language.

Teachers and learners are beginning to see that language—not just the English language—is a fascinating subject in its own right, as the *Languages Book* (1981, ed. Raleigh) produced by the English Centre (ILEA) shows. Through the *Languages Book* and similar material learners are encouraged to reflect on the nature of language and languages, on linguistic diversity in certain countries and communities, and in particular on their own bilingualism, bidialectism or biliteracy. This naturally leads on to consideration of different media, that is speaking and writing. Bilingual learners can be asked to consider how much or how well they read and write, as well as speak, another language. The Linguistic Minorities Project developed a questionnaire, primarily to find out about patterns of bilingualism among a sample of secondary school children in multilingual schools. As the Project team (1983) points out, however, it can also be used as a language awareness exercise in the classroom, with children thinking and talking about their own uses of language and languages (cf. Text 2, for an extract from the questionnaire).

Teachers in multilingual and multicultural classrooms can draw on resources not available to teachers of monolingual groups. Where there is a diversity of languages and dialects spoken, with many individual learners speaking several languages or dialects, the data are available for interesting cross-linguistic comparisons, including the features of different writing systems. For instance, where bilingual children can read and write in their mother-tongue, even if only a few words, they can talk about it to the others in a class. Chinese learners might discuss in simple terms how an ideographic system works; children can be encouraged to bring into the classroom any kind of written material in the mother-tongue to present and talk about to the rest of the group. Indeed, there should always be books and other written material in a range of different languages already in the classroom.

Consideration of the different media of speaking and writing leads in turn to a consideration of different styles. As we can see, it was largely the characteristic style of certain kinds of texts that created difficulty for some of the second language learners in the Case Studies. We can encourage learners to see how the use of different language and/or languages in different ways for different purposes ties in with the choice of medium. For instance, the written medium may be seen as more appropriate where the addressee is not known and information needs to be filled out or elaborated, as in a letter of complaint to the manager of a large firm. Looking at speaking and writing and their related ranges of style—formal, colloquial, literary—leads naturally to some discussion of the linguistic features which mark these styles, such as certain kinds of syntax. The teaching of grammar is thus put in a meaningful context.

Similarly, the concept of literacy itself can be discussed; what it means to be a reader in Hong Kong or Pakistan; how literacy needs will differ between urban and

TEXT 2

9 Languages in your district

49 Near where you live, does anyone speak any language(s) besides English?   yes ☐   no ☐   don't know ☐

50 Are there any signs and notices in languages apart from English near where you live?   yes ☐   no ☐   don't know ☐

51 If you ticked YES to either question 49 or 50 above write the names of the languages in the box. ☐

Now please go to the last page, page **10**

rural communities. In some countries or communities it may be only a minority who learn to read or write; literacy may not be thought necessary or desirable for certain groups, such as women. With older learners, at least, literacy can be discussed as part of both individual personal behaviour and of social and political structures.

A language awareness project

At a middle school (8–12-year-olds) in West London, a language awareness project developed by Jean Brewster (1983) has been set up—one of an increasing number of attempts to show how language is worth studying in its own right, as the subject, not just the medium, of discussion.

The vast majority of the students in the school are bilingual in Punjabi and English (with some Hindi and Urdu). The general aim of the project team, which consisted of school staff and three lecturers at Ealing College of Higher Education, was to raise the children's awareness or language through getting them to consider various language uses, skills, styles and media, including non-verbal communication such as gesture. There were three constituent projects:

Communication   for 1st-year pupils, 8–9 years old.
Advertising   for 2nd-year pupils, 9–10 years old.
Reading   for 4th-year pupils, 11–12 years old.

The projects provided teaching material for between 6 and 12 hours each. The teachers either fitted the work into their usual 'topic' slot (about 1–2 hours per week) or taught the material continuously over three afternoons. The overall aims of these projects were:

(1) To start the children thinking about language, what it is for and how it works.
(2) To improve the children's own linguistic competence by developing appropriate language and learning skills.
(3) To encourage the children to co-operate on collaborative learning tasks.
(4) To teach the children how to work independently.

The reading project was for 4th-year pupils (11–12) and was based on authentic texts in English, used to demonstrate a variety of text-type or genre and function. Similar texts in different languages were also used, e.g., Greek, German, Arabic. Below are three sample activities, designed to encourage learners to reflect on the function of print, purposes in reading, their attitude to reading and the features of different styles of text.

Activity One: Why do people read?

If you couldn't read . . .
Write down some of the things you wouldn't be able to do, e.g. find out what's on TV:
    . . . .
    . . . .
    . . . .

Activity Two: Matching text extracts

Decide which of the following parts of texts fit together: as you do so consider:

—the content, what the text is about
—the style. e.g. very formal, like speaking, use of slang words
—the type of text, e.g. novel, advertisement, newspaper article
—the tone of the text, e.g. serious, funny, ironic.
—graphic features, e.g. size of print, italics, bold type.

Examples might be:

TEXT 3

D is matched with E because:

the **content** is political/current affairs (therefore newspaper is a likely source);
the **style** is informal (therefore popular newspaper);
the **type** of text is editorial, marked by the function: opinion giving (opinion signalled by 'comment');
the **tone** of text is ironic (Mirror is a newspaper critical of Conservative Government);
the **graphic features** show underlining, bold print (typical of *Mirror* editorials)

Activity Three

Look at the green cards (which form part of the material, e.g. recipe (1), advertisement (2), school textbook (3), comic (4)). Here you will find a lot of bits of reading matter. Look at each one and decide why someone would want to read it. Each piece has a number. Write the number in the appropriate column on your tree diagram.

To find out something in particular	To learn more about the world	To pass an examination	For enjoyment	To learn how to do a particular job
E.g. (2)	E.g. (3)?	E.g. (3)	E.g. (4)	E.g. (1)

This kind of work can be used to introduce and accompany early literacy teaching at various levels of sophistication. The material quoted above was designed for older children, but even with 5- and 6-year-olds language can be talked about; its uses, meanings and constituent parts can begin to be explored.

Language awareness helps all learner-readers. It is a cart-and-horse situation, however, because an awareness of many features of language, and concepts such as word and letter, develop through reading itself. Nevertheless, continued language awareness and language development work in the multilingual classroom should give valuable support to early reading.

Part of being language aware is seeing reading not as an isolated activity but as integrated with other language related work in the classroom. In the next section I shall give closer attention to ways in which reading may be placed in the context of work on other language skills.

Integrating the Language Skills

Reading and writing

Reading and writing are often seen as skills which go hand in hand, each supporting the other, especially for the learner. There are, however, some difficulties in maintaining this view. Firstly, in real life the circumstances of reading and writing are different. Reading and writing do not usually accompany each other. Only in school are we required to read in order to write something—often writing the answers to comprehension questions, occasionally merely copying from the blackboard. In real life we do not usually read something in order to write; writing is a natural corollary only to certain specific kinds of reading task, such as making notes on texts to be recalled for examinations. Nor do we write with the major purpose of reading our text ourselves; we usually write for and to someone else. Reading and writing are not, as Stubbs (1980) expresses it, 'mirror images'.

We do not read and write the same sort of things; in everyday life, for instance, we read all kinds of instructions and warnings of various kinds, as well as books and newspaper articles, but we rarely write them. Moreover, we do not on the whole read and write for the same purposes; we read for fun, relaxation or the need to do something, such as mend a puncture. We are far less likely to write for these reasons. Most importantly, being a reader and being a writer are associated with very different social or professional roles in the everyday life of adults, at least. Few of us would identify ourselves as writers; most of us who live in literate societies aspire to be readers.

Despite all this, there are also good reasons for including some writing in early literacy classes. Firstly, although I have suggested that becoming a reader should take priority, survival literacy must mean being able to write one's name and address and perform everyday writing tasks such as making notes and lists. Secondly, learners expect to be taught to write: reading and writing collocate for most people. Moreover, learners are aware that the school system values the ability to write well, though this is often perceived only in terms of neatness, spelling and use of standard English grammar. More important, perhaps, is the wish of students to explore and make clearer their own ideas and feelings through writing, as the *Write First Time* student was doing through his poem about Mrs Thatcher (Chapter 1). Writing is thus valuable in itself, helping to give adults, in particular, a feeling that they are asserting power over the written word. In Chapter 8, I discuss some ways in which readers can also be writers.

Listening and speaking

While not wishing quite to dismiss the traditional association of reading and writing, I believe that a more fruitful association of skills in the very early stages of literacy is between reading, listening and speaking. Particularly for E2L learners still actively acquiring the second language, early reading is best developed from work in listening and speaking skills. I have argued that the spoken and written media show significant differences (Chapter 2); nevertheless, for most of our learners a base competence in English is best established through the spoken medium, in which E2L learners, unlike some EFL learners, need anyway to learn to operate. An ability to control simple structures in listening and speaking, and a prior knowledge of certain vocabulary fields, is the best springboard into the new medium, and represents the kinds of ability and knowledge with which native speakers approach the task of reading. Moreover, without a firm base in speaking it is difficult to see the relationship between spoken and written language, important for a learner who is new to literacy.

This is not to say that the content of early oracy in the L2 should exactly match that of early literacy. Survival spoken language and survival reading and writing skills will be different; we need to **say** 'Good morning!', 'How are you?' and 'Excuse me', not to read and write them; while we need to **read** 'Keep out', 'Danger', 'Bus Stop', and to **write** 'two pints of milk' or a note to the teacher.

Listening tasks can be seen as both preparatory and complementary to reading; both skills involve predicting—in both cases, that is, we are continually using the evidence of what has gone before to predict what comes next. Effective listeners make use of similar strategies to those used by effective readers. For example, we listen in different ways for different purposes, and the listening strategies can be developed through certain exercises. One might, for example, get the listener to listen selectively for certain information, listen with a view to summarizing the essential part of a message, listen in order to report the gist to someone else, and so on. It is a good idea for E2L learners particularly to listen to a story on tape as they follow it in their books. They might wish to do this several times before they read it themselves either aloud, recalling the rhythm of the original, or silently. Reading is thus a natural accompaniment and extension of listening.

Too often a reading scheme is introduced in classrooms with a high proportion of second language learners simply because it is the scheme used by that particular school. There is no attempt to relate the structures and vocabulary already introduced orally to the new medium or, conversely, to anticipate the content of reading by selecting some of the sentence patterns and vocabulary in class reading materials as a basis for oral language work. From the very beginning, and with all ages of learners, reading can be accompanied not just by listening tasks but by talk; a class discussion or teacher–pupil dialogue in the case of one-to-one learning may be opened up about the meaning of certain printed messages or the content of books, eventually encouraging the sort of silent dialogue between individual reader and writer which I mentioned in Chapter 3.

I suggest here some language activities which might help learners become effective listeners, more fluent, confident talkers and willing discussants.

Activities to Integrate Listening, Speaking and Reading

Pictures

Pictures offer an important route into early reading and from the beginning learner-readers should be encouraged to exploit fully the help that they may give. Wordless picture books, where a series of pictures tells a story, give learner-readers the idea of narrative before print is introduced at all. Picture books are particularly appropriate for L2 learners, who can be helped to interpret a narrative through pictures. L2 learners may initially wish to vocalize the picture narrative in their first language. Once texts are introduced, the accompanying pictures are useful for getting readers to look ahead and predict the outcome of a story. They can also support and clarify any culture-specific references in the text. Then, when print takes over the major role in developing the narrative, the pictures and other visual information continue to offer valuable support.

Single pictures, too, can tell a story. Part of the activity of skimming a newspaper, for example, is predicting content from pictures, the aim of which is to excite curiosity and to prompt us to read the text. We can choose newspaper pictures which relate to our learner's own experience, likely to be from the local newspaper and reflecting some concern or controversy in the local community with which our learners will already be familiar. In this way, the content of an accompanying text can be anticipated and discussed before it is read.

Problem solving

We can introduce an activity which is more familiar to our learners than ourselves (such as, with Indian learners, making chappatis) in order to describe a process that went wrong. The learners must listen carefully to establish the error or missed step in the process. Directed listening of this kind can prepare learners for reading for a particular purpose.

For adult learners one might set the following kind of listening task:

Tom wanted to claim Supplementary Benefit. You can get this if the money you have coming in is less than you need to live on, and you are not in full-time work.

He went to the Social Security Office and said that he couldn't manage on the pay he got from his job as a cleaner. Even though he worked from nine to five, and overtime as well, he could not earn enough to keep his wife and kids.

The man at the office said that John could not get Supplementary Benefit. Why?

We could go on to quote several more imaginary claims. As well as sharpening listening skills and offering opportunity for discussion, the task helps the learner to better predict the content of the actual form when he comes to read it:

TEXT 4

What is supplementary benefit?

It is cash you can get if the money you have coming in is less than you need to live on.

You can't get it if you are in full-time work. But if you have any children you may be able to get FIS (Family Income Supplement) instead. Get leaflet FIS.1 from a post office or social security office.

You can claim supplementary benefit if you are:
- over pension age
  or
- unfit for work
  or
- bringing up children on your own
  or
- unemployed and can't get work
  or
- working only part-time
  or
- needed at home to look after a disabled relative.

Did you know:

● You don't need to have paid national insurance contributions.

● Savings up to £2000 won't affect your benefit at all.

● Owning your home won't stop you getting benefit.

● If you get supplementary benefit, you and your family can get other things free – like school meals, milk for the under-fives, visits to the dentist, glasses and prescriptions.

If you want to know more:
Ask at your social security office. Or go to a Citizens Advice Bureau or other advice centre. Detailed information is given in *Supplementary Benefits Handbook*. You can see this at your local library.

Story-telling

Probably the most effective way of integrating speaking, listening and reading, is through story-telling. This can take several forms. One can read a story inviting the learner/learners to give missing predictable items or say in general terms what happens next. Various 'bids' can then be accepted or rejected as more or less probable—as good or not so good guesses—before the reader continues. I find older learners as well as children enjoy listening to stories in this way. Non-readers are thus introduced to and encouraged to reflect on some of the conventions of the written medium. Younger children are familiarized with the 'Once upon a time . . ., . . . lived happily ever after' conventions; older learners—with some of the more sophisticated features of written discourse.

Learners can also retell stories to which they have listened, with picture prompts helping them, if necessary, to recall the key incidents. As an extension of this, one can encourage learners to tell their own stories, not just to 'talk about themselves', but to organize what they have to say into a story-telling genre. Story-telling requires that speakers be much more explicit than they would be in most verbal contexts; it can therefore act as a bridge between the learner's everyday use of language and a more organized, elaborate style characteristic of written language.

Approaching the Text

Let us now turn again to some of the features of written texts and consider how we might extend our learners' ability to deal with different levels of meaning in texts.

One tends, in describing the characteristics of texts, to go from smaller to greater units. Indeed, my description in Chapter 2 was along those lines. However, as a teaching approach it is more satisfactory, I believe, to start from the whole, moving on to consider smaller components of texts, such as words and parts of words, at a later stage and preferably during one-to-one reading with a learner. This means that in preparing a class for the reading of books, one should first consider a particular text as a whole. In doing so one should look, firstly, at the context of the communication (for example who wrote it or for whom); secondly, at the overall function of the text, whether it is to amuse, inform or direct; and finally, at the topic (cf. Chapter 1).

One further important way of raising appropriate reader expectations about any text is to consider its genre. It is this feature that we shall consider next, looking at classroom activities which may help to develop in learners the concept of genre.

Genre

Poorer readers tend not to have a very clear notion of genre, largely because—like other reading-related and text-related concepts—it develops largely through reading itself. Though an awareness of genre is common to every mature reader, the concept of fiction or non-fiction, and more specifically of thriller, romance or biography, may not be very clear to learner-readers. In the brief warm-up to my reading session with Sarla (cf. Case Studies 6) she did not pick up the idea I was hoping to get at, namely, that the book *Running Man* was an adventure story.

CW.   What do you think it's about?
S.   Children.
CW.   What sort of story does it seem to be?
S.   They must be playing hide and seek.

There are various ways in which classes may be guided towards an understanding of genre. The organization of different kinds of texts can be discussed: how information is arranged—e.g. under days of the week (as in *TV Times*), or in order of eating (as in menus), and so on.

When it comes to stories, learners might be asked themselves to classify sets of books for the class library under headings such as animal stories (with a moral such as that it is bad/wrong to be lazy, greedy, tell lies), fairy stories (with fantastic characters such as witches and fairies), stories about real life, or religious stories (e.g. the Divali Stories for Hindus).

In looking at a range of simple books for learner-readers, both fiction and non-fiction, I have found they can be broadly grouped as follows:

—fictional narratives, which describe particular events, such as a visit, a journey, a fight, something being lost or found;
—non-fictional narratives or descriptions, such as biography or auto-biography, which describe either particular events or habitual events (what used to happen);
—fables and folk tales, where the pragmatic rules of 'normal' texts are broken; the impossible becomes possible—animals talk, death is not final;
—transactions, such as going to the market, a visit to the dentist, going to the clinic;
—processes, such as how to mend a puncture, making a kite, recipes.

In getting learners to try out their perceptions about kinds of stories, and how they can be expected to develop, teachers might try an exercise suggested by Florence Davies (1982). Learners pick out, from the early part of a story, what they see as a key sentence which anticipates the outcome of the story (cf. *Wild Elephant Raid*, Text 5, on page 105). Alternatively, students can be asked to predict roles and behaviour when presented with the key characters in what is recognizably a fairy, folk or ghost story. An example might be:

Many years ago, there was a rich landlord who was very mean. No one liked him. He wanted to marry the daughter of a farmer who owed him money.

(Opening of Norwegian folk tale)

One might, at this point, invite groups or individuals in a class to speculate about the characters' personal qualities, roles and actions in the story. For this tale, as characters, we would have: Rich landlord—Farmer—Farmer's daughter—Farmer's mare (whose role is the least predictable). One might then give students one or two clues; for example, it is crucial to the story that the animal is a mare and not a stallion. However, the aim is not, of course, to predict what does happen so much as to speculate what might happen.

Structure

E2L learners are likely to need some extra help with certain characteristics of text structure at sentence level and beyond. At a very early level one can play with simple word order, asking learners to judge what 'sounds right', thereby encouraging E2L learners to develop their intuitions about what is English and to exploit the syntactic resources they already have. For example:

John ate an ice-cream greedily
John greedily ate an ice-cream
John an ice-cream greedily ate
An ice-cream ate John greedily

and so on, possibly asking learners to put the versions in some order of 'silliness'.

Learners may also need help in coping with more complex syntax. As Kohl (1974) says, 'the ability to deal with complex sentences develops through reading a lot and through experience with building and modifying sentences'. Likely areas of continuing difficulty are ellipsis and reference items, which I turn to now.

TEXT 5

WILD-ELEPHANT RAID

by WILLIS LINDQUIST

1 Haji tried to sleep at the top of the bamboo watchtower on the edge of the rice fields. Suddenly a well-known smell came to him on the breeze from the jungle.

2 "Elephants!" he whispered, "and very near too."

3 Then Haji saw them. Large elephants and small slipped quietly out of the jungle to feast on the villagers' rice. The boy bent forward, hoping to find in this large herd his lost elephant, the mighty Majda Koom.

4 When the boys in the other watchtowers saw the elephants, they began shouting and throwing stones. Suddenly one of the stones hit an elephant. There came a scream and a crash as one watchtower was pushed over.

5 "It's Majda Koom!" cried Haji. "They made him angry with their stones. Now he's charging the towers."

6 Boys leapt for their lives as the enraged elephant rushed down the line of towers. Soon the huge beast

Ellipsis

Features of ellipsis create particular difficulty for all poor readers and particularly for E2L learners. Help in predicting the following kind of item is useful: '. . . when she returned with Prince Charles for a holiday at the end of their Australian tour this year, even though the British Press stayed away, the Europeans . . .' (from 'What Diana's Job Really Means', *Woman* magazine).

Reference

Learners may need help with reference items, such as *one*, *this* and the use of the definite article, *the*. For even with early readers an understanding of how items refer back and forwards in a text is crucial; they cannot otherwise connect the relevant parts of the text. I was using the story in Text 5 which is part of the Science Research Associates Reading Development Project, trying to get my literacy class to pick out a key sentence in this early part of the text on which to base our predictions about the outcome of the story.[1] We finally agreed on: 'The boy bent forward, hoping to find in this large herd his lost elephant, the mighty Majda Koom!' But an unanticipated difficulty arose. None of the group had connected *the boy* with *Haji*, the hero of the story. They appeared not to have picked up the role of the definite article as referring back to someone already mentioned. On this occasion I proceeded to go through the whole text, identifying—or getting the learners to identify—the ways in which (a) Haji, and (b) the elephant were referred to (e.g. the animal, the beast, the mighty tusker, etc.) In such circumstances it is extremely useful to go through a text with the students, exploring the range of ways in which key persons, places or events are variously referred to, discussing how it is that we are able to identify the newly mentioned and the already known or 'given' respectively.

The use of cloze

Finally in this section, let us consider how cloze, the device of deleting either content or structure items from a text, can develop learners' competence in using structure and meaning to fill in what is missing.

Cloze is now a fairly well-established tool for testing in reading. As a testing procedure it involves the deletion of words from a text at regular intervals (typically every fifth or tenth word). More recently, cloze procedure has come to be seen as a valuable way of extending learners' reading strategies in the teaching of reading. In this case a selective deletion process is likely to be adopted. This means that only certain kinds of words are omitted, for example only content words or, more specifically, only content words which are powerfully cued in by the context.

Using cloze procedure, Grant and Moony (1980)[2] set up a pilot study on reading in a multilingual school in Southall. Prior testing (using the Neale test) had revealed that nearly all the children—both monolingual and bilingual—scored significantly better on word recognition scores than on comprehension. In other words, the results of the tests suggested that though the children could read words in isolation, they were less effective in reading for meaning.

Grant and Moony were interested in discovering if the use of cloze procedure in teaching might close the gap between mere word recognition and reading for meaning. They used a selective cloze procedure, omitting only highly predictable content words. More interestingly, they systematically introduced the reader to three search strategies:

Strategy A—meant using the cues within the sentence itself, e.g. 'It was cold, so he closed the . . .'.

Strategy B—meant using the cues from preceding sentences in the text, e.g. 'He hurried down the road until he reached his own front door. He fumbled in his pocket but he had lost his . . .'.

Strategy C—meant using the cues from sentences which occur later in the text. The reader needs to read ahead, e.g. 'Mum and Dad were taking him to the c . . .. He wanted to see all the elephants and clowns.'

Twice a week the researcher discussed a cloze passage with individual children, who read for approximately 15 minutes from one of the three kinds of cloze texts mentioned above. Over a period of 5 weeks, the readers were required to employ strategy A for the first week, strategy B for the following week, strategy C for the next week. For the last 2 weeks the cloze texts demanded a mixture of strategies. There was a control group in which individual children merely read aloud to the same researcher for the same time each week.

We noted that a weakness showed by most of our young learner readers (Chapter 4 and cf. Case Studies) was an apparent reluctance to search the text, to move backwards and forwards. On the face of it, Moony and Grant's use of cloze in teaching would appear to encourage just those searching strategies which are absent in not-so-good readers. Indeed the results were encouraging. The regular one-to-one teaching using cloze texts resulted in the elimination of the original difference between reading accuracy and reading comprehension. In other words, the children were now more effective in reading for meaning.

It is important to emphasize that a crucial feature of the experiment was the teacher-learner discussion about the text. Where the child could not provide an appropriate word, the teacher discussed the text with the child and pointed to cues within the text. The teacher's role was to help the learner maximize the information already in the text, and at the same time to draw on what he already knew from experience—about circuses, or how to open doors, for instance. The implications of such an approach (as I have tried to suggest in Chapter 4) are that the quality of the process is more important than the product. It is not getting the right answer that counts.

This is also true when cloze is used as a group activity. Lunzer and Gardner (1979) point out how effective it is for groups to work together, discussing what kinds of item are acceptable in the context. Joanna Studdert (1980) shows more particularly how helpful this activity is for the learner whose mother-tongue is not English. As she points out, if one or two second language learners are part of the group (with at least two mother-tongue English speakers) the discussion of context and vocabulary gives the non-native speakers great support. Once again, the aim is not to find the 'right' answer—there are likely to be several acceptable alternatives—but to encourage learners to reflect on what is possible in the particular text and what is possible in written English texts generally, taking into account the structure of English and the style and genre of the text.

Though cloze exercises are most commonly used with the content words or items omitted, it is possible also to draw learners' attention to structure words or items. For the native speaker these are highly predictable in simple sentence structure because the range of options is small. E2L learners, however—even those who have lived and studied in an English-speaking environment for some years—appear not to predict structure items as competently as indigenous peers judged as having roughly the same reading ability. One might, therefore, give E2L learners more help in predicting structure words or parts of sentence structure, especially if these are omitted or typically different in their own speech. Learners can also be made more generally aware of sequential constraints, that is, of what kinds of word classes follow which others, e.g.

Toussaint . . . born . . .   . . . Island . . . Haiti . . .   . . . West Indies. His parents . . . slaves.

Vocabulary

How many meanings?

One can take a word—any word—close to the learner's interests and preferably contributed by himself, and consider whether it has one or several meanings. A difficulty young learners often have is that they assume that one word equals one meaning, and also that one sound equals one meaning (cf. Yasmeen's comment on *new/knew*, Chapter 2).

Word families

Another technique is to discuss how a word can be added to or changed to form new words related in meaning. An example might be RACE–RACIAL–RACIST–MULTIRACIAL. In this way we can build up lexical fields, drawing on contributions from the class. Learners can then see how words with related meanings have shared visual features rather than shared phonetic ones, e.g. *race* and *racial*. In other words good readers know (cf. Chapter 2) that shared visual characteristics tend to equal shared meaning characteristics.

Incidentally, good spellers recognize that related words are spelled alike though pronounced differently (see Chomsky, 1970). For example, we may not know how to spell *adoration* though we know what it means. After all, the second syllable might be spelled -ar- as in *declaration* or -ir- as in *inspiration*. Each syllable sounds the same; but we spell the word as we do because of the rule that the stem spelling stays constant: *adore–adoration; declare–declaration*, even though the sound of the second syllable changes. If Yasmeen had realized that word families are related in this way she might have been happier to accept the spelling of *sign*, relating to a word already familiar to her—*signature* (Case Studies 5).

Which words go together?

Learners can be encouraged to see what sorts of words go with which others. For it is not knowing words of high frequency as such which may help the reader, but the expectations of how frequently these words combine with others. The more learners can be helped to read in chunks, by seeing phrases rather than words as meaningful wholes, the sooner early fluency can develop. Such phrases are, to quote Southgate *et al.* (1981), 'part of the linguistic and cultural tradition of a speech community'. Hence they tend to present difficulty to non-native-speaking learner readers, as we can see from Ravinder's difficulty with 'cup and . . .' (Case Studies 4). The expectation of what can follow can be built up through simple word games, which encourage learners to collocate—put together—items, many of which are culturally based, e.g. fish—and chips, a pint—of beer, cup—and saucer, Christmas—pudding/cake/tree/carol.

Enriching vocabulary

While vocabulary fields must be developed for all the content words, it seems that in narratives the verbs are particularly important since they carry the action along. It was the verbs that Nadeem and Sarla (Case Studies 2 and 6) struggled with most, simply because they did not know the possible means of talking about different ways of holding things, moving or speaking. Particular help, it seems, is needed in building up groups such as:

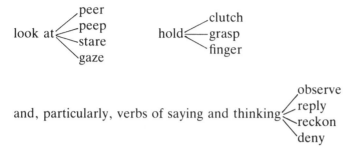

One can then discuss what kind of adverbs are likely to accompany the verbs we have chosen, e.g. peer—shortsightedly, stare—rudely, clutch—anxiously, and so on.

Classifying vocabulary

One can encourage learners to classify. I selected the headings below from an advertisement by a large department store during sales:

LINGERIE   MENSWEAR   FURNITURE

Learners might either be given words to classify under the headings, or be asked to think of as many words as they can to group below the words given. Classification exercises help the reader to see meaning relations in texts. More specifically, the learner is here being encouraged to reflect on his own experience as a shopper, before coming to read the actual text, reproduced in Text 6.

TEXT 6

LINGERIE

LONG LENGTH NIGHTIES
Nylon nighties with shoe string strap, in pink only.
Sizes W, WX   Special purchase **£4**.99

SILHOUETTE BRAS
With under wire, in white or honey, cup D & DD
When perfect £6.99   Seconds **£4**.99

BERLEI NON-SLIP COTTON BRA
Cotton bras in white only, A & B cup.
List price £5.99   Now only **£4**.99

MENSWEAR

TONIC SHIRTS
By Levi, in polyester/cotton, sizes small, medium and large.
Normally £8.99   Now only **£6**.99

PURE WOOL WAISTCOAT
Knitted button through waistcoat, assorted colours & sizes.
Normally £15.99   Now only **£9**.99

FASHION TROUSERS
By Avante, in polyester/wool, with side pockets. Sizes 30, 32, 34 & 36.
Normally £15.99   Now only **£9**.99

REVERSIBLE CASUAL JACKET
In polyester/cotton, with zip front and side pockets, navy/grey,
Sizes 36, 38, 40 & 42
Normally £29.99   Now only **£14**.99

FURNITURE

BEDSIDE CUPBOARD
A larger than average bedside cupboard, finished in teak effect and white with storage space and single drawer.
If perfect £30.00   Seconds **£16**.95

CHARTA CHESTS
A 35" 4 drawer chest finished in green wood grain effect (self assembly).
Normally £79.95   Now only **£41**.95
OTHER SIZES AVAILABLE AT BELOW ½ PRICE

CHARTA WARDROBE
A full length 2 door wardrobe in an attractive green wood grain effect (self assembly).
Normally £104.95   Now only **£51**.95

Concepts and functions in texts

There is more to texts than their constituent structures and vocabulary. Extended texts express certain concepts and functions in characteristic ways, and learners may need some help with these levels of textual meaning.

Concepts

As well as understanding the concepts expressed by content words or vocabulary items, readers need (cf. Chapter 2, p. 26) to understand both the conceptual meaning and the use of structure items such as *of course* and *in fact* (cf. Sarla—Case Studies 6). The reader needs, too, an understanding of causal relations, hypothesis, sequence and comparison, and how these are typically encoded in written language. For instance, the notions of comparison, cause/effect, and simultaneity are all expressed by *as* in the following:

> He is *as* tall *as* John.
> *As* it was late, he had to hurry.
> *As* he was passing the corner, he heard a strange noise.

For young E2L learners, as for native speakers, certain language structures and their related concepts will be developed through a whole range of classroom activities involving, among others, deduction, reasoning and hypothesis. For instance, certain kinds of game naturally lend themselves to the introduction of certain concepts and the ways these are typically encoded in English. An example might be, for hypothesis, the desert island game, i.e. 'What would you do if you were stranded on a desert island?', where prompts would include—food—warmth —entertainment, etc.

Unless certain key concepts are developed through classroom talk, E2L learners may be in some difficulty when they come across these same concepts expressed in written texts.

Functions

We have said that the first thing we should ask of a whole text is: what is it for—to warn, persuade or simply entertain? Readers also need to identify, in reading, as they do in spoken contexts, various functions within the text. I am referring here to social functions, such as the language of complaints, requests, leave-taking, and so on. These can be practised as part of pre-reading through role-play of situations, particularly transactions, in which certain language functions naturally occur, e.g. shopping or going to the dentist (the language of requesting, greeting/leave-taking, stating problems). Learners can be helped in this way to cope with transaction-type texts, particularly since many early reading texts are of this kind, especially reading for adults, e.g. 'Abdul's Tooth', 'Baby's Bottle', 'Mohinder goes to Market'.

Many of these situations can be described in terms of scripts (cf. Chapter 3, p. 37). By rehearsing some of these scripts, whether transactions (e.g. buying something), processes (e.g. making something) or events (e.g. visiting someone in hospital), E2L learners can predict the typical stages when they come across them in their reading texts. Confidence can be built up with scripts that are familiar and therefore have very predictable stages, such as buying shoes or making a kite. Also, if the reader is familiar with the basic script, he can appreciate departures from it; for, as noted in Chapter 3, it is the unexpected that makes stories interesting.

In rehearsing some of the scripts dealt with in the students' reading material one can check how far the learner's script (for making tea, for instance) synchronizes with that described in the text. In role-playing situations like restaurant visiting, going to the clinic, a birthday party, one can check how far the learners' scripts match the typical scripts of such situations in 'British culture' texts.

A Sample Text

I selected at random an early reader (Ladybird, *The Little Red Hen*), to see what pre-knowledge of overall content and organization of the text and particular structures, vocabulary, concepts and functions would help the learner to anticipate the content.

Overall content and organization of text

Folk story genre signalled by the 'Once upon a time' convention, which requires a happy ending. Simple past narrative but non-specific time and place. Similar event repeated four times, with similar outcomes. The expected about-turn of the finale is typical of folk tales, as is the attribution to animals of human characteristics, such as speech. There is a moral which brings the story close to the fable genre. At the same time, the story charts a series of steps in a process.

Structures

Basic SVO word order, e.g. 'The little red hen found some grains of wheat'.

Subordination with—who
that (introducing noun clause)
to (in order to)
as (= when)
Mainly simple past tense
Active voice, apart from: when X was
had been $\Big\}$ -ed
Y . . .

Vocabulary

For example, grain, wheat, mill, miller, grind (ground).

Concepts

(i) Sequence—an understanding of what constitutes a process. The process described in this story can be thus represented: grain › wheat › flour › bread.
(ii) Purpose, signalled by 'to' (in order to).
(iii) Consequence, signalled by 'so'.

Functions

(i) Expressing intention: 'I shall plant the grain myself'.
(ii) Asking for help: 'Who will help me?'
    —refusing: 'Not I'
    —agreeing: 'I will'.

(Clearly 'Not I' is a literary variant of the more colloquial 'Not me').

The organization and content of this story would seem to confirm the importance for a reader of having an understanding of different levels of meaning in texts. In other words, readers are helped by:

(1) An understanding of the content and organization of different genres and their typical characters, roles and outcomes. More important than an understanding of the specific features of texts is an awareness of how whole texts hang together; in particular, for early learners, how stories are structured. What kinds of outcomes can be anticipated? We know that Snow White cannot really die, that Ginger and Sharon will not be allowed to get away with their deviant behaviour (or will reform!) and that the Little Red Hen will finally get the better of her lazy friends.
(2) An understanding of concepts such as sequence, consequence or comparison, and how these are typically encoded in English grammar; for example, 'first . . . then' or 'so' or 'not so . . . as'.
(3) An awareness of language functions and how these are typically expressed in certain texts. The reader needs to understand, for instance, that the 'Not I' (or 'Not me') function in the story *The Little Red Hen* is a rather rude refusal.
(4) A competence to predict at sentence level the basic sentence patterns common to simple reading material.
(5) Some knowledge of the vocabulary field. For example, if the topic is travel: bus, train, aeroplane, horse, fly, ride, drive, etc.

A Sample Lesson

I shall conclude this chapter by considering how, within one particular lesson, we might accommodate the need to develop an understanding of the features of texts—their structures, vocabulary and the concepts and functions expressed in them—with the need to integrate the E2L learner's language skills.

I have chosen to take **topic** as the organizing principle in the two model lessons presented here. The key sentence structures of English can be introduced and practised in the context of topic work, and selected because they encode basic concepts such as sequence or hypothesis.

As well as an awareness of how concepts are typically encoded in English grammar, E2L learners need an awareness of the functions of language—how we use language to establish social contact—to make requests, complain, apologize and so on, and what we use language to do, in order to achieve things in everyday life.

As an extension of this, learners need to be aware of how social interaction typically progresses, particularly those everyday transactions which they will have to be able to handle. Familiarity with simple transactions—who says what kind of thing to whom and how—will clearly help the learner to anticipate the stages of such transactions in reading texts.

Finally, learners should be encouraged to build up a vocabulary for the topic, drawing on their existing knowledge, so that the core vocabulary represents the shared experience of the group. This can then be extended by new vocabulary introduced by the teacher. It is possible to organize language work around a topic in such a way as to both develop general language competence and provide a good foundation for early reading.

MODEL LESSON 1

Topic	Introduce topic	Concept	Function	Structure	New vocabulary
Food growing preparing	Remind learners of simple processes they are familiar with, e.g. making the tea. Learners listen to a description of a process: grain › bread.	Sequence *Exponents*: —fill the kettle with water, then put the kettle . . . —The farmer plants grain, the grain grows into wheat . . .	1. Giving instructions 2. Making polite requests 3. —Agreeing 4. —Refusing *Exponents*: 1. Put the kettle on 2. Who will help me 3. —I will 4. —I'm sorry ⎫ I can't —I'm afraid ⎭	*Revise*: Imperative *Introduce*: Simple present Will . . . can/can't	*e.g.* grain wheat grind bake

Suggested methodology:
—Learners can instruct the teacher or each other through the stages of a simple, familiar process, using the already known imperative. Then they can transform to simple present, third person, e.g. 'Every morning Dad makes tea. First he . . . then he . . . (opportunities to compare scripts will arise here).
—The story of the making of bread might be introduced through pictures. The students can then reconstruct the process, prompted by the sequence of pictures, using simple present tense.
—The language of requests can be practised through role play or pair work, with picture cue cards of grain, wheat, bread, etc. This activity anticipates the similar social functions introduced in the text *The Little Red Hen*, e.g. who will help me PLANT—the grain; who will help me CUT—the wheat etc. Key vocabulary is also thus introduced.

Follow-up work:
Other processes introduced, e.g. how tea gets to the packet; processes in simple present reconstructed to form simple past tense narrative.

Follow-up reading:
1. Breakthrough to Literacy, *A Cup of Tea.*
2. Ladybird, *Little Red Hen.*

I have argued in this chapter that developing early literacy necessarily involves an understanding of certain reading-related concepts and functions. The need then follows to devise tasks and exercises which help learners to discover both what print is and what it does. Secondly, I have considered ways of encouraging an integrated approach to the development of all the language skills, so that reading as a classroom activity is not seen as separate from talking and listening in particular. Thirdly, I have suggested certain kinds of classroom work which may help learners appreciate some of the key features of written texts.

In the next chapter we look beyond these very early stages at the learner tackling much more extended texts inside and outside school. Once learners have embarked on reading, how can they be helped to become more effective, flexible and confident readers?

MODEL LESSON 2
For adult beginners one might introduce the same basic concepts/structures in the context of a more adult topic

Topic	Introduce topic	Concept	Function	Structure	Vocabulary
Homes home decorating	Draw on learners' experience of home decorating. Learners listen to a description of the process of wallpapering.	Sequence *Exponents*: —put paste on the wallpaper, then . . . —X puts paste on the wallpaper, then he . . .	1. Expressing likes and dislikes 2. Expressing necessity 3. Making suggestions *Exponents*: 1. I like pink wallpaper —I prefer blue 2. We need —some new wallpaper —a roller —some paste 3. We can —paint it pink —mix two colours	*Revise*: Imperative, Like/Prefer *Introduce*: Simple present Need/Can	*e.g.* wallpaper roller paste to stick

Suggested methodology:
—Learners can be invited to discuss and compare likes and preferences, e.g. I like plain wallpaper—I like/prefer patterned wallpaper, carpets, etc.
—Learners plan the task of decorating in terms of (a) requirements—'we need'; (b) suggestions—'we can' (with pictures as cue cards).
—Topic is introduced by asking learners to instruct each other through a familiar process, such as preparing to paint or wallpaper a room, e.g. fill a bucket with water . . .
—After listening to the process described (simple present use) learners order cards (both pictures and sentences) to give the stages of the process. These might be so designed as to prepare them specifically for the content of the reader *New Wallpaper*, eg.:

Hardip puts paste on the wallpaper.	Mohinder puts the paste in the water.
Hardip cuts the wallpaper.	Mohinder stirs the paste with a stick.
Hardip measures the wall.	Mohinder fills the bucket with water.

Follow-up reading:
1. Community Education Project, Coventry Education Committee, *New Wallpaper*.
2. Breakthrough to Literacy, *Mending a Puncture*.

Notes

1. I am indebted to Florence Davies for the choice of the particular text, (adapted from *Burma Boy*) and for the idea of selecting the key sentence.
2. The eventual aim of Grant and Moony was to establish whether it might be possible to narrow the observed disparity between word recognition scores and comprehension scores in the case of spina bifida children. The Southall Study was a pilot study.

7

Extending Reading

In the last three chapters I have focused largely on the beginner-reader in the process of acquiring reading competence in English. How might we help learners, in particular E2L learners, to extend their reading skill adequately enough to cope with the demands of secondary school and higher education, if they are of school age? If they are adults, how are they equipped to handle the demands of everyday life and jobs? How do learners like Joyce and Hillyard move beyond survival literacy?

In this chapter I shall consider how reading can be seen not just as what we are teaching, but as a way of teaching across the secondary curriculum. I shall suggest ways in which we might help to make classroom reading an activity to which readers bring a clear sense of purpose and a flexible and reflective style of reading. Finally I shall consider reading for work and pleasure outside the context of school.

Beyond Beginning Reading

I suggested in previous chapters that what have sometimes been considered to be more advanced reading skills are in fact involved in effective reading from very early on. An HMI document (1980) notes: 'Once children have acquired the early reading skills, they should begin to learn to predict what may appear next in a piece of writing, to use various contextual clues . . .'. However, all reading is predicting; in maturing as readers, we learn more about the reading process itself and, through reading, acquire richer sources of knowledge which help us to predict on a number of different levels. But from the beginning reading involves both predicting and the use of various contextual clues: one word constrains the next; sentences and paragraphs constrain following sentences and paragraphs.

The same HMI document continues; 'During the secondary school years pupils need to become aware not only of the overt meaning of what they are reading but of the many kinds of oblique meaning.' Once again, an awareness of 'oblique meaning' is important from the beginning of reading. It was just this kind of oblique meaning which created difficulties for Balwinder (Chapter 4). However, it is true that (as the same document continues) in the case of older learners, attention can be drawn more to nuances of tone and attitude; also class or one-to-one discussion may centre more on features of exaggeration, prejudice and fact versus opinion. What is sometimes called 'critical reading' comes very much into its own.

Reading as a Way of Teaching

Once children get to secondary school they are expected to be able to read. It is taken for granted that reading has been dealt with in junior school. Indeed, with the emphasis on a skills approach which suggests that there are a finite number of discrete reading skills which can be 'learnt', it is sometimes assumed even by middle school teachers teaching the 8–12 age group that children have acquired their reading skills in the infant school, and that reading has, therefore, been taken care of. Teachers of children over the age of 7 or 8 will sometimes in fact say that they 'know nothing about reading'. This sense of a demarcation of responsibilities is even stronger in the secondary school, and across the curriculum. Maths and biology teachers, for instance, do not see that it is their business to 'know about reading'.

Yet, becoming an effective reader is a continuing and open-ended process. The business of learning to read has only begun in the junior school. We are all learning to read—to be more competent readers of income tax forms or train timetables, for instance. Once children are in secondary school, effective reading is involved in all subject areas; reading is not therefore merely the concern of the English teacher. Good readers have one of the most powerful tools there is for learning, whether it is learning about mathematics, biology or cookery.

To say that all subject area teachers should be sensitive to reading development needs does not mean that they should teach reading as such—or, at least, not directly. Michael Marland (1977) suggests rather that reading should be seen as a way of teaching. In an American experiment quoted by Harrison (1980), an English specialist took over a mathematics class to teach a 2-week unit on linear equations. Without any prior knowledge of algebra, the English teacher took the children through the unit, emphasizing the concepts of linearity and dependence, and stressing the meanings of key words and the relationships between ideas. After 2 weeks the class and a control group taught by the head of mathematics were tested. The results showed a clear advantage to the group taught by the English teacher. Of course, a number of factors may account for this, but the experiment does at least raise the question that help with the reading of specialist texts may be required if the subject-related concepts are to be fully understood. The English teacher was using reading as a way of carrying out the teaching of mathematics.

Reading and Learner Autonomy

The English teacher quoted above was, in helping her learners' general reading competence, also helping them to achieve greater autonomy as learners.

Most people would agree that developing reading is crucial in promoting independent learning. However in their survey, *The Effective use of Reading* (1979) Lunzer and Gardner found that relatively little time was spent on reading in the classroom. Looking at 10–14-year-olds, they found that already at top junior level the salient language activity was writing, if indeed we can properly call much of the writing done—often merely copying from the blackboard—a true language activity. In secondary age groups (1st and 4th year) the major language activity was listening to the teacher.

One reason that teachers favour writing is that with writing, children can be perceived to be doing something, in a way not usually apparent with reading. Reading is likely to be reserved for homework, and often, in fact, to be more difficult than any supervised reading done in class. We need to provide suitable opportunities for more extensive reading in the classroom itself. To counter the view held by teachers and students alike that somehow reading is not work—that it something which fills the odd moment—tasks may be designed to precede or accompany the reading. These tasks should aim to reflect the natural purposes and process of reading discussed in earlier chapters. They should be both intellectually demanding and related to the particular reading text—whether novel, newspaper article, a biology book or a social science text—and aimed at encouraging a flexible and reflective response to reading. An ability and willingness to reflect on what they are reading was, concluded Lunzer and Gardner (1979) a major characteristic of good readers. It is just this ability and willingness which should be encouraged from the very beginning of reading, and which plays in increasingly important role in accommodating new learning in the secondary school.

At the same time class teachers should provide occasions for more than short bursts of reading. As Lunzer and Gardner (1979) point out, 'how can a diet of work cards and blackboard notes prepare a child for the very heavy demands of textbooks in the later years of secondary schooling?' One might ask, incidentally, how can such a diet prepare an adult or young adult for out-of-school needs—the demands of income tax forms, the Highway Code or a hire purchase agreement? Reading gives us autonomy not just as learners in school but as everyday members of society.

Reading Across the Curriculum

The language of instruction

It is clear that reading skills are required to cope with all subject areas in the school. This is less apparent in the junior school than in the secondary school. Even in junior school maths, however, quite sophisticated reading skills may be required in order to do the maths problems. Teachers in multilingual classrooms frequently comment that some L2 learners can do the mathematics but cannot follow the instructions or rubrics. The language is occasionally more complex than the mathematics, as perhaps this example from a maths book for 9–10-year-olds illustrates:

> At the same time next day Paul and Susan again counted the traffic and made a bar graph to show the number of each type of vehicle. To save time, instead of making small drawings, they used squared paper, letting one square stand for one vehicle in each case . . .
>
> (T. R. Goddard and A. W. Grattidge, *Beta Mathematics 3*)

While this is not a particularly difficult text for most 9- or 10-year-olds, there may well be L2 learners, competent to do the maths, but who are perplexed by features in this text such as the concealed negative in 'instead of making small drawings' (i.e., they *did not* make small drawings). Similarly, there may be difficulties, for cultural minorities, which are nothing to do either with mathematics or knowledge of English. For example, five of the six illustrations and captions in Text 7 are open to some cultural misunderstanding.

Asian children tend not to have seaside summer holidays or birthday cakes; Christmas will not be celebrated with presents by many ethnic minorities, the pierced heart and St. Valentine's day is open to further cultural misunderstanding. And what about Chinese New Year?

TEXT 7

Write in the correct month for each picture.

Your birthday _____	Your holiday _____
The longest day _____	Christmas _____
St. Valentine's Day _____	New Year's Day _____

Arrange the months you wrote in order.

1 _____   2 _____   3 _____

4 _____   5 _____   6 _____

Measurement: days and months

(Howell, Walker and Fletcher, *Mathematics for Schools, Level 1, Bk 6*)

Similar difficulties with the language of instructions may arise later on, in secondary school. The question quoted here, for instance, is fairly typical of the rubric of science examination papers:

It is suggested that in order to keep up the temperatures of a greenhouse in winter a hollow *metal* container, *blackened* on the outside and with *holes* in the *lid* and near the *bottom*, is placed in the centre of the greenhouse (a greenhouse is a structure with a glass roof and sides in which plants are grown). Give and explain the physical ideas behind this suggestion paying particular attention to the five words in italics.

An attempt at a rewrite of this question by physics teachers and myself at a largely Asian West London High School, read as follows:

> A greenhouse is used for growing plants and has a glass roof and glass sides. If you want to keep up the temperature of a greenhouse in winter, you should put a container in the centre of the greenhouse. This container should
> —be made of *metal*
> —be *blackened* on the outside
> —have *holes* in the *lid* and
> —have *holes* near the *bottom* of the container
> Why is it important that the container should be like this? Pay particular attention to the words which are in italics.

In this case, difficulty about some of the features of the language of the original were only hypothesized and very generally discussed with some teenage Asian learners in the school. One could set up experiments with sets of E2L students of comparable general ability in both science and English, whereby, within a given time, one group would be asked to answer the original question and a second group the re-written version. In this way one might establish whether in fact the style and language of examination questions affects performance; staff at the school were fairly sure that it did. What is also interesting is to involve students themselves in discussion of features of rubric, possibly getting them to re-write questions, comparing and evaluating different versions, writing questions for each other to answer, and so on.

Subject-specific language in reading texts

All writers of textbooks and examination papers should aim for clarity; there is no justification for complex, convoluted prose. Nonetheless, secondary school students will need to come to terms with certain features of both syntax and vocabulary that characterize the language of different school subjects. In science subjects, in keeping with the need for objectivity, there will tend to be a use of impersonal forms, such as the impersonal pronoun *one*, or the passive rather than active voice, for example, 'Blood is carried round the body in tubes' rather than 'Tubes carry blood round the body' (cf. page 121). This kind of style may be quite unfamiliar to the student coming into secondary school, who is used to a rather different kind of language, typified by this junior school science textbook:

> What makes thunder and lightning? Lightning is really just a huge electrical spark. In the winter, if you scuff your feet on a wool rug and then touch a metal lamp, there will be a tiny spark. This spark, in its small way, is like lightning. And it is caused by electricity.

In style, this language is closer to the language we might expect to hear. As we have seen, this can present difficulties in itself; features of texts, though typical of speaking, such as *really* and *of course* may be obstacles for poor readers when encountered in written texts. Nonetheless, the writer is attempting to personalize the text through the use of 'reassuring' sorts of words like *really* and *just* and the personal pronoun *you*, and by relating the new information directly to the everyday world of the reader. Later on in secondary school science textbooks, such features are rare.

Subject-specific vocabulary may create even greater difficulty than formal impersonal style. We need to ensure that students have grasped the meaning of the core vocabulary of the subject area, the specialist terminology. A likely difficulty are polysemous or homonymous (cf. Chapter 2, p. 23) words. Poorer readers, as already suggested, tend to be less aware of the range of meanings that a single word may have. Pupils may think they know the word simply because they knew it in another context. In a study carried out by Page (1977) on the language of science, second-year pupils from a sample of schools were given a list of words which their teachers agreed they should have met. The children were asked if they understood what these words meant. They were then asked to write an explanation of these words. The results are shown in Table 1, and show a fairly wide discrepancy between

TABLE 1   *Pupils' understanding of scientific words (n = 186 pupils)*

	Claim (%)	Correct (%)
dissolve	98	51
mass	71	39
evaporate	93	66
distil	76	5
condense	70	33
inflammable	95	74
deposit	71	20
residue	26	11
crystallize	77	53
anhydrous	7	1
fuse	54	5
solution	49	25
molten state	85	46
reactive	56	31
non-luminous flame	53	45

claimed and real understanding, which suggests that some care needs to be taken in introducing subject-specific language; though the **words** may be known in other contexts, the **meanings** are new.

L2 readers are likely to have greater difficulty with polysemous words. Ray Williams (1981) found that polysemous words included in a vocabulary test administered to secondary school Hong Kong pupils offered strong evidence of the confusion that such words are likely to cause L2 readers. Williams concludes that readers of subject-specific material need to be familiarized with the way certain language items are used. They need, that is (and this is my own attempt at a familiarization!) to be led into an understanding of how a word or expression is being used in the particular context. Some writers are very sensitive to likely confusion; Perera (1979) gives an example of a writer who has anticipated the possibility of her reader attaching an inappropriate meaning to a word, e.g.

> The scientist is a curious person—not of course soft in the head—but curious about things, wanting to know why they do this or that.

Pictures and diagrams

Pictures and diagrams can also give important help in introducing key vocabulary. Where pictures or charts are not provided in the text itself, teachers can contextualize the new key vocabulary by bringing in relevant illustrations—pictures, diagrams or charts to support the text, or rather (and I take the term used by Williams (1981)) to 'interact' with the text. For example, information might be used from the text to complete the labelling of a diagram; at the same time the diagram can give help in completing a cloze text, as shown in Figure 1.

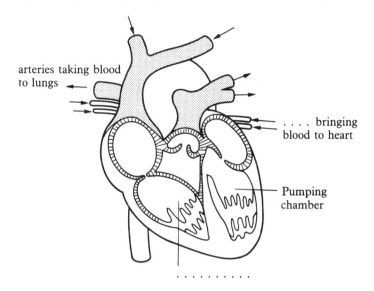

arteries taking blood to lungs

. . . . bringing blood to heart

Pumping chamber

FIGURE 1 *Diagram of heart.*

Blood is carried round the body in tubes known as _____, _____, and capillaries. Blood is pushed through the arteries by the _____, which acts as a pump.
The blood flows through different parts of the body in capillaries and back to the heart through the veins.
The heart is made up of two _____. One pump sends the _____ to the lungs to get oxygen.
When the blood comes back to the _____ the second _____ forces it out to all parts of the body.

The pupil, as Michael Marland (1977) notes, needs help in synchronizing graphics and texts; and the balance between graphic and non-graphic information requires care. A proliferation of charts and pictures may actually distract the reader. In the case of pictures, in particular, culture-specific information can confuse L2 readers. This is particularly the case with cartoons, as Figure 2 perhaps illustrates.

The organization of subject texts

It has been shown that texts may be characterized not just by certain kinds of sentence structure and vocabulary, but also by the kind of information they present. Johns and Davies (1983) have drawn up a classification of what they call 'topic types', based on the sorts of information certain kinds of texts typically contain. These topic types are perhaps misleadingly named, as they cross the

'But honey, if I loved Racquel Welch, I'd have married her wouldn't I?'

FIGURE 2   *Accompanying a text on Marriage and the Family*; Modern Society, Social Studies for CSE

boundaries of subject disciplines. As Johns and Davies observe, the following topics appear on the surface to be quite unrelated: *a suspension bridge, a flowering plant, a skeleton* and *a blast furnace*. However, they all describe physical structures; and descriptions of physical structures consistently feature information about:

(1) the parts of the structure;
(2) the attributes of the parts;
(3) the location of the parts;
(4) the function of the parts.

It should be added that (1) is obligatory and the others are optional; in other words a physical structure text must name the parts and will probably though not necessarily give the attributes, location and function of the parts.

The reader is referred to Johns and Davies for a full list of topic types; if we keep here to the example of physical structure texts it does appear that they are readily classifiable along the lines proposed by Johns and Davies, as the text on 'the ear' in Figure 3 shows:

The ear in mammals

The ear is divided into three main regions. The outer ear consists of a tube which passes from the side of the head to the eardrum. Usually there is also an external ear, or pinna, surrounding the outer end of the tube. The pinna is made of cartilage and skin.

    The middle ear is an air-filled cavity in the skin which lies inside the eardrum. It is connected to the back of the throat by the eustachian tube. Three small hairs called ossicles form a chain across the middle ear. The outer ossicle is attached to the eardrum and the inner one fits into the oval window.

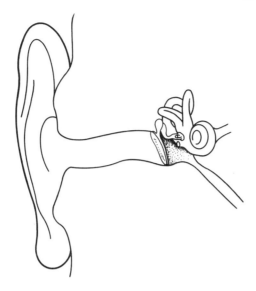

FIGURE 3   *Diagram of ear*

Students can then complete Table 1. Once completed, it forms a useful summary of the key information contained in the text which can be surveyed at a glance.

TABLE 1

Structure/Part	Location	Attribute	Function
The outer ear	from side of head to eardrum	like a tube	. . .
Pinna	. . .	made of cartilage and skin	. . .
The middle ear	inside the eardrum	. . .	. . .

So, in subject-specific reading pupils can be shown what kind of information to expect in different kinds of texts; they can be helped to discover relevant information more effectively than by simply seeing all texts as strings of words or sentences, where one starts at the beginning and reads on to the end. They can be helped to see that there is an information structure which typically characterizes certain kinds of text.

Teacher-made materials

Perhaps teacher-made materials might resolve some of the difficulties presented by published material? Apparently this is not always so. Writing clear prose is not easy and there is no reason to suppose that a good subject teacher will necessarily write well even about her own subject. When the *Effective Use of Reading* team (1979) assessed the level of difficulty of teacher-produced sheets they found, for example, that one set produced for a first year, mixed-ability secondary group was comparable in difficulty with the standard 'O' level textbook in the same subject.

There is a further difficulty about work cards which has already been mentioned, namely that they do not on the whole allow for extended reading in the way that books do; nor do they encourage learners to use source material flexibly. Textbooks properly used will probably not be read from beginning to end but searched for material relevant to the readers' needs and interests. Work cards do not on the whole help learners to make use of a wide range of information sources.

Where teachers do wish to produce their own work cards they might be guided by Perera's useful assessment (1979) of those features of textbook language which create difficulty for secondary school learners. This description can guide teachers both in selecting textbooks and in writing work cards. (The examples listed are my own.) Potential difficulty, suggests Perera, exists:

(1) at word level —familiar words with special meanings, e.g. *solution, deposit* (cf. p. 120).
—technical vocabulary, e.g. *anhydrous* (cf. p. 120).

(2) at sentence level —long noun clauses as subject of sentence, e.g. 'And with the progress of evolution, *what is now the shining genius of an eminent few* might become a common possession of the many' (cf. p. 132).
—sentence patterns characteristic of formal writing, e.g. concealed negatives, as in 'instead of drawing pictures' (cf. p. 117).
—altered word order, e.g. 'By intelligence we mean a style of life' (we mean a style of life by intelligence)(cf. p. 131).

(3) at text level —for instance, the use of logical connectors exclusive to rather formal speaking or writing, e.g. 'The attraction is the energy that the wind will give us free. In reality, of course, . . .' (cf. p. 130).

Making such a list of typical difficulties in subject-specific texts does not mean, as Perera points out, that textbooks or work cards should be written in the simplest possible language. Learners, especially L2 learners, will best extend their linguistic repertory through reading stylistically diverse material, including very formal texts. However, it is helpful for teachers at least to be aware of areas of potential difficulty and to be alert to too great a mismatch between learners' current language and reading competence and the linguistic level of the text.

Critical Reading

In all school subjects, including sciences, what is involved is not just an understanding of the specific characteristics of certain types of texts but an ability to read widely and critically. Good reading is active reading; it involves comment on the text at all levels, from the simple comments by Mark (Case Studies 1) to the critical, 'mental' comments on the quality or clarity of a writer's thinking by more sophisticated readers. But good reading is not just active; it is interactive. Readers need to be encouraged to see that there is nothing necessarily fixed about the meaning of a text; that texts are open to various interpretations. This is particularly the case with literary texts, where obliqueness and ambiguity may be part of the writer's message.

From the beginning of learning to read, learners should be invited not just to 'retell the story' but to offer their own interpretation of texts. Occasionally, such interpretation is bizarre, or incomplete in its concern with exclusively surface or literal meaning, as we saw with Balwinder in Chapter 4. But encouraging learner-readers from the beginning to interpret and evaluate events and behaviour is one way of promoting reflective reading. Older children may, in small groups, discuss and compare their interpretation of a poem or short story. Moy and Raleigh (1981) show how effective this can be with mixed-ability groups. They videotaped a typical group activity lesson in which a first-year, mixed-ability class in secondary school were tackling an extract from a story called *Geordie* by David Walker. The class was divided into groups, with four in each group. Each group was required to answer specific questions about the text. The questions were calculated to draw on the students' critical ability and involved evaluating the author's intended meaning rather than 'finding the right answer'. With multicultural and multilingual groups one might select pieces of writing which assume diverse kinds of cultural knowledge and attitudes. Individual students can, therefore, draw on different areas of knowledge and experience, matching these up and comparing them with the knowledge and experience of other students. Interesting differences in inter-pretation may emerge due to cultural background factors, as we saw with the wedding stories in Chapter 3.

Criticism in reading is a concept that has been associated with the reading of literary texts in the English class. However, I would suggest that critical reading might be extended in the English class and indeed in other subject areas to cover a wider range of written material. Literary texts will then take their place alongside magazine and newspaper articles, political pamphlets and advertisements. It might be argued that we are moving towards some form of political education in thus extending the range of texts thought suitable for class discussion. I would answer, firstly, that learners need the opportunity to consider, discuss and be influenced by as wide a range of contemporary written genres and styles as possible; secondly, as claimed earlier, that literacy is necessarily political. Print is powerful. The printed word can not only reach an audience of millions, as can other media such as television, but it has greater durability than spoken communication.

Encouraging Reflective and Critical Reading

Let us now consider more closely some ways of encouraging reflective and critical reading in the classroom across different subject areas. This will involve us in a reconsideration of some of the resources which, it was suggested (cf. Chapter 3) experienced readers bring to reading, and some of the strategies they use during reading itself. It will also involve us in challenging one still widely accepted interpretation of 'comprehension' as a classroom activity, which might be summed up as follows:

Readers are given a piece of text to be read, frequently with little or no discussion of the context in which the text was originally written or the author's purpose and supposed readership. Students read the text with a view to answering a series of questions which follow in either open-ended or multiple-choice format.

Such a procedure cannot be said to reflect what actually happens when most of us read in normal (i.e. out of the classroom) circumstances. We do not come cold to a text with neither interest nor purpose and then proceed, retrospectively, to ask ourselves certain questions about it. Reading occurs in a context, both a wider social context and the more immediate context of the reading event itself.

Of course, the classroom itself is a context with its own particular constraints; it is probably neither possible nor desirable for classrooms to reflect real life. Nonetheless, the activity of reading might be made more meaningful to students if there were seen to be, as in out of class contexts, a purpose and interest in reading the text. In other words, we need to consider how we can offer strategies to help our readers both to tackle a text with appropriate expectations and purpose and to interact with the writer, conducting an active critical dialogue with the text. In the next two sections I shall consider firstly how we might motivate readers in their approach to the text; secondly how we can encourage an active engagement with the text during reading itself.

Tackling a Text: Pre-reading

We want to give the reader a purpose in reading, a positive approach to the task and confidence that he can bring enough knowledge of the language and world knowledge to get something out of the task. We need to show learners that we read different texts in different ways for different purposes; when it matters to read for detail and when it does not; and what kind of detail is important. Finally we need to help them to draw on relevant areas of knowledge and experience.

Providing a purpose

While it is not always possible to select texts in which a whole class is interested, we can motivate learners as individuals by getting them to ask their own questions about the subject-matter. This is, after all, what we do in real-life situations. By getting readers to raise their own questions one has hopefully motivated them to read to find the answers. They are encouraged to think about things they would like to know or are curious about, or which affect their interests. If one takes a text about 'Consumers' Rights', for instance, the sorts of question students are likely to come up with are:

—How long does a guarantee last?
—Can I always get my money back?
—Is it better to write or talk to the manager?

They then scan the text to find the answers to their own questions. Clearly they may not find the answers, but they are reading to find out something that they personally would like to know. One has individualized the activity. Moreover, it is as important to draw attention to information which is omitted from texts as it is to consider what is included.

In extended texts or books one can get students individually or in groups to do a survey of the text, i.e. an initial skim read, looking at chapter headings, pictures, captions etc., which will raise questions or allow statements to be made or views expressed which can be confirmed or disproved by a closer look at the text. Students are encouraged to anticipate outcomes about the text. This procedure, sometimes known as survey–question–read–recite–review, is discussed more fully by a number of writers, notably Lunzer and Gardner (1979) in *The Effective Use of Reading*.

Matching purpose with text-type—reading different things in different ways

One is not likely to read a telephone directory from cover to cover. Yet there is evidence (cf. the sixth-former quoted by Marland, 1977, who in looking for a particular piece of information in a book started reading at page 1), that even otherwise good readers do not have flexible strategies. To overcome this problem, one can give learners various pre-reading tasks which involve either **scanning** for particular information (much as with 'finding answers to your own questions' above) or **skimming** to get the general idea or gist.

Scanning can be encouraged through different kinds of competitive game in class. Two popular ones are:

—Give groups copies of the *Yellow Pages*. The winner is the first to find a dentist in Ealing, a 24-hour plumber, and so on.
—Give groups the day's newspapers, with questions like: Where can you get a three-piece suite for less than £300?, or 'What gave the bishop a red face?' Better still, groups can work out their own questions from the newspaper, to ask rival groups.

In the case of skimming one might organize the following activities:

—Get a number of leaflets and ask individuals or groups to look through them as quickly as possible to say what they are about (leaflets in other community languages can also be used with biliterate learners).

One can set a more particular task such as:

(1) Which leaflet will help you to claim supplementary benefit?
(2) Which tells you what to do in cases of racial discrimination?

Building confidence

One can show readers how a relatively difficult text need not be intimidating; that one can extract the information one wants from quite a formidable text. If one takes a text on 'Tenants' Rights', for example, a reader might approach the text with a specific problem which he hopes and expects the text to answer, e.g. 'My neighbours keep me awake till 3 o'clock every morning. What can I do?' As it happens, the answer to this problem is accessible in the text, through the general organization of the content and sub-headings in particular, though the linguistic difficulty of the text is considerable. One can show readers how to find out what they want to know from even quite difficult texts, well above their general reading level. For this reason among others (cf. Chapter 8) readability studies are not always to the point. Most reading is selective; we do not need to read all of the parts of a text equally carefully. What we need to help readers with is how they can get at the parts of the text which are important to them.

Reminding readers of what they already know or think

We can get readers to organize their knowledge or views prior to reading a text by encouraging them to assemble pieces of existing knowledge and to reflect upon them. Often it is not that readers lack the world knowledge to bring to a text, but that they need to be reminded of how much they do, in fact, know. Then we can encourage them, once they embark on the text, to check off mentally their prior knowledge, preconceptions and opinions against those of the writer. In a text about social class in Britain, for instance, we might have the following kind of pre-reading exercise:

> What tells us most about a person's social class?
> Put in order of importance: (a) in your own culture/community; (b) in British society generally:
> —how you dress
> —how you speak
> —how well-educated you are
> —where you live
> —how much money you can earn.

Or, if we take the social science text on marriage mentioned earlier (page 122), these kinds or pre-reading tasks might serve to 'warm up' the students:

> (1) which is the best way to choose a marriage partner?
>   (put a ✓ beside those you think are the best; put a × beside those you think are not so good).
>   —at work
>   —through friends
>   —through shared hobbies
>   —at church
>   —through one's parents arranging the marriage
>
> (2) Make notes on what you think are the advantages and disadvantages of the following kinds of marriage.
>
>   *Advantages*   *Disadvantages*
>   —one husband/one wife
>   —one man, several wives
>   —one woman, several husbands
>   —arranged marriages
>   —'love' marriages

Before reading the text, pairs or groups can discuss their own ordering, and cultural differences as well as personal views will doubtless emerge, with discussion of arranged marriages and so on. An 'after reading' column may be added as a check, both to compare the writer's view with the reader's and to note whether the reader has changed his views subsequent to reading. Clearly one can exploit the resources of the multicultural classroom by getting learners to draw on diverse cultural experiences and attitudes.

With a 'facts' text or indeed a 'facts' lesson a true/false pre-reading task can lead students into the content of the class. The following pre-reading quiz was designed for a general science class (the same CSE group who tackled the text/diagram on the heart, cf. page 121). Once again adjusting original views after reading highlighted their awareness of what had been learnt.

Pre-unit quiz	Pre-reading True or false	Post-reading True or false
1. A normal heart rate is about 70 beats a minute.		
2. Most athletes have fast heart rates.		
3. Cold showers are good for you.		
4. Heart attacks can be caused by eating too little fat.		

With such pre-reading tasks one is creating a readiness to evaluate while reading; also some kind of 'before and after' exercise highlights the readers' awareness of learning, indicating what it is they did not know or had not thought of before.

Reading as Interacting: While Reading

We turn now to consider more closely some activities whereby readers might be encouraged to bring into play certain kinds of knowledge and opinions during the reading of the text itself. This involves us in considering what are sometimes known as 'while-reading' exercises.

Activating knowledge of the language and of the world

Many E2L readers may still require help with the more complex reference items. We saw how the function of the definite article apparently stumped the beginners' literacy group mentioned in Chapter 6. At a later phase of reading development readers can be asked to relate items like *such* and *these* to their referents in the text. This is complicated by the fact that they may refer not just to other single words, but to chunks of text—parts of sentences or whole sentences, or even whole paragraphs (my own use of 'this' above refers back to 'relate items . . . in the text'). Further work may need to be done also with co-reference; that is, the referring to the same person, event or place in different ways. Examples were noted in Chapter 6 (page 106). To give several further examples here: In the Norwegian folk tale (cf. Chapter 6 page 104), to make sense of the narrative we need to know that *landlord—ugly old miser—the old miser—my/your/his master*, and *the old landlord* are all the same person. Similarly, in this extract from a junior school history book, readers need to see that craft = glider; 'They built three *gliders*, each better than the last. Between them they made over 1000 flights and learnt how to control their *craft* in the air' (Oxford Junior History, Speed: *The First Aeroplanes*).

Cloze has already been mentioned as a helpful teaching (as opposed to testing) tool. With more advanced learners one can occasionally omit items of structure—not just within the sentence but between larger stretches of text. Logical connectors—items such as *however, on the other hand, moreover*—which link ideas in a text, tend to create particular difficulty for second language readers. These linking words can be systematically omitted from a text, with students in groups invited to discuss and opt for a connector that fits the text not just syntactically but logically. An alternative here, incidentally, is to give a range of options in the form of multiple choice items, e.g.

Workers in Britain have a securer life than they did
(a) ⎧and   ⎫ no greater equality (b) ⎧moreover
    ⎪but   ⎪   ⎪however
    ⎨as well as   ⎬   ⎨similarly
    ⎩including   ⎭   ⎩of course
they treat the class battle as a comic opera.

(Adapted from Michael Mann 'The Working Class' *New Society* 1976; quoted in Barr. *et al.*, 1981)

Many secondary school learners, both L1 and L2 readers, remain very unclear about the meaning of these connectors, many of which are characteristic of very formal speech or writing. They need to be given the opportunity to discuss options in a context.

Larger chunks of texts can be omitted, with students asked to fill in with phrases or sentences which satisfactorily complete the meaning, again comparing and discussing different versions.

Another idea is to chop texts up, with students either using a mask or being 'fed' the pieces of text. The text is stopped at natural breaks and at relatively predictable points, where there is enough information in the preceding part of the text to allow for a sensible prediction as to what might follow. An example might be as below.

TEXT 8

There is a burgeoning of windmills. They are springing up in the fields and large gardens, some big enough to make a useful contribution to the energy needs of the household and others so small as to be only entertaining experiments. Recently the world's governments have shown an interest. The United States and Canada, West Germany and Israel, Japan and the United Kingdom, all . . .

From the text above what features do these countries have in common that is relevant here? Read on . . .

. . . have plans for wind-driven electricity generators.
There is even a project for a very large windmill on the South Downs that will heat greenhouses. The attraction is the energy that the wind will give us free. In reality, of course, . . .

What point is the writer going to make about the real situation?

. . . you no more get free energy from the wind than you get free steam power because someone happens to give you a bucket of coal. You must harness the energy in both cases. And although your windmill's raw energy, unlike coal, is free, you still have to harness it in the most economical way for your particular needs. Which is why you may choose a . . .

Can you say, in very general terms, what comes next?

(Adapted from an article in *The Sunday Times*, 1978, quoted in Barr *et al.*, 1981)

It is important to emphasize that it is the sensible guess that counts. However, one L2 reader was able to predict not just generally but precisely what followed 'which is why you may choose a . . .'. She predicted the exact words of the text 'a bicycle-wheel windmill' having recently seen a TV programme on windmills which mentioned bicycle-wheel windmills. Stopping the text in this way can encourage students to draw very directly on recent experiences and share these with the group before moving on through the text. In order to predict, one is forced to focus on what is relevant in the preceding part, rather than on incidental or peripheral content. This is an analytical task, involving, like cloze, hard and detailed study of the text, but if accompanied by class or group discussion it is much enjoyed by students.

Another variation on the theme of seeing how texts connect together is to give groups of learners texts which have been cut up, which they then reassemble. The bits of text may be anything from a few sentences (to build into paragraphs) or paragraphs (to build into complete longer texts), Moy and Raleigh (1981) and Owen Watkins (1981) recommend this as a way of promoting both a close attention to the text and group discussion in which knowledge of English, knowledge of the structure of texts and knowledge of the world are all brought into play.

Conducting a dialogue with the text

With expository texts, readers can be given the first part of the text and then invited to ask questions of it. A suitable text to choose for this activity is one in which a writer is making a controversial point. Indeed, as discussed in Chapter 3, writers of such texts typically proceed by anticipating reader objections and mentally ticking them off, as they write. This is the writer's part of the dialogue (Widdowson, 1979). We can encourage students to enter into their part of the dialogue if we stop texts at points which particularly invite reflection; such points may come—not just after the initial presentation of a case—but at any stage in a text, as the writer develops her argument.

This paragraph, for instance, commences the summing up of Holt's book *How Children Fail*, and may serve to make the point here:

'When we talk about intelligence we do not mean the ability to get a good score on a certain kind of test, or even the ability to do well in school; these are at best only indications of something larger, deeper and far more important. By intelligence we mean a style of life, a way of behaving in various situations, and particularly in new, strange and perplexing situations. The true test of intelligence is not how much we know how to do, but how we behave when we don't know what to do.'
(John Holt, *How Children Fail*)

Prompts to encourage learners to bring their own views and experience to bear on the text so far might be as follows:

The second paragraph begins. 'The intelligent person . . .
—Anticipate how Holt develops his argument
—What do you think being intelligent is?
—How do teachers and schools decide who is intelligent?

Reading as evaluating

As we read we are continually involved in evaluating on a number of different levels; we make judgements about both content and style, checking the views and opinions expressed with our own. Let us finally look at how learners might be encouraged to evaluate certain kinds of content, style and presentation in texts.

Evaluating intellectual and affective content

Provocative texts likely to invite strong responses can be chosen by teacher or students. Issues such as abortion, marriage and children, or teenage unemployment are likely to be things about which people have opinions. To reflect the mental (or sometimes verbal) cry of 'yes'/'true' or 'rubbish' which naturally accompanies critical reading (and listening), one might provide a margin in which students can express their response. ✓ could mean agree (with the writer), ✓✓ strongly agree, ✗ disagree, ✗✗ strongly disagree. While it is difficult to offer examples out of context, statements likely to provoke a margin response of this kind might be this one from Bertrand Russell's *Has Man a Future:*

TEXT 9

> Man has not only the correlative capacities for cruelty and suffering, but also potentialities of greatness and splendour, realized, as yet, very partially, but showing what life might be in a freer and happier world. If Man will allow himself to grow to his full stature, what he may achieve is beyond our present capacity to imagine. Poverty, illness, and loneliness could become rare misfortunes. Reasonable expectation of happiness could dispel the night of fear in which too many now wander lost. And with the progress of evolution, what is now the shining genius of an eminent few might become a common possession of the many. All this is possible, indeed, probable, in the thousands of centuries that lie before us, if we do not rashly and madly destroy ourselves before we have reached the maturity that should be our goal. No, let us not listen to the pessimist, for, if we do, we are traitors to Man's future.
>
> (Bertrand Russell, *Has Man a Future?*)

Evaluating bias and prejudice

Learners can evaluate bias in newspapers, comparing, for instance, the way a news story is reported in different ones including those for minority groups, such as *West Indian World*. Even simple newspaper headlines can make a clear and pertinent point about bias, as these two perhaps show:

Sri Lanka holidays hit as mobs kill and loot
BRITONS CAUGHT IN RIOTS
(*The Standard*, 27 July 1983)

Tamil prisoners die in rampage
(*The Guardian*, 27 July 1983)

It is particularly important for students to be alerted to racial prejudice. A black student of mine could read, i.e. decode *discrimination* in a newspaper headline, but to my great surprise he did not know what it meant. Words like *discrimination*, *unemployment* and *immigration* should be among those that leap from the page for ethnic minority students in particular.

As a way of thinking about the nature of prejudice, one can do simple 'collocation games'. What words can go with what? Does it matter which words we use? Is it true that one word is as good or as bad as another. Is being called 'nigger' no worse than an Englishman being called 'pommie' by an Australian? (as claimed by the head of the Police Federation, *Panorama*, 18 July 1983). Sexism, classism and racism can be very simply revealed, as Lakoff shows (1974), through 'deviant' collocations. For example:

* 'I got into conversation with a charming young nigger on the train.'
* 'Hordes of attractive, elegant women attended the fashion show' (cf. text below).

Simply thinking of how many negative or positive words there are to describe men, women, homosexuals, heterosexuals, blacks and whites can be revealing. There are, one finds, simply far more negative ways in English of describing someone who is black than someone white, just as there are more—usually negative—ways of describing someone who is criminal or lunatic than someone who is law-abiding or sane.

When it comes to looking at whole texts, students can be asked to underline recurring collocations and discuss their effect. Part of critical reading is an awareness of the power of words and their cumulative effect as a text unfolds.

Text 10 shows the front page news story in the *Sun* on 12 December 1983.

TEXT 10

WOMEN AT WAR

By DAVID GRAVES

THE WILD women of peace brought mayhem to Greenham Common missile base yesterday.

Violence erupted as a massive 25,000 gathered to demonstrate against Cruise.

Three policemen were hurt, including an inspector knocked unconscious when protesters tore down a section of perimeter fence.

The CND demo — which followed Saturday night's nuclear holocaust film The Day After — was intended to be peaceful.

But it ended with almost 60 people arrested in ugly clashes *Continued on Page Two*

with 1,000 police and hundreds of troops, drafted in to guard the base near Newbury, Berks.

Injured Inspector Michael Page, 30, was cut on the head by a crashing concrete fence post.

An ambulance battled for an hour to reach him through the hordes of women. He was recovering in hospital

Another officer suffered crushed ribs and a third a cut head.

The demonstration marked the fourth anniversary of the NATO decision to site Cruise and Pershing missiles in Europe.

Most of the arrests were made when the fence was torn down.

A police chief said last night: "The CND are offering perfect cover for those who want to break the law."

Britain the Day After
—See Centre Pages

The *Sun*, Monday 12 December, 1983

Students might be asked to consider how the word 'women' collocates in the text with other words, whether adjectives, nouns or verbs. For example:

Adjectives	Nouns	Verbs
wild	war	tore down
ugly	mayhem	
	protesters	
	clashes	
	hordes	

This kind of text study offers an opportunity to introduce the notion of connotative meaning; that is, words may denote similar things (have a very similar 'core' or dictionary meaning) but have a very different connotative meaning, in some contexts particularly. Why for instance has the writer here selected *tore down* rather than *pulled down* or *hordes* rather than *crowds*? Students might consider the range of vocabulary choices available to a writer as the text evolves and what determines one selection rather than another at each point.

Evaluating style

We have suggested that an awareness of style, that is of the syntactic and lexical features that typically characterize certain kinds of writing, is helpful to learner readers. One might present students with a language awareness exercise in which they are asked to assign a text sample to a particular stylistic category. Teachers can incidentally gain the opportunity to judge how aware their learners are of a range of written styles. More important however, is the opportunity given to students to discuss their reasons for making a certain choice. Examples might be:

(a) 'Peter has been in the record business for nine years'. 'I started as a record plugger. I must admit I didn't like it much'.

Is this from:

(1) a newspaper report
(2) a letter to a friend
(3) a school textbook
(4) an interview in a magazine?

(b) 'On the brink of death Sally felt her mind reel under the awful realization that Melanie had set out to kill her'.

Is this from:

(1) a newspaper report
(2) a friendly letter
(3) a story in a magazine
(4) a letter in a newspaper?

Evaluating material for other readers

Older learners can be encouraged to evaluate material for other reader groups in a range of different ways. They can, for instance:

—Evaluate the content of reading material written for younger children, discussing the linguistic and cultural context and commenting on classist, sexist or racist stereotyping (incidentally this activity might lead into writing stories for younger children, too, thereby providing an authentic purpose to writing, so often missing, as with reading, in the school).

—Evaluate forms and leaflets written for particular groups or the general public to consider:
the likely target audience; the purpose of the document; how generally readable it is.

Finally they might design their own forms, thinking of how to make the language accessible to the target readership and considering such things as graphic features and layout, as well as vocabulary and syntax.

Vocabulary: Still Worrying About the Words

However much we, as teachers, try to suggest that effective reading is more to do with the sorts of processes just described than with knowing vocabulary, many learners even beyond beginning reading may still see reading difficulty in terms of 'not knowing the words'. Of Brendon Kelly's class of 12-year-olds (cf. Chapter 1), nearly all felt that word meaning was the most difficult thing about reading (indeed almost a quarter of the class talked of difficulty in terms of not knowing how to 'pronounce the words'). Obviously the reader with a wide vocabulary is advantaged and in Chapter 6, I suggested some ways of extending learners' vocabulary. However, the fact remains that the best way of extending vocabulary is through reading itself; and vocabulary work should aim to develop the strategies for doing this. Many traditional vocabulary exercises, rather than encouraging learners to discover new meanings from context, simply test whether words are already known. An example may be this question from an Ordinary Level English examination:

Which one of the following words is closest in meaning to 'guileful' as used in line 12?
A—evil
B—sinister·
C—twisted
D—sarcastic
E—sly

If you already know the word, E is clearly the only possible option here. You do not need to look at the text, which does not in fact give strong contextual support in this case. If our aim is to teach helpful comprehension strategies, rather than test what is already known, then we want to help our learners acquire vocabulary in the course of reading; to show them how meeting a word in context or a number of contexts helps us induce a core meaning for it. Students should never be asked comprehension vocabulary questions, the ability to answer which depends on prior knowledge of the word.

It is the anxious reader who worries about not knowing the words. Therefore one of the first things we might do is show students that we, too, do not know all the words, but that we can nonetheless read pretty well for our purposes most of the time, and that looking up words is the last resort of the successful reader. We can bring into reading groups examples of texts which contain words for which we would be hard put to give a dictionary definition (though we might have a rough idea). For myself, examples would be the words *dialectical* and *albescent* in these contexts:

> Mr Roy Hattersley does try to be another Harold, though he places himself in something of a dialectical difficulty by favouring Wilsonian compromises at one minute and Gaitskellite stands at another.
>
> (Alan Watkins, 'Political Diary', *Observer*, 31 July 1983)

> The world looked with interest at the man who first showed Monroe's entire albescent physique.
>
> ('The Silver Spoon Girls Stir it up.' Jessica Berens, *Cosmopolitan*, August 1983)

Pupils and teachers can share and discuss uncertainties about word meanings. Members of the class can bring in unusual words (or words used in unusual ways) which they have come across in their reading. One starts with the rough meaning of the word: is it something good or bad? Does it describe appearance, behaviour, thinking and so on. Dictionaries are then used to confirm or disprove guesses.

What one is doing is encouraging maximum use of context before students check for an exact meaning in a dictionary. For everyday reading purposes we may not anyway require a precise dictionary definition. Of course, dictionaries are important in class, to encourage a healthy curiosity about words; but context comes first.

One might use a cloze exercise to get students, not to guess the missing word, necessarily, but to think of what semantic features it must have, supporting their decisions with evidence from the text. For example:

> She employed a team of . $\times$. full-time for 15 years

Students can consider whether × is

> human v. non-human
> animate v. human (i.e. could × be animal?)
> natural v. man-made
> positive v. negative

Students are thus encouraged to explore the text, preferably in groups, for evidence which points to the distinctive features of the missing item. The idea is not necessarily to guess the missing word. Indeed, the words selected for omission can be just those words which have a high redundancy rating; that is, they are not key meanings in the text nor do they make any particular point about the style of the passage or the writer's attitude. In these cases a dictionary-type definition is over-specific for the reader's purpose.

A variation of the idea of encouraging students to reflect on the properties of unknown words is to have multiple-choice items embedded in the text at places of likely unknown words. Texts can be as simple or complex as the general reading level of the group requires. Here is a very simple example in which the story of Donnovan (cf. Chapter 8) is adapted for this purpose:

(In preparation for a party) . . .

Donnovan's grandfather made some carrot juice and a great big rum punch

punch is {
something you wear
something you clean with
an alcoholic drink
a non-alcoholic drink

Students will draw on both the clues in the text and their own experience (here of parties) to arrive at the most likely definition. The idea is to show readers how we learn new words and meanings through reading itself.

We can also show students how meanings are accumulated as one progresses through a text. New words, particularly if they are central to an understanding and/or appreciation of the text, tend to be repeated, whether they refer to important persons, things or events in narrative texts or important concepts in expository texts. One can stop the text at the first introduction of the likely unknown word and invite rough guesses, possibly with the support of a multiple-choice format, to guide the reader towards selecting a meaning which fits the text so far. Again this kind of exercise can be done with any kind of text at any level of reading difficulty.

In Paul Scott's novel *Staying On* the average reader may not know what the word 'mali' refers to on its first introduction in the text. The immediate context is:

> Presently Ibrahim (one of the servants of the house) went out by the back to look for the young mali. The mali was nowhere to be seen.

The evidence from the text enables us at this point to make some rough judgement as to what a 'mali' is. Is a mali for instance a kind of

machine?
animal?
person?
clothing?

Opting for two or three as possibilities, we reserve judgement until—on the next mention of the word—the text helps us to fill out the meaning:

> He went to the servant's quarters in the rear compound and found the young mali trying to repair the leak in the old water-can.

Good reading entails being prepared to tolerate uncertainty until the text offers us further clues.

I have said that some words are more important than others. These are sometimes called the key words, which represent what the text is about. The teacher can pick out the key words from a text, not in order to give the meanings but to find out what a student associates with the word. The word may be part of a newspaper headline, such as STRIKE. One can get the class to free-associate, thinking of as many words as possible that come to mind associated with the word *strike*, eg.

	jobs
	unemployment
STRIKE	dismissal
	sack
	unions

Better still a whole headline or caption can be given, for example

BL shuts Bathgate Factory

which might call up the following associations

redundancy
unemployment
workers
workforce
management, etc.

In this way an appropriate lexical field is built up before learners embark on the text.

As mentioned in Chapter 2, it is more accurate to talk not of words but of meanings or concepts. Judith Langer (1981) introduces the useful idea of 'key concepts', in connection with subject-specific texts. She makes the point that all students have some relevant knowledge about the subject—knowledge which can be 'called up' and organized during the pre-reading phase. Teachers can help students retrieve prior knowledge of a subject through a pre-reading procedure, consisting of three phases:

—tell us anything that comes to mind (for example with the word . . .)
—what made you think of that?

and then (following class discussion)

—based on our discussion, have you anything new to say about . . .

In the first phase the teacher selects a key concept from the text to start group discussion. The students then freely associate. The second phase involves students in thinking of how they arrived at the association. The third phase represents the shared rethinking of the concept and what is associated with it after group discussion. Where new key vocabulary, especially that specific to a new subject, needs to be introduced before reading, it should always be clearly contextualized, whether by the key concept discussion or by a visual demonstration (e.g. the equipment used in a scientific experiment) or through pictures or simpler mini-texts which introduce the key vocabulary prior to the main text. Students need not so much to be taught new words as to be orientated towards the kinds of meaning certain texts will contain.

Finally, it is clearly not enough to see meanings, whether at word or sentence level, in isolation. Interpretation involves reading and relating across the text. Unknown words/concepts, even if not repeated, may be clarified later in a text. One can show students how this happens by occasionally giving them texts which have 'prompts' in the margin. For example:

. . . she's the only one in the family to admit to	
twinges of conscience	How *much* does her
. . . I feel a *bit uneasy* about that	conscience trouble her

(from Barr *et al.*, 1981)

Readers are directed towards the parts of the text that will give them the clue. Or they might themselves be asked to indicate (through underlining, for example) which parts of the text they have used to arrive at a working definition of an unknown word.

Much of the work on texts described here will be done in the English class, but some of the principles of pre-reading and while-reading-type exercises might be applied in other subject classes. To repeat Marland's words, 'The teaching of reading can become an effective way of teaching the subject matter, and the associated concepts.'

Literacy for Life

We shall conclude this chapter by considering some contexts for literacy beyond school, that is literacy needs for work and leisure in a society which demands increasingly sophisticated literacy skills of its members.

Minimal functional literacy will be related to surviving in one's place of work, and forms the basis of language training programmes in the workplace, such as those offered by Industrial Language Training Units. In the first instance the ability to find one's way round a place of work will depend on being able to follow signs and directions and understand safety regulations. This is what we have called survival literacy. Beyond minimal literacy, however, there is the need to understand more complex job-related written language. One can usefully prepare packs of reading materials that relate to a particular job, or get students themselves to think of as many things as possible that they need to read as part of performing a particular job, including socializing in the lunch hour and belonging to a trade union. This kind of practical literacy work is obviously relevant to people in work, but can also be done with learners at school or on Youth Training Programmes. A group of young trainee hairdressers on a Youth Training Scheme together compiled this list of job-related reading texts:

> appointments book;
> price list;
> instructions on products;
> hairdressing journals for general interest;
> instructions in journals on how to do styles;
> advertisements for new products;
> record cards giving information about customers.

An alternative is to ask students to make a 'literacy diary', noting what reading or writing tasks they are required to do in the course of a working day.

Many of us are likely to need not just reading skills for work, but reading skills for being out of work. Unemployment, as well as employment, requires us to be able to read in order to take advantage of the rights or opportunities available to us. We are likely to be involved in scanning job advertisements in newspapers or shop windows, skimming through leaflets that might affect our interests, and carefully reading things that clearly do affect our interests.

Forms, in particular, present certain linguistic and cultural difficulties for L2 readers. While some forms are now well-designed, giving information and instructions in a clear, accessible style and format, others continue to be almost impenetrable, even to good readers, as it seems to me is this extract from Form CH 11, 'One Parent Benefit':

> Are you getting, or have you received during the last twelve months, or are you waiting for the result of a claim for industrial death benefit for a child at the lower rate (where no industrial injuries widow's pension is, or was paid to you)?

Even in the context of the other information in the form it is very hard to answer a simple YES or NO to such a question.

L2 readers will need some help in coping not just with the linguistic features of forms as, indeed, do many L1 readers, but with certain cultural assumptions about life-styles. For example, the social structure of a family from the Asian sub-continent is very different from the simple family unit of the West. The head of the family is the oldest male, regardless of whether or not he is the breadwinner. Cousins are 'brothers', and naming systems may be different. Information about family groupings may therefore create some cross-cultural difficulty. For anyone adapting to a different language and social structure, the demands of bureaucracy are formidable.

Similarly, being an effective consumer in so-called 'advanced' Western countries involves one in ever more complex reading skills. Simple *Which* (the magazine of the Consumer's Association) reports—or adaptations of these—can form the basis of more advanced material for consumer skills work. One might—with adults, for instance—ask the group to list what they would look for in, say, buying a bike such as:

    cost;
    appearance;
    technical impressiveness.

They might then, in looking at a range of advertised models, consider how they rate against these criteria. Or they might make their own shopping lists for household products and then do a scanning exercise through advertisements for the products of different supermarkets in order to select the cheapest brands.

In this chapter I have hoped to show how readers beyond beginner level can be helped to be more critical, reflective and confident. The aim has been to suggest ways of developing reading strategies which will help them cope with educational needs across the curriculum and with situations in everyday life.

We need now to turn again to perhaps the most important reason for reading of all—reading for pleasure. Whether one chooses to talk of educating for unemployment or more euphemistically perhaps of educating for leisure, reading for pleasure must score highly. It is first of all possibly the only free form of entertainment, given the availability of public libraries. It is something you do on your own, but it also offers a potentially enormous range of things to talk about to other people. You can share impressions and opinions of your reading with others, ask for advice about books on certain subjects and so on. Much reading for pleasure is 'short-burst' reading of comics and magazines. Whole books offer opportunity for more sustained reading for pleasure. In the next chapter I shall look at the role of books and at what criteria we might use in selecting books, for the L2 learner-reader in particular.

8

What to Read

In talking of what to read, I am ending where perhaps I should have begun. For if we can put the right things to read in the way of our learners, we are more than half-way to getting them to become readers.

While there are rich sources of reading material all round us, it is books that, on the whole, offer opportunities for more sustained reading, allowing people to see themselves as real readers. Children see reading as the entrée to an adult world (reading 'makes you grow up' as 5-year-old Baljit said (Chapter 1)); adults want to join the club of parents who read stories to their children or those who visit libraries or belong to book clubs. As David Milner (1983) says, 'The book as a source of information and knowledge has a mystique and an authenticity which is unrivalled by other cultural media.' We want to get our learners as soon as possible to see themselves not just as readers, but as readers of books.

In this chapter I shall consider some of the criteria we might use in selecting books for multilingual classes, books whose structure and content do not intimidate early readers; books which do not stereotype or patronize minority cultures and, above all, books which are fun to read.

Finally but most importantly, we can consider the enormous flow of popular literature around us—romance novels, comics, magazines and newspapers. How do they, if at all, reflect a culturally and linguistically diverse society?

The Content of Books

Writers as readers: making your own books

I started, in Chapter 1, by saying that the content of early reading should come from learners themselves. There are no such things as 'easy' or 'difficult' words; there are high or low content words for individual learners, or rather there are words or collocations which express powerful meanings for the reader. How can we get at these high content words—words which, when they are met in reading, will have what Zimet (1980) calls 'recognition value', and will leap from the page?

There are several ways in which the students' own words can help to launch them into reading. Firstly, one can ask students to recount a particular experience or describe a familiar process, such as making *puri* or raising pigeons. This can be taped. One can then, acting as scribe, produce a written version of what the students have said. A difficulty presented to the teacher when transcribing the students' own words is how to conventionalize them according to the requirements of the written medium. Particularly in the case of E2L learners, it is probably best to modify the learner's spoken version, filling out the structure to produce predictable, well-formed sentences for them to read back.

The advantage of such an approach is that in the case of a reading class or group, a coherent readable text, even a proper book, may emerge from an experience which the group has shared. An example was the shared recollections of a visit to the students' college by Prince Charles. Contributions from the group included what he wore, who he spoke to, and what he said. The result was 'The day Prince Charles visited the Pathway Centre'.

An alternative is for learners to write their own books. With second language learners with very little spoken or written English one might begin by getting them to write simple biographies describing their appearance, likes and dislikes and so on. This is particularly suitable for adult learners who have a lot to say but limited means in English of saying or writing it. They can bring together the English they do know in the context of simple SVC or SVO sentences. The structures are given; the content is their own. They may, of course, need the help of more fully bilingual fellow-students to get a translation into English of some of the words they want to use. For example, they can slot items like *war, violence, the bomb, jobs, husband, girl-friend, fish and chips* into simple sentence contexts. And it is not only L2 learners who will welcome the opportunity to write about themselves, but other students who are beginning to explore the possibilities of literacy. William, a young Afro-Caribbean student, had missed schooling and was now, aged 18, learning to read and write. He wanted to say these things about himself:

I am	slim
	handsome
	lovable
	tall
	black
I like	girls
	Jamaican food
	Indian food
I want	a job
	a house
I hate	violence
	discrimination
We want	jobs
	employment

Eventually, simple biographies like these or more elaborate ones can be put together into a collection of personal stories to be read by the whole group. Alternatively, with students who come from a range of different cultural backgrounds, they may each contribute a folk story. The taped oral rendering of the stories can then be transcribed and 'translated' into written story form by a teacher. In fact, the spoken story mode translates more successfully than other forms of speech into the written story mode.

The value of this kind of language experience approach is that in putting together these simple personal profiles, experiences or stories, students feel that they have something worth saying and writing, and also something that someone else might want to read.

Real books

While language experience approaches have a place in any reading class of adults or children, they do present difficulties, already touched upon in Chapter 6. One is that the dual writer/reader role is not one which we commonly take on in real life. We usually want to read not about our own but about someone else's experiences, ideas and feelings. Simply reading back what one has written or produced with the support of a teacher, either individually or as part of a group, is not an authentic reading experience, in this one sense at least. We know what we think, feel or have experienced. We want to share with a writer new feelings, ideas and experiences, which may be very remote from those of our immediate social group. Reading allows us, as Rosen and Rosen (1973) describe it, to 'converse with more voices than we hear from the speakers round us'. Aspiring readers need to have a sense of what it is that reading uniquely enables us to do.

How can we make the reading experience a 'real' one for our learners? How can we get them to feel that they are exploring new experiences and ideas through reading? At the simplest level we can ensure that the reading realia introduced to students has an authentic communicative function. For this reason I preferred in Chapter 6 to talk of **messages** rather than words in the context of introducing a basic sight vocabulary. Written language, from one-word messages to whole books, should be seen to communicate something. If readers are to be encouraged to engage with print—to interact with the text—there should be a foundation for such an interaction in all the reading material we introduce to our students.

We need, too, to consider the identity of the writer. With some kinds of writing, the personal identity of the writer is irrelevant. Examples of this kind of writing are signs, notices, gas bills or income tax forms. Because of their anonymity, such writing has been called 'institutional' writing (Davies and Widdowson, 1974). In other kinds of writing the writer does take on an identity, and we noted in Chapter 3 how an identity is also attributed to the reader. We might qualify this here by saying that writers have not single but multiple identities, any one of which may be highlighted in different kinds of texts, depending on content and genre; it may be more or less relevant what sex the writer is, of which ethnic group or of what political beliefs. In adult reading, at least, we are aware of what we might call the writer's 'voice'. A sense of both writer identity and writer purpose is one of the hallmarks of 'real' books.

In books written for small children the writer's identity is likely to take second place to the events of the story. Nonetheless, active young readers soon begin to express their favourite reading in terms of favourite writers; they are likely to move away from talking about reading preferences in terms of 'horror stories' or or 'funny books' to 'Roald Dahl' or 'C. S. Lewis'; and it is certainly possible to introduce to children books which are real in terms of their function. Real books inform, entertain or have a moral. 'Reading books', on the other hand, are written primarily to teach reading. Educators write reading books. Real books are written by people who would describe themselves as authors.

There is no reason why real books, in the sense I have described, should not play the major role in early reading instruction for children. Jill Bennett (1979) believes that children should be introduced to real books from the start of reading; she sees story as the basis of everything. Story books can be read out loud, giving children a sense of story, in the way that most reading books do not. Stories have an organization, a beginning, a middle and an end; reading books, as I discuss later in this chapter, may be no more than strings of sentences. We want to get learners to see books, or any texts, as wholes. Even simple books of no more than twenty words can be given some narrative shape.

Children move into the reading experience through hearing stories read out loud, and for E2L learners the sense of story can be developed through hearing stories told in their first language. Here there is an important role for parents of language minority children, who might either come into the school to read to the children or tape stories for the children to listen to. As reported to me by Linda Smith, one young Asian girl on a Youth Training Scheme had great success in a Barking school. She worked alongside the regular classroom teacher, telling and reading stories in several community languages and translating and explaining where necessary. In this way the bilingualism or trilingualism of young people in the community can be used to good effect. White, monolingual children can also be encouraged to take an interest in these stories and follow them through gestures and pictures, much as beginner E2L learners are required to do in the case of listening to English stories.

Listening to an experienced reader reading out loud undoubtedly has an important part to play in familiarizing learners with kinds of texts and kinds of stories. Perera (1981) interestingly suggests that even teachers of older children might occasionally read non-fiction subject texts out loud in a class, helping students to get used to the more complex structure and rhythms of formal prose.

I would only add a note of caution here, with regard to stories, at least. Some stories lend themselves far more easily to being read aloud by a skilled reader than by a beginner. For instance, certain kinds of dialogue can be lifted off the page by a good reader reading out loud, but perplex the learner who is still struggling to make the appropriate links between speaking and reading. One solution to this may be to have two versions of the same story (cf. *Reading through Understanding*). The teacher reads out the full version of the story, after which the learner reads a simplified model of the story. As the child reads his own version, however, the simpler text is enriched by recollection of the experience of hearing the full version.

With adult learners, choosing real books presents greater problems. Books written for the general adult market, whether fiction or non-fiction, whether do-it-yourself, romantic fiction or thriller, will simply be too difficult for the adult learner-reader. Just the same, I believe that, as is the case with children, story is the basis of everything. Adults, like children, enjoy simply written fables and folk tales, and as discussed in earlier chapters, these have, for E2L learner-readers particularly, the added advantage of structural repetition and a predictability of outcomes.

Structural readers

Are structural readers of the kind often written for foreign-language learners to count as real books? Structural readers may be either original fiction or non-fiction and are characterized by carefully controlled vocabulary and sentence patterns. Much depends on the quality of the content; if a story has strong narrative interest, for instance, the reader is likely to be persuaded that the book offers an authentic reading experience and not just an opportunity to improve his English. On the whole, structural readers have a useful role to play in guiding readers into second language literacy; features such as consistent tense and predictable syntax give helpful support. However, if a story line is reduced to the bare bones, events may then become too condensed for reader comfort. As I discuss more fully later in this chapter, short does not necessarily mean simple. Making texts easier for L2, and indeed for L1 readers, may involve adding to and elaborating texts rather than reducing them.

Occasionally, well-known books, including the classics, are abridged and simplified in order to make them more accessible to L2 readers. Some might object to this 'mucking about' with the classics. In defence of simplified readers, however, it might be argued that there are only so many good stories to go round; in simplifying *Great Expectations* or *Wuthering Heights*, writers are easing the path for those who want to read the classics. The mere fact of reduced length, larger print, different format and illustrations makes them less daunting; and, of course, one hopes that at a later stage students may be motivated to read the original books. Many structural or simplified readers have found their way into classrooms for indigenous 'remedial' learners. It may be that remedial teachers feel that the structural readers do not make the same assumptions about their readership as do books written particularly for indigenous adult or adolescent poor readers; these tend to assume that their readers will identify with delinquents or down-and-outs of various kinds. It is an assumption which many poor readers understandably resent. They may not be able to read very well, but they do not want to see themselves as social deviants.

So good stories, either original or adapted, which are structured with an eye to the E2L learner-reader, also have an important part to play in literacy teaching to older children and adults who are native speakers of English. But what is it that makes a good story? A full discussion would take us far beyond the scope of this chapter. A few points may suffice here. Firstly, the material should, for early readers, be familiar, but not too familiar. We need to know about the basic scripts described, for example what happens when people go shopping, go to the dentist or get a parking ticket. But we do not necessarily want to be taken through the stages. None of us wants merely to read about what happens in everyday life. However, reading books as opposed to real books tend to describe just that, taking readers through supposed everyday events in their own lives. They may be 'real life' but they are not 'real books'. Real life can be the backcloth to the story but not the story itself. In a good story something must happen, something exciting, funny or frightening. There must be a climax. Even for the very early reader it is possible to give the kernel of a good story, as Cliff Moon shows so successfully in his simplified fables. Text 11 shows a sample page.

The role of pictures

I have already mentioned how important pictures are in supporting and filling out written texts, particularly for early learners. Too often pictures are merely decorative. We need to look for pictures—and diagrams and charts—which interact with the text, each supporting and reinforcing the other.

While the pictures should relate closely to the text, the text should not be there

TEXT 11

The hare ran and ran.

The tortoise crawled and crawled.

(Cliff Moon, *Hare and Tortoise*)

simply to describe the pictures. Some early reading books begin with captions rather than self-contained simple texts. For example, to accompany a picture of a table with a sheet over it and a teddy bear under it, we have as text 'What is in the house?' (cf. Text 12) or, in the case of a picture of a dog playing. 'He is playing with the dolls and the toys', followed on the next page by 'the dog can play with the baby in the house'. It is true that the pictures provide the information in the text for the learner-reader. The difficulty is that there is no continuity of text; there is no motive to turn the page,

Even in early reading one picture should follow the other, just as one part of the text naturally follows on from the preceding part. Pictures can then help learners to develop a sense of sequence, crucial to an understanding of narrative. Some reading materials, in particular *Reading through Understanding*, have very

TEXT 12

what is in the house

(E. Bradburne, *The Dog in the House*)

imaginatively incorporated picture sequencing into the suggested teaching procedure. *Make-a-story*, the material for 5–8-year-olds, contains full-colour picture cards which, when sequenced, tell the story. The picture sequence allows the learners to anticipate the events.

True stories

Many books for adult learner-readers have adopted the true-story format. The books record the lives and experiences of the usually poor and working-class students who have attended adult literacy classes. Many of these stories, told by the students themselves, are very good; they are moving and funny, with a powerful sense of the writer's identity. However, there are occasionally difficulties for readers with different cultural backgrounds and values. Annie Spike, in *A Woman's Work* (Centerprise, 1978), describes her idea of a good time: it is a day's outing, or 'beano', with her mates from the factory. The whole script is likely to mystify the second language reader, however, as I have tried to suggest here:

TEXT 13

And you go on your beanos—
Your days out
You all put
a few bob together
over so many months,
then hire a coach (OK so far)
and go off down to Southend
You stop at a halfway house
all get a bit drunk
and have a knees up (?)
To me Beanos are fantastic,
out with your hats and streamers
and the blokes are so blind drunk
they've lost their memories (? ?)

(Annie Spike, *A Woman's Work*)

Now linguistic and cultural minority learners are beginning to tell their stories in published form. The book that Ravinder was reading (Case Studies 4) was one of these, called *Back Home* by Ranjit Sumal, and published by the Commonplace Workshop. It is a story that people who have left their country of birth to settle elsewhere will relate to; but, as Anne Johnson says in the introduction, it is also a story with a universal theme. Leaving home is something most of us do at some point in our lives. This is a story of a particular life and a particular journey, but, as Anne Johnson says, 'all the stories of the journeys and lives of working people have much in common'.

The Commonplace Workshop is a very small publishing company which publishes writing by ordinary people living in the West London Borough of Ealing. Many of these mostly young writers are poor, working-class and black. They look back to early childhood in their homeland, or describe their experiences of growing up in a white, largely hostile society, as this poem by Paul George, a Grenadian, does:

TEXT 14

SPLIT IMAGE

I looked in the mirror once,
I saw a black face.
Who are you nigger?
I questioned.
What right have you
To be in this here land?
You don't work
The voice replied.
Same right as you have,
Black boy

(Paul George, *Memories*)

Publications such as those produced by Gatehouse or Centerprise have a slightly different purpose. They aim to give adult literacy students a voice of their own by giving them the opportunity to recount stories of their own lives and experiences in print. The books are also intended to be read by other adult learner-readers, and it is this which may present certain difficulties; for while the content of many of these biographies or autobiographies is interesting, the language of some of them creates particular difficulty for second language learners. The nature of these difficulties is discussed in the next section, The Language of Books.

Sex, race and class as portrayed in children's books

A powerful and increasingly voiced objection to much of children's literature and reading books is that the characters are overwhelmingly white, middle-class and male; although girls are featured, they are frequently the supporting cast. Boys are given the leading roles. They tend to take the initiative; girls follow suit. So for instance, in the *Television Castle* (Sparks Readers) it is Robert who is seen to act, while Ruth is the onlooker:

Robert climbed up the tree and looked in the window

It is Robert who makes most of the suggestions too:

Let's try to get in at the back

Mums and dads, too, have clear traditionally defined roles, so that even in the *Nippers* series of reading books, which have in many ways succeeded in moving away from conventional reading book language and content, Mum nags while Dad acts.

The impression gained from the text is reinforced by the pictures, where boys are seen to be doing things much more frequently than girls, who stand passively by. Much the same is the case between black and white characters. The white children on the whole, as shown in both the text and pictures, play the lead roles. The black children are faces in the crowd. Chinese children rarely figure at all.

The exception to the dominance of white male characters is in those books written for a particular minority group, such as books for adult, home language tuition. This is the situation where adult E2L learners are taught literacy and language in their own homes on a one-to-one basis by volunteers. These books have a closely identified target readership. For example, a set of readers produced by the Community Education Project (Coventry Education Committee) have been written for Asian women. There has been a clear attempt to identify reader need, and one cannot, in fairness, object to sex stereotyping where the women reading the books are likely to find themselves in just those situations which the books describe; going to the clinic, for example, or going shopping. These books have a useful place; their readers will have some prior knowledge of the 'scripts' they describe, which they can then bring to bear on the text. At the same time, useful everyday transactions and key vocabulary can be rehearsed and practised respectively in the reading of the books. They are a helpful bridge to real reading;

they cannot, however, in the long term replace those books which, in the telling of a good story, reflect a culturally diverse society in a natural, unselfconscious way.

To sum up, the objection to the content of books is on three counts. Firstly, there are simply far more male than female characters, and proportionally more white than black characters. Secondly, when blacks and women do feature, they are not the lead characters. And the third objection, which I turn to now, is that both blacks and women take on predictable roles in stories.

Admittedly, writers are in something of a 'no-win' situation; they are condemned for portraying the stereotype, down-trodden, passive girl or woman or the socially or educationally alienated young black; at the same time they are open to accusations of a different kind when women are seen to be 'behaving like men' or blacks 'like whites'. Moreover, there is inconsistency as between the criticism of the portrayal of sex role and class behaviour. Books are criticized for putting women in typically women's roles—shopping, cooking and so on; but most women do take on these roles in real life. The argument against this, which I would accept, is that 'reading is not like real life'. Reading should not just reflect contemporary reality but challenge current life-styles and values.

If books are attacked, and rightly so, for allowing women a very limited set of behaviour options, why, when it comes to class, are working-class families almost always portrayed as scruffy and dishonest, with Mum in curlers, and milk bottles on the table (again the pictures reinforce the stereotypes). The assumption seems to be that older, 'remedial' readers, for whom this type of book appears to be written, will identify with Ginger (cf. Chapter 3) who is a bit of a delinquent with Dad in prison and so on. This is fine as long as other images of working-class people appear in the general range of reading material.

Ethnic minorities also tend to be presented in restricted social contexts, almost exclusively in urban, working-class environments. Once again, this is unobjectional, as long as other images of black people appear in books. To say that these images reflect reality is, as we have seen, beside the point. For stories—real stories—do more than reflect reality. They should cut across the grain of the everyday and predictable. In doing so, they both avoid sex, race or class stereotyping and give us a good story.

The Language of Books

Books that 'teach reading'

Books that set out to teach reading are frequently not so much books as strings of sentences which do not connect to build up any kind of text with a beginning, middle and end. A sense of the progression of a text may easily be lost if the over-riding aim is to show the phonic regularities of English or introduce learners to a particular set of sight vocabulary. In fact, it has been observed that some reading books can actually be read backwards with little or no loss of meaning! A random page taken from a Ladybird reader shows how, on this particular page at least, the lines could just as well be read from bottom to top:

TEXT 15

> Here they go, in the car
> Daddy is in the car with Peter and Jane
> We like it in the car, they say
> Go on, Daddy, go on
> We want to go on and on
> This is good fun, they say
>
> (Ladybird, *Key Words Reading Scheme*)

Texts like this can start or stop at any point. Learners are thus encouraged to think that reading also can start or stop at any place in the text, and that we read words or lines or pages and not continuous text. But we want to give learner-readers a reason for turning the page; we want to find books, including even very simple books, which make it hard to stop at the end of the page.

At word and sentence level, too, the language of books that concentrate on the decoding aspects of reading is often bizarre, bearing little relation to any other written or spoken variety of English. There is a special language of reading books which is peculiarly uncommunicative, sometimes known as 'readerese'. Even their titles tell us very little. What can we anticipate for instance about a book which is called *Paint Away?* All it tells us is that the writers are concerned to present the letter clusters *ai* and *ay* as the homophone (ei). Indeed, a major aim of the text is to include as many words as possible which contain this particular sound, taking Received Pronunciation as a model. The final two lines are typical of the text:

> It's no longer a rainy day
> So paint away, paint away

The emphasis is on words—in this case words that look different but sound the same. Such reading approaches attend to the substance of reading rather than looking beyond surface characteristics of texts to features of syntax and meaning.

Look and Say approaches also attend to the surface text. For instance, if we take the sentence:

TEXT 16

>   (1)   (2)
> We like going round your farm like this
>
> (Ladybird, *Key Words Reading Scheme*)

Like (1) and *like* (2) are identical in substance, that is they are graphonically identical, but they are grammatically and semantically quite distinct. *Like* (1) is a content item—a verb—whereas *like* (2) is an item of structure—a conjunction. Sentences of this kind in early reading result not in the learning and reinforcement of new words but, for a non-native speaker of the language particularly, in total confusion.

In fairness, it has to be said that many learner-readers respond well to phonically biased and *Look and Say* reading books, that is those books which set out ostensibly to teach reading. Some of the phonically biased books (despite my earlier strictures) do in fact manage to allow for fun with words, playing with rhymes, even at times producing plausible narrative. The difficulty is that it is hard to maintain the fun element over a whole series of books, as some phonically biased reading schemes attempt.

The most famous representative of the **Look and Say** approach, *Peter and Jane*, remains popular for several reasons, I believe. Firstly, the books are attractively illustrated and easy to handle; secondly, they provide a text, or rather series of pages which, however stilted and odd the style, allow very early readers the opportunity to move quickly through them. Learners are not exactly reading for meaning—for there is little meaning to be had—but they are getting through pages of print. The 'readerese' acquires a momentum of its own. My learner, Peter, after a few weeks only of learning to read from scratch, got through an early *Peter and Jane* book. No matter that it was with considerable support from myself; no matter that the book was fairly nonsensical (as Peter was quite aware for he laughed as we read 'He jumped up up up'). No matter that it was anyway written for 5-year-olds rather than for someone of 40. He had read a book for the first time, and that in itself represented a considerable achievement.

Nonetheless, the difficulty with the word-centred approaches typical of reading books is that, because they tend to concentrate on the phonic or visual characteristics of individual words, readers are not encouraged to see the text as a coherent whole. While I have suggested that some reading books are almost a genre in their own right, with a unique kind of predictability, they bear no relation to any other variety of written or spoken language. Real texts which tell real stories or describe identifiable processes, events or transactions, preferably with an element of surprise, are on the whole easier to read than strings of sentences.

Secondly, books which teach reading tend to have very low-interest content, with low-interest vocabulary for most learners; they may be common words but, as discussed in Chapter 2, words like *dog, toy* and *shop* do not excite the imagination or call up rich associations as do, for instance, *dragon* or *flying saucer*.

Thirdly, reading books are not informed by any sense of writer purpose, or at least not one which is accessible to the learner. It is not clear whether the writer or writers aim to inform us of certain facts, tell us a funny story or allow us to have fun with words. If writers write books to 'teach reading' it is not surprising that young readers see the purpose of reading books not to enjoy the story or learn about something but to 'learn new words' or to 'learn reading'.

In conclusion, books that aim to teach reading through paying close attention to the look or sound of words are particularly unsuitable for L2 readers on several counts:

—They tend to encourage a mechanistic view of reading, which many L2 learner-readers have anyway.
—L2 learners are denied the opportunity of extending their experience of English, its structure, vocabulary and textual organization through clear predictable texts, with a beginning, a middle and an end.
—Phonically biased readers in particular are unsuitable for L2 learners who, as discussed in Chapter 6, are likely to have a different set of homophones from RP speakers. Indeed, phonic schemes which are designed for basically southern English RP speakers present difficulties for speakers of other accents than RP, as well as for non-native speakers. At the very least, the point of the phonic organization, will be lost. For example, though *where/wear* will be

pronounced differently by most Scottish speakers, for whom they are not homophones, the pair *cot/caught* are homophones for Scots but not for RP speakers.

Books that 'teach the language'

In EFL/ESL teaching contexts one comes across reading texts whose sole aim is to practise the structures and vocabulary introduced through speaking. As proposed in Chapter 6, work on listening and speaking skills can lead naturally into certain kinds of reading texts, preparing students for some of the typical features of written narrative or the descriptions of processes or transactions contained in written texts. At the same time, however, a reading text, of whatever length, should stand on its own as an authentic piece of communication. It must have something to say to us. In some language teaching materials, reading is presented merely as an opportunity to practise a particular **sentence** pattern, such as the present continuous. Here is an extract from a reader in the Scope teaching material:

TEXT 17

This is London airport
It is Sunday. It is ten o'clock
This is Ali's father
This is Ali's uncle
They are at the airport
They are wearing coats
They are wearing coats
because it is cold in England
They are at the airport
They are looking at the planes.

(*Scope*, Reader 6, *Ali's coming to England*)

At the worst, EFL texts are communicatively quite empty, stating what the reader already knows, as does this reading passage from a text book for Arab learners of English:

TEXT 18

1. This is the first lesson of Book Two. You can now read a little
2. English. You are in the classroom. That is your teacher in
3. front of the class. Can you see the teacher standing at the
4. blackboard? The teacher is now getting chalk and books out
5. of the cupboard. How many windows do you see in the room?
6. You are sitting at your desk.

(Stannard Allen *et al.*, *English for Arabs*, Book 2)

The text lacks coherence. 'You can now read a little English' seems to have little to do with the following sentence 'You are in the classroom'. Nor is it easy to see how the teacher's activities in lines 4 and 5 relate to the number of windows in the room. Once again, what we have is not a text, but a string of sentences.

Even where real (i.e. new) information is given in 'EFL' texts, we are not always offered a plausible piece of text. This example is taken from an American book for E2L learners:

TEXT 19

Text B
Mr and Mrs Lee live in Chicago. They are going to Jamaica on their vacation. They're going by plane and they're staying there for a month. They aren't staying in a hotel, they are staying with friends.

(Manuel C.R. dos Santos, *In Tune*)

Texts like this are over-informative. We are unlikely to be very interested in what the Lees *are* doing; do we really need to know what they *aren't* doing (i.e. staying in a hotel). Of course, the negative statement is there to allow practice with the negative, present continuous tense; and while such texts may legitimately serve the purpose of reinforcing areas of the language system of English for second language learners, they cannot really count as reading. They are not likely to motivate learners to become readers in the second language.

Books that are like speaking

Books which try to represent the way we speak create particular difficulty for early L2 learner readers. Texts may, for instance, display contractions or ellipsis, as in this extract from one of the *True Life* Gatehouse books, written by an adult literacy student for other adult literacy students:

TEXT 20 (Josie has been talking about her mother and father)

> Even told me I didn't have to read and write
> because of the simple reason I was a girl, and would grow
> up to be married and have babies.

(Josie Byrens, *Never in a Loving Way*)

Never in a Loving Way was told by Josie herself and written down by her teachers. The story reads like a very close rendering of Josie's own spoken version. Doubtless, Josie's teachers did not want to lose the author's authentic voice through any editing or restructuring. This is understandable, but the result is an occasional loss of coherence in the written form. On reading the story along with a student, I myself thought there was a mistake on coming to this new paragraph. The elliptical omission of the subject (before 'Even') creates extraordinary difficulty here, especially when the preceding part of the text does not make it wholly clear whether Josie is talking about her father or her mother. The content of the story is interesting and moving. It is a pity, therefore, that the language does not guide the reader along. Some editing and restructuring would not spoil the authenticity of this and similar 'real life' stories and would make them more accessible to a wider range of adult learner.

Writers for children, also aiming to make the written text more natural, that is more like informal speaking, create similar difficulty by omitting structure words such as pronouns and verbal auxiliaries. For example:

TEXT 21

> Its winter now, said the farmer
> Got nowhere to go wintertime Pa said
> Chucked off the airfield

(Geraldine Kaye, *Christmas is a Baby*)

Here pronouns such as *we* and auxiliaries such as *have* and *been* are omitted (*we have* got nowhere to go . . . *we have been* chucked off the airfield).

There are several reasons why omitted structure, including such features as contracted forms (cf. Yasmeen, Case Studies 5), creates difficulty for learner-readers, particularly E2L learners. Firstly, as noted in Chapter 2, learner-readers realize early on that there are distinctive differences between what we typically speak and what we read. Secondly, the very early learner, reading in 'reading aloud style', with little of the pace of natural speech, will make little sense of writers' attempts to characterize spoken usage. Finally, in the case of some E2L learners, colloquial English style may not be in their own repertory of spoken English styles, so this kind of writing is even more inaccessible for them than for native speakers.

Colloquial usage in written language, especially where some of the sentence structure is omitted, actually makes reading harder for learner-readers. In this sense shorter does not mean easier. The more structure we have, the more redundancy. Redundancy is the term used to describe the fact that all language, whether spoken or written, gives us more than the minimally necessary information. For instance if one says 'See him yesterday?' the question mark in written language signals the question form. This information is duplicated if we add more structure to the sentence, that is an auxiliary and a pronoun: '*Did you* see him yesterday?' E2L learners depend on this extra information. In fact it is often what is missing from texts, rather than what is on the page, that makes for reading difficulty. Easy listening and reading for the early E2L learner are dependent on fully structured language.

Books in non-standard English

I have argued against books for early learners which are like speaking in the sense that they present written forms of colloquial speech. They are attempts to convey a certain **style** of speaking in writing. What about books written in non-standard **dialect**? While I would certainly wish to present a case for high levels of literacy in the standard language, this does not in principle preclude the use of non-standard English in reading material for classroom use.

In the United States, less so in Britain, there has been considerable interest in producing books written in black English—or more particularly, in the case of the United States, in Black Vernacular English. The argument for these is attractive, and many linguists, as for instance Stewart (1969), have argued persuasively in favour of early reading materials written in the children's own non-standard dialect. In making available books written in a learner's home dialect, one is bringing book language closer to the student's own spoken language. He can then more readily, it is argued, predict the syntax and vocabulary of the text.

However, while in principle it is possible for any non-standard dialect to be used as a perfectly adequate vehicle for writing, there are several difficulties raised by dialect reading books. Firstly, there is no agreed orthography for non-standard varieties of a language. This is not to say that one cannot quickly become established. Conversely, the loss or decline of an orthography may mean that what was once arguably a language comes to be perceived as a mere dialect. A recent translation of the New Testament from Greek into Lowland Scots is an attempt to give new vitality to this particular variety (Text 22).

However, until such an orthography is generally recognized, learner readers will be confused by attempts to produce written versions of dialect. This is particularly the case if attempts are made to characterize pronunciation as well. Shaw, in Pygmalion, was forced very soon to abandon his attempt at a full representation of

Eliza Doolittle's cockney dialect (Text 23).

TEXT 22

Awa in a manger

"Nou i that same pairt the' war a wheen herds
bidin thereout on the hill an keeping gaird owre their
hirsel at nicht. Suddent an angel o the Lord cam an
stuid afore them, an the glorie o the Lord shined about
them, an they war uncolie frichtit. But the angel said
tae them : 'Dinna nane afeared : I bring ye guid news
o gryte blytheness for the haill fowk — this day in
Dauvit's Toun a sauviour hes been born til ye Christ
the Lord! This d gate ye s'ken it is een as I say : ye will
finnd a new born bairn swealed in a barrie an liggin
intil a a heck'."

(*The Guardian*, December 1983)

TEXT 23

THE FLOWER GIRL.   Ow, eez yɔ-ooa san, is e? Wal, fewd dan y' dɔ-ooty bawmz a mather should, eed now
bettern to spawl a pore gel's flahrzn than ran awy athaht pyin. Will ye-oo py me
f'them?

If we turn more particularly to the case of British Black English, one difficulty in
producing an orthography is that there would appear to be considerable variation in
the language used by the Black British. It is difficult to predict exactly which
linguistic features are typical of the speech of a range of users, as one must do if one
is to publish books for non-standard speaking readers. As discussed in Chapter 5,
speakers of Creole are likely to show individual differences in the parts of the Creole
continuum they operate; or they will have varying degrees of Creole features in a
mainly indigenous variety of English. Moreover, it will be remembered that the
Reading through Understanding project team found that the spoken language of the
black children they studied differed little from that of their white peers.

In the light of the above points, writers who present features of non-standard
English, such as Black English, may find that they are not so much representing as
caricaturing typical phonological or syntactic features oi the language variety.
Unless great care is taken in the selection of an orthography, the result of attempts
at a written representation of non-standard language may be offensive to the users
of the particular variety.

A further point is that non-standard spellings are not reinforced outside the
classroom. Nearly all print on TV, in advertising and on street signs will be in
standard English. We want to encourage learners in the early stages of reading to
relate school reading with reading in the real world.

Finally, a powerful objection to providing dialect reading books for some
learners, is that they are thereby singled out as 'different' if they are in a classroom situation; and it is difficult for minority groups with low status in their
community or in society at large to be convinced that different provision does not
mean inferior provision. Admittedly we should work towards changing attitudes. In
the meantime, account needs to be taken of how learners themselves perceive their
own needs in present circumstances. Roxy Harris (1979) makes the point that while

some students may wish to read and write in Creole—keeping in mind the difficulty that Creole English has been an oral language rather than a written one—'In the majority of cases West Indian students will not be willing to do this. If this is so, their wishes must be respected.'

An alternative strategy which I have argued for in this book is to introduce non-standard dialect speakers to standard English books but to allow them to read out loud in their own dialect. In fact, as suggested in Chapter 5, most West Indian learner-readers can predict the forms of standard English in texts as long as they are of high frequency in most varieties of spoken and written English and obscure quasi-literary expressions are initially avoided. As we saw, Hillyard, whose first language was French Creole, was able to predict the language of standard English texts very effectively. Indeed, the very fact that the English writing system does not show a one-to-one correspondence with the pronunciation of any one group of speakers of English is here an advantage. Speakers of English with many varieties in pronunciation are able to use the one writing system; and standard English syntax is only likely to create difficulties, I believe, if the learner is required to reproduce the standard syntax in reading aloud rather than rendering the text in equivalent dialect forms.

So does non-standard English have a place in reading instruction? I believe its place is not in the very early stages of reading, but a little later. Then dialogue can be introduced preferably through oral story-telling; the characters in a story will then be heard to speak Cockney, Glaswegian or some variety of Black English in line with their identity in the story, and learner-readers can begin to understand how people's speech is conventionally conveyed in writing.

For older readers beyond the earliest stages, learners of all language or dialect backgrounds can be introduced to poetry and prose written in varieties such as Black English. They can also observe how writers may at different times and for different reasons draw on different linguistic resources. For instance, Eric Huntly (of the Walter Rodney bookshop) notes that Linton Kwesi Johnson usually writes not in Creole but in a phonetic variety of British Black English; elsewhere, however, he writes in Creole—and also in standard English. Other West Indian poets like James Berry write both in standard English and in Creole. The choice of medium relates to what a writer wishes to say on a particular occasion. There is an exciting diversity of language media here. Nor is there any risk, as I believe there is with dialect reading books, that the use of Black English will be perceived as patronizing or inappropriate; for in these cases it is part of the writer's voice, central to what she is communicating. It shows the whole community of readers, not just black people, that Black English is a fresh and exciting medium and sometimes the only way in which black writers can say what they have to.

Books in two languages

Several bilingual or dual-text books have recently made a welcome addition to the still rather small number of books which have particular appeal to linguistic minority learners. Folk tales have been told in various minority languages and English by people drawn from the community. One result of a collaboration between parents from different language backgrounds and a teacher, Eve Gregory, based in a Newham School in East London, was a collection of four dual-language *Folk and Fairy Tales*, available in English and Punjabi, English and Urdu and English and Gujerati.

A much larger project based at Middlesex Polytechnic (*Reading Materials for Minority Groups*) aims not just to promote the publication of dual-language folk tales but to become 'a repository for community folklore'. The first story produced by Middlesex Polytechnic itself is *The Tiger and the Woodpecker*, a beautifully illustrated book available in seven languages with English. It was this story which was referred to in Chapter 2 (page 30).

It seems to me that the books have several different potential uses. Firstly, they are very helpful material for 'language awareness' work (cf. Chapter 6). They offer a context through which all learners—bilinguals and indigenous monolinguals—can discuss features of the unknown languages. Even without knowing a language at all one can begin to work out some of its distinctive features from a written script, where there is support from a known language; and discussing features of the unfamiliar scripts also highlights awareness of the features of the already known script.

A second use for dual-language books for young bilingual learners is as material to be taken home and possibly read aloud by parents. Parents who are monoliterate in the minority language can then either read the familiar version aloud or even attempt the English version. The books are a way of bridging literacy between home and school.

A third use which I can vouch for is with older learners who are literate in their mother-tongue but not yet in English. A recent class of E2L learners were anxious to get started on L2 reading, but their spoken language competence offered them as yet little support. They were skilled decoders but simply did not know enough English to read for meaning. The familiar language and the familiar stories helped them to move from the known to the unknown.

Choosing Books

Is it possible finally to arrive at some kind of checklist of criteria for choosing books? I have in mind here early L2 learner-readers, particularly those working in the multilingual/multiracial classroom, who are looking to books both as a source of pleasure and learning and as a means of extending their mastery of the second language.

Some criteria

Good stories

The best kinds of texts to get learner-readers started are simple narratives with a clear story line. Stories can build on scripts which are basically familiar to the learner but there must be something beyond the everyday. Real stories aim to excite, surprise or move the reader. The unexpected, even fantastic, is what makes stories interesting.

Pictures which reinforce the story-line

In very early reading books the pictures alone should tell the story and give a sense of a sequence of events or stages in a particular process or transaction. Pictures can then be used to preview the text and introduce the key vocabulary. They should not be merely decorative, and should also avoid stereotyped images; there are still too many Mums in curlers, boys having all the fun, and black faces in the crowd.

Cultural diversity

We should look out for books which simply have far more black and brown children and adults in them in a whole range of roles; we want to see them acting as characters in good stories, whether they are nurses, detectives or bus drivers.

We want to avoid role stereotyping so that Dad cooks supper, boys cry, girls take the initiative and the teacher or doctor is black. Stories which depart from the predictable scripts are anyway more interesting. Many writers have seen the appeal of the tom-boy character—including Enid Blyton—though, of course, boys behaving like girls is simply 'not on'.

We do not necessarily want to ban the sexist and racist books. Writers like Enid Blyton have had a rough ride in recent years. There are charges of racism in her books, by a number of people (cf. Dixon, 1978 and Hoffman 1976). Agatha Christie, too, is thought to be racist; anti-semitic in particular. So is Shakespeare, however much we fudge the issue; and Bob Dixon rightly points out, 'There is no need for anyone to accept racism in literature, not even if expressed in deathless blank verse.' Nonetheless, writers, good and bad, write in line with their own ethnic, class and sex identity and with widely-held views about class, sex and race current at the time of writing. Rather than ban Shakespeare, or even Enid Blyton, perhaps one can try and open up discussion, with slightly older readers at least, about the factors which affect a writer's view of the world. One solution to racism and negative stereotyping of all kinds in books is to use the content as the basis for dicussion.

This is not to say that we should be sanguine about the racist or sexist content of books. There is a case for censoring certain books, particularly for very young learners who have not yet developed a judgement about who it is that writes books and why. However, it might be best to concentrate our energies on writers who are writing now, and not just the writers of children's fiction, but the whole of popular writing, including newspapers and comics and the whole range of popular fiction.

Clear, predictable structure

In the early stages of learning to read, E2L learners in particular are helped by texts which show the key sentence patterns of English, such as SVO (e.g. she saw a policeman); SV (she screamed) and SVA (she ran away). It is important to avoid unusual word order and inconsistent tense use; for example a mixture of simple present and simple past tense, in very early books. Even apparently simple sentences such as 'Up he went', by inverting the normal word order (SVA, He went up) unnecessarily defeat the expectations of very early readers. L2 learner-readers need to build on the core sentence patterns of the second language. They are helped to move forward in the text if a tense natural to narrative is used, such as the simple present or simple past. The present continuous, which features often in books written for E2L learners, is not in fact appropriate for story-telling narrative.

An eye to careful structuring need not make the story any less real. For instance, the structure of the opening sentence of this reading book for children is, I believe, extraordinarily difficult for any learner, and I cannot see that it adds anything to the story:

> That day, when Paul got Mum an Easter egg, was the day Susan ran away.

It is easier for the learner to get launched into this text if he is able to identify:

WHO?	did WHAT?	WHEN?	WHY?
Susan	ran away	on the day Paul got Mum an Easter egg	She ran away because . . .

As well as taking account of typical word order in English, writers of books for early readers might consider highlighting some of the other grammatical characteristics of English. A focus on regular past tense verbs in the course of presenting a narrative can help L2 readers to arrive at the generalization that -ed on the end of verbs marks past tense; or perhaps a number of examples can be given where the doer of an action is given, so that readers can generalize that -er is the item of language which tells us that this is a noun and is likely to denote a person performing an action, e.g. *teacher, walker, loser, winner* and so on.

Once dialogue is introduced it should be clearly and consistently presented. Simple question/answer or comment/response pairs, where the words of the first speaker constrain those of the second, best introduce readers into the way speech is conveyed in writing. These kinds of exchanges occur naturally in folk stories and fables, for example:

> What big eyes you have Grandma
> All the better to see you with

Well-selected vocabulary

High-content vocabulary, as already discussed, gives the learner-reader a better start than bland, low-content words, such as *come* or *get* or *here*. These words are both visually and semantically less distinctive than *explode* or *smash*.

The building up of vocabulary fields within one text can help learner-readers to see how words form families, e.g. *Japan–Japanese, explode–explosion, mountain–mountainous.* If writers can naturally, in the course of the story, allow vocabulary to cluster in this way, learners can be helped to gain some insight into how the English writing system works. When coming across new words they are also encouraged to look for visual similarities with already known words.

Books that are resources for learning

The educational content of books, even early reading books, is important. Fiction,

as well as non-fiction, should offer learners the opportunity to extend their knowledge and the incentive to move on to further reading on the same topic. This is not to say that early books should be didactic in any explicit way; rather that they should be seen by readers as potential tools for learning, for finding out about strange animals, different countries and so on. Many adult readers enjoy fiction not just for a good story but because they are incidentally learning about sheep farming in Australia or tribal customs in Papua New Guinea. If a story presents a problem to be solved, no matter how simple, then that too sharpens motivation and interest.

Clearly at high school level, and in the case of silent reading, a whole class may be given the same book to read; discussion and evaluation then follows and some ideas for organizing this were suggested in Chapter 7. What about class reading books at an earlier stage, that is in junior or middle school? It is in fact useful to have sets of books for both group reading and integrated language skills work in the classroom. In this case, as we discussed in Chapter 6, the reading of a text, silently or aloud, may follow on from a particular lesson or may precede a group activity.

In ordering sets of books, one needs to consider how exploitable they are as resources for learning. Does a book or part of it lend itself to any of the pre-reading or while-reading work of the kind described in the previous chapter? Does it naturally lead on from a language class on making butter or shopping? Might it precede or follow a class visit to the zoo or a museum? Most importantly, does a particular book, even if it is fiction, relate across the curriculum to the content of a biology or geography lesson?

Functionally diverse books

While I have concentrated so far on stories, particularly for early learner-readers, we need eventually to ensure a more varied reading diet. We will need to show how books have a range of functions, from sheer entertainment to helping us to do things like fix our motorbike, to giving us new knowledge and ideas. Different kinds of books should gradually be introduced to readers in the classroom. Different genres and topics will present learners with their associated styles, so that technical, literary and colloquial varieties of written English can gradually be introduced.

A book which works

Any checklist of things to consider in selecting books or other reading material can only provide a very general guide, for there is no formula for a good book. For a start, what works with one individual or group may clearly not with another. Still, when one comes across a particular book which seems to go down well with a number of readers it is worth perhaps considering why. One very small but successful book with most young adults beyond the very early stages of learning to read is *Donnovan*, by Carol Bergman.

Donnovan is the story of a young West Indian who has recently come to Britain to join his mother, leaving his grandfather behind in Jamaica. Donnovan is homesick; he misses Jamaica and his grandfather; he day-dreams in school. He thinks about flying kites back in Jamaica. So his English teacher asks him to write a story about flying kites. The story is a great success and leads on to animated discussion in class about ways of making kites.

It is a simple story, so what is the appeal? I think the story probably works for these reasons:

—The leaving home theme has universal appeal.
—The theme of kites and kite-flying is of particular interest to most Asians and West Indians brought up respectively in India or the West Indies.
—There is high content vocabulary for West Indian learners. Hillyard had no difficulty reading words like *guinap, mangos, yams* and *souse*. They had high recognition value for him.
—Donnovan is allowed to tell his own story about making the kite. The experience comes alive in this way and the story within a story format gives some extra narrative interest.
—Stereotyping is avoided. Donnovan is not portrayed as a disaffected young Black. He tells Grandfather that he has joined the air cadets!
—There is an educational content; the process of making a kite is described. Following Donnovan's story, the rest of the class offer suggestions for kite-making materials.
—The ending is upbeat and, uncharacteristically for books written for teenage poor readers, shows Donnovan achieving at school. 'Donnovan was feeling good. All the rest of that day he worked hard in all his lessons.'!

The reading scheme

I have so far referred mainly to individual books. Perhaps one should consider books as part of a scheme of reading? Some of the books I have mentioned are in fact part of commercial reading schemes where learners are led through a series of levels or grades. It might be argued that one should see individual books in the context of the scheme of which they are part. However, readers read books, not schemes. Children do not say 'we read a marvellous scheme last year'. We should be more interested in whether our learners say 'That's a good, silly or funny book,' than whether teachers think that X or Y is a good scheme. We can encourage people to become readers through enjoying good books, not by 'going through a scheme'; and whether part of a scheme or not, books should stand up as autonomous pieces of communication.

The debate continues, and doubtless will for some time, over whether it is possible to 'get away from the reading scheme'. Work with adult non-readers seems to suggest that it is not necessary to put learners through a series of hoops in this way. However, in a large class of small children many teachers feel that a reading scheme provides a helpful guide to the level which individual children have reached in their reading development. Some would argue, too, that the presence of the reading scheme gives children themselves a sense of progress and achievement. My own feeling is that it can encourage an inappropriate attitude to reading. Five-year-old Mary, a very good—and competitive—reader, racing through a series of reading schemes at school, was asked what would happen when she had 'gone through all the schemes?' She reflected for a moment before answering, 'Well I suppose I could start all over again'!

If, in spite of these difficulties, a school does opt for a reading scheme, what criteria might they use in selecting one? Some schemes or sets of reading material have been designed with a particular group in mind; *Reading through Understanding* (1978) is not so much a scheme as a 3-year curriculum development project designed largely for West Indian learners. However, the writers make the important point that the material was not designed exclusively for West Indians and indeed would hopefully be used in all-white schools. The teachers' notes point out:

> To teach an Indian, Chinese or West Indian child without any reference to his or her ethnic identity and cultural background is contrary to a child-centred philosophy. And to teach *any* child without reference to the cultures of the other ethnic groups is seriously inadequate, for such a narrow education cannot promote the respect for other cultures which is essential to the development of a harmonious society.

Over and above this, however, is the point that neither black nor white children, nor adults, want to read exclusively about their own milieu or day-to-day lives. As mentioned earlier in this chapter, we read largely to find out about other people's lives and experiences. Reading is a window on other worlds. The problem with *Peter and Jane* is not so much that they represent middle-class values and life-styles with which only middle-class children might identify, as that they exist in a no-man's land with, as Mary Hoffman (1976) puts it, 'all unpleasantness smoothed away. The dog has no teeth, the siblings no rivalry, the house has no connection with main drainage.' Everyone does what they are supposed to and everyone likes or loves each other. 'Peter and Jane go to school with Pam. Pam sits with Jane in school. Pam likes Jane and Jane likes Pam'. How much more interesting it would be to read . . . 'but Jane hates Pam'!

An alternative to using a single or several reading schemes is to use a readability guide such as that provided by Cliff Moon (1974), who has built up comparative lists of selected reading books, which cover thirteen stages of reading and incorporate many of the established reading schemes.

The advantage of Moon's grading is that the concept of readability on which his lists are based depends on the **interaction** between the reader and the text. While there are a number of well-known readability measures, the difficulty with most of these is that they consider only the text itself. They also tend to equate sentence length and word length with difficulty. As we have seen, it may be short sentences rather than long which create difficulty for learners because of what is omitted from sentence structure. Also, long words—as well as being more distinctive visually—tend to be more distinctive semantically, and may not in fact create difficulty as long as the reader readily identifies the meaning. Secondly, with conventional readability measures no account is taken of culture-specific difficulty for L2 readers. Finally, allowance is not made for interest level, although research has confirmed what a number of teachers have informally observed, namely that learners may read well beyond their assumed reading level if the interest level is high.

It seems, then, that there can be no absolute yardstick in assessing readability, which is largely to do with an individual response to a particular text. Only by noting, as Moon does, how a number of individuals have responded to a particular text, can one make some assessment of its general readability level, as compared with other texts. In setting up a class library, books can be classified and graded using either Moon's guide or the checklist of points given in this chapter. Usually some form of colour coding is used, with a wide range of 'real' children's fiction and reading books offered at each level. As well as providing for a range of content one can try and assure a range of genres—to include folk tales, fables, rhymes and poems and non-fiction, such as travel books and simple biography or history.

Newspapers, Magazines and Comics: Reflections of a Popular Culture

Print is all around us, a part of our social, professional and private lives, and being able to handle it is part of effective functioning in everyday life. Much experience of print is 'short-burst' reading at a survival level—the reading of traffic signs, street signs, slogans and notices. However, most learner-readers aspire beyond this minimal level of literacy. Adults may have been getting by with rudimentary skills for a number of years, but they still want to identify with real readers, that is those who are seen to read newspapers, books and magazines. Put simply, they want to be like other people—normal people who can read; and children too will seek to emulate the reading behaviour of those around them.

In the case of the reading behaviour of E2L learner-readers, several sorts of identities may be at stake. They are likely to want to learn to read in their mother-tongue in order to maintain links with family and friends. As we saw in Chapter 1, certain roles within the family may require certain reading activities. Adults will wish to read the mother-tongue newspapers, for instance, to keep in touch with issues in Poland or the Punjab or Hong Kong.

However, cultural and linguistic minorities will also want to be able to read a wide range of English-medium material. They want to see themselves as part of the broad community of readers. They want to read women's magazines, local and national newspapers in English, articles on music, fashion and cookery. After all, the same political, economic and social issues affect them.

And yet, mass popular literature largely ignores the existence of cultural and linguistic minorities. Popular newspapers, unconsciously perhaps, exclude ethnic minorities from their club of readers. The interests and tastes they reflect are predominantly those of a readership which is perceived as white and working-class, represented by bingo, pop stars and TV soap operas. Clearly, many of these tastes and interests are shared by ethnic minority working-class people, but not all. There are few references to minority culture life-styles, with the possible exception of Reggae music, which has been adopted by some young whites. The overwhelming assumption is that everyone speaks English as a mother-tongue and that everyone is white. The tabloid national newspapers, like much of British popular culture, are slow to absorb the notion of cultural diversity. One looks in vain through the popular daily newspapers for any evidence that many communities in Britain are now multilingual and multicultural. The scripts which they describe are highly culture-specific.

Serious news affecting ethnic minorities is largely absent from the tabloid press, and when one turns to the popular literature read by children and teenagers, ethnic minorities are under-represented or negatively portrayed. Comics, for instance, remain notoriously ethnocentric and full of racist caricatures. A look at contemporary titles and themes suggests that little has changed since Laishley in 1971 examined 150 issues of 15 different comics over a 6-month period. Only 20 stories included non-white characters and not one of them was a hero. Laishley (cf. Laishley, 1972) concluded that none of the comics reflected a multicultural and multilingual readership.

There are several implications for linguistic and cultural minority readers of the narrow cultural perspective taken by popular literature. Firstly, much of the content simply is inaccessible to many potential readers, at least unless they are very familiar with the range of typical behaviours of the indigenous majority culture. Secondly, and more importantly, an opportunity is lost to give a more representative, livelier and more diverse popular literacy. The existence of L2 readers in a community or society should be seen as the opportunity to widen the horizons of the majority readership.

In the same way, the existence of culturally and linguistically diverse classrooms should be seen by teachers as an opportunity to broaden and enrich the curriculum; and where reference can be made to languages and literacies other than English, teachers are helped to give a new momentum and interest to reading, as both the content and medium of much classroom teaching.

9

Case Studies of Learner-Readers

Introduction

In this chapter I look at the reading strategies of six learner-readers, ranging in age from Mark, aged just 8, to Yasmeen and Ravinder aged 19. Most of them are learning to read in a second language and their competence in English varies from the case of Mark, who is a native speaker of English, to Yasmeen who had, at the time, been living in an English-speaking environment for less than a year. Yasmeen and Ravinder are already literate in their mother-tongues of Urdu and Punjabi respectively. In the last case, that of Sarla, I have tried to show how there appeared to be some development of reading strategies and general approach over a period of time.

What follows are transcribed interactions, from tapes, between learner and myself as teacher, representing what might be typical of a one-to-one teaching situation. The aim is to look at the respective roles of teacher, learner and text in such a situation. I have selected extracts from fairly long one-to-one taped sessions with a view to highlighting some differences in learners' responses to text difficulty and to looking also at the teacher's role in correcting or lending assistance. Ideally, one would wish to show not just a range of learner strategies but also a range of teacher strategies, as shown by different teachers (though cf. Chapter 4 for an account of the interaction between Dorothy and Di and their respective learners).

Some of the learners I know better than others, and obviously the way the reader felt about me personally, the whole reading event and its purpose and individual temperament, must be taken into account.

Teachers listening to the tapes have commented that the texts are simply too difficult for the learners. There is no easy answer to this objection. The learners had all chosen the books themselves, except for Mark. The class situation was either one-to-one or, in the case of Yasmeen and Ravinder, that part of the literacy class where students are asked to read on their own, vocalizing or not, as they prefer, while the teacher spends her time in turn with individuals.

There is no doubt that the kind of description and analysis given here takes time. However, if done even occasionally it can serve two major purposes. Firstly, it is salutary from time to time to put our own teaching behaviour under the microscope; secondly, close scrutiny of certain learners, thought to be achieving little, can sometimes show them using more positive strategies than we had given them credit for. It may at least make it a little clearer what are the favoured strategies of a particular learner, and how far they can be seen to work successfully.

NB: The system of transcription is that described on page 53 of this volume.

Case Studies

1. MARK

Mark is a native speaker of English. At the time his reading was taped he was aged just 8, and studying in a class of about 25 in a working-class school in west London. He is reading here from a book in the class reading scheme. (T – Text)

The interaction

Mark   C.W. (Teacher)

T. Lindy and Billy lived in town. They had
M. Lindy and Billy lived in town. They had
T. never thought of living anywhere else
M. never thought of living anywhere. **Easily**[1]   anywhere? . . .
anywhere easily
. . . *is that easily?*   think about the meaning, start
                                                  again and you'll get it this time.
                                                  'They had . . .'

T. They had never thought of living anywhere
M. They had never thought of living **away**[2]   ANYWHERE . . .?
                                                  anywhere . . .?
                                                  begins with E.
                                                  No? ELSE—in any other place

T. But one
M. But one . . .[3]
I know that word but I've forgot what it is.   EVENING
T. evening their father gave them a great surprise.
M. evening their father gave them a great **special**[4]
. . . *is that special?*   It doesn't make sense does it?
                                                  'Their father gave them a
                                                  great . . .?' begins with S

T. Surprise. One minute he was reading the paper
M. *Surprise. One minute he was reading the paper
T. while Lindy
M. **white**[5] . . . Lindy — *Miss, my mum's name is called*   WHILE
Linda.
T. and Billy were looking at a big book of pictures
M. and Billy were looking at a big book of pictures
T. The next minute he was asking them —
M. The next minute he was asking them
Miss, what's that line for?   That's just to show that this is
                                                  what he's going to say

T. How would you like to live right out
M. How would you like to live right out
T. in the country
M. in the country — *Miss, my Dad likes to live there.*
T. Lindy and Billy thought he was joking
M. Lindy and Billy thought he was joking
T. No it is not a joke, said Mother
M. No it is not a joke, said Mother
T. Father has not been well, so the doctor
M. Father has not been well, so the doctor
T. wants us to live on a hill where
M. wants us to live on a hill where

Mark   **C.W.** (Teacher)

T.   we can get fresh air and sunshine

M.   we can get fresh air and **shiny**[6]   and what?
       shiny   that doesn't make sense does it?
                                         'The doctor wants us to live on a
                                         hill in the country where we can
                                         get fresh air and . . .'

T.   sunshine. We have found a house that

M.   *sunshine . . . sunshine. We have found a house that

T.   seems exactly right

M.   s . . . seems (pause) **excellent**[7]   No, it looks like 'excellent'. That
                                         word is (pointing to the next
                                         word) 'right' EXACT . . .?

       ly — *exactly   Yes good

T.   exactly right for us said Father

M.   exactly right for us said Father

T.   As soon as your school holidays begin

M.   As soon as your school holidays begin

T.   we shall move into it. Lindy and Billy stared

M.   we shall move into it. Lindy and Billy **started**[8]   No, not 'started'. They were
                                         'surprised' remember. They . . .?

M.   They . . .

       Miss, I'll start from here again.   Good

T.   we shall move into it. Lindy and Billy stared

M.   we shall move into it. Lindy and Billy **st**   What do you do when you're
                                         very surprised? They looked at
                                         their father in amazement. They
                                         [st] . . .

       stared*   good

T.   They could not believe their ears

M.   They could not believe their **eyes**[9] — *ears

T.   Did Father really mean that they

M.   Did Father really mean that they

T.   were to leave their own home

M.   **were to leaving**[10] — leave their own home

T.   and live somewhere else

M.   and live somewhere else — *Miss, how come it's
       different here?* (referring to 'else')   That was *anywhere* else

T.   Can't we just go on living here said Billy

M.   Can't we just go on living here said Billy

T.   But Mother answered

M.   But Mother (pause) . . .[11]   What's that word?
                                         But Mother . . .?

       'anyway' Oh, it hasn't got an E in it,
       anyway hasn't.   What do you do when someone
                                         asks you a question?

       *answer

T.   answered that the most important

M.   answered that the most **elegant . . . ill . . .**[12]   Have another look at the word.
       I'll start from here, 'just go . . .'   No, start from here. It's always
                                         best to start from a new
                                         sentence.

T.   Can't we just go on living here said Billy

M.   Can't we just go on living here said Billy

T.   but Mother answered that the most . . .

M.   but Mother answered that the most   im I-M-

T.   important thing is to be well

M.   *important thing is to be well

Mark

T. Now packing was such . . .
M. Now packing was **sure**[13]

    fun
T. such fun that soon both children were busy helping
M. such fun that soon both children were busy helping
T. As busy people are usually happy
M. As busy people are . . .[14] happy
T. Lindy and Billy soon found themselves
M. Lindy and Billy soon found them . . .[15]

T. laughing and cheerful
M. laughing and . . .[16]
    giggling

    ful — *cheerful
T. Lindy and Billy soon found themselves
M. Lindy and Billy soon found them . . .
    Miss, I've never learnt that word.
T. laughing and cheerful
M. laughing and cheerful

C.W. (Teacher)

No, what's that word? (pointing
to next word) 'Now packing
was . . .? SUCH

USUALLY

What's that word? (pointing to
'laughing')
What goes with 'laughing'
— laughing and . . .?
— yes, but it means 'happy';
what's another word for happy?
[ch] . . . What's that bit at the
end of the word? . . .
Good, yes, lets go back

SELVES

The analysis

No.	Miscue	Level of miscue	Source of miscue	Learner response	Teacher prompt
1.	Easily (else)	graphic	T: as a reference item (referring back to 'town') highly predictable to adults; less so for children	M. drops voice on anywhere; 'Easily' appears to start a new sentence; he is attempting to impose meaning	suggests – think about meaning – start again gives initial letter gives
2.	Away (anyway)	graphic (fits preceding context syntactically/ semantically)	T: confused by following word ELSE	—	gives (M. has just read this correctly)
3.	— (evening)	—	?	asks T.	gives
4.	special *(surprise)	graphic (fits preceding context syntactically/ semantically)	T: collocation 'give surprise' does not immediately come to mind	queries his own miscue gets word with T. prompt	gives meaning prompt gives initial letter
5.	white (while)	graphophonic	T: connectors more typical of writing may create difficulty	—	gives
6.	shiny *(sunshine)	graphophonic (fits preceding context syntactically)	S: 'Fresh air and sunshine' collocates well. M. is not predicting effectively from preceding text	gets word with T. prompt	backtracks for M.
7.	excellent *(exactly)	graphic (fits preceding context syntactically/ semantically)	T: this adverb is an unpredictable item here	gets word with T. prompt	directs attention ahead in text gives first two syllables
8.	started *(stared)	graphic/syntactic	S: M. fails to follow through idea of 'surprise' — or read ahead (which would help)	chooses to go back and gets word with T. prompt	gives meaning prompt gives initial consonant sound

No.	Word	Cue type	Comment	Response	Teacher prompt
9.	eyes *(ears)	graphic/syntactic	**slip:** immediately corrected	—	—
10.	were to leaving (were to leave)	syntactic	**slip:** M. temporarily confuses two synonymous structures 'were to leave/were leaving' — as a native speaker immediately self-corrects	—	—
11.	— (answered)	—	**S:** back-tracking would help. Billy's question anticipates an answer.	**S:** offers 'anyway' as a bid then, looks closely at word and comments on letter E; gets word with T. prompt	gives meaning prompt (ask→answer)
12.	elegant . . . ill *(important)	graphic/syntactic — picks up end of word	**T:** not predictable from pre-ceding context **+** **S:** However, reading ahead might have helped, cf. 'to be well'	**S:** offers to back-track; finally gets word with initial syllable prompt	suggests – look at word – go back gives first syllable
13.	sure (such)	graphic (also fits preceding context syntactically/ semantically)	**T:** such = 'so much' not familiar to children	—	points to word ahead, then gives
14.	— (usually)	—	**T:** adverbs less predictable (cf. exactly)	no attempt	gives
15.	them . . . (themselves)	—	**T:** syntax of text beyond M.'s competence	no attempt at second syllable of word	directs attention ahead in the text finally gives
16.	— *(cheerful)	—	**T:** unknown word? (not in childrens stylistic repertory)	responds to T. prompt with eventual success	encourages collocation 'laughing and . . .?' gives initial sound, draws attention to final syllable

Comments

The text: The text creates some difficulty for Mark because certain items of structure are beyond the language competence of children of a certain age, though wholly predictable for adults, such as 'else' and to find . . . 'oneself doing something'.

There is also a rather coy kind of readerese, e.g. 'packing was such fun' that is remote from children's experience of language. In fact, most of Mark's miscues are text-provoked.

Mark: Mark does not attempt a phonic decoding of unknown words. He is aware that back-tracking can help him to get the unknown words, though he goes back to rather random points in the text. He is also occasionally prepared to wait for a cue from me. However, he does not miscue with nonsense words, or with words that do not fit the preceding context either semantically or syntactically.

What is particularly encouraging is that Mark has the confidence to initiate comment on the text: he relates the content to his own experience, and he asks about features of the text, such as the dash and the recurrence of 'else' in the text. What is most interesting in terms of the language that Mark uses is the kind of questions that he makes use of:

What's the X for?
Is that X?
How come it's different here?

It is this language for learning that L2 readers need to be helped to acquire.

C.W.: I tend to move, quite unconsciously, in my prompting from meaning–structure–graphic or phonic features; e.g.

think about the meaning—
start again (i.e. fit it into a structure)—
begins with E
(I also occasionally give the initial sound as prompt—as a last rather than first resort)

I do not give Mark a chance to repair his own miscues, tending to come in far too quickly—as soon as he has miscued, in fact; for example, I might have given him the opportunity to reject for himself the miscue 'special' as he read on.

Moreover I do not, as is so often the case with teachers, give credit where it is due. 'Special', which I dismiss as 'not making sense', is in fact not a bad guess.

2. NADEEM

Nadeem is 11, in the top junior class of a multiracial school in north-west London. He was born in Britain though speaks Urdu at home. Nadeem is a near-native speaker of English though a few miscues here are attributable to his use of spoken English. He is reading an extract from *Mr. Potter's Pigeon* by P. Kinmouth. Mr. Potter's pigeon is missing—

The interaction

Nadeem	C.W.
T. Lupin walked across the garden	
N. Lupin walked across the garden	
T. and rubbed himself against Mr. Potter's legs	
N. and **rubbēd**[1] himself against Mr. Potter's legs	
T. purring loudly. Mr. Potter bent down and	
N. purring loudly. Mr. Potter bent down and	
T. stroked him. 'A cat will always be a cat', he	
N. **shooked**[2]*—stroked him. 'A cat will always be a cat', he	
T. observed with a long sigh.	
N. **obstervade—absorbed**[3] with a long **sign**[4]	What does that mean? (referring to (3)) It means 'he said' that's all it means, really. 'With a long?— What's a 'sigh'? When do you sigh?
Like you sign a letter	No not *sign*, Sigh—with a long sigh.
stroke	No, it's when you go 'Ah'.
T. Just as he was	
N. Just as he was	
T. thinking that Lupin looked especially	
N. thinking that Lupin **lookin'**[5] **specially**[6]	
T. well-fed, Mr. Potter heard a whirring of	
N. **fed**[6] Mr. Potter heard a whirring of	
T. wings above him and he looked up eagerly	
N. wings above him and he looked up eagerly	What do you think the 'whirring' was?
he was worrying because he thinks the cat ate the pigeon	So he's worrying do you think— that word wasn't 'worrying', it was 'whirring'. 'Mr. Potter heard a whirring of wings above him.' Now what's a whirring of wings? So what was it do you think?
patting	
Pigeon	Pigeon, yes.
T. There was this pigeon sitting calmly on the	
N. There was this pigeon sitting **climbly**[7] on the	
T. roof of the shed	
N. roof of the shed	What's this word? How was he sitting? Do you know that word? —CALMLY
T. calmly on the	
N. calmly on the	
T. roof of the shed, as if she had never been	
N. roof of the shed, as if she had never been	

Nadeem   C.W.

T. away. Mr. Potter raised his hands, the
N. away. Mr. Potter raised his hands, the
T. pigeon flew down into them and he
N. pigeon flew down into them and he
T. pressed her soft grey back against his
N. pressed her **softly grey**[8] back against his
T. cheek. 'You've come back for the race,
N. cheek. 'You've come back for the race,
T. then?' he said with a chuckle, and the
N. then?' he said with a chuckle, and the
T. pigeon blinked her beady black eyes
N. pigeon blinked her beady black eyes
T. That night Mr. Potter slept well. He
N. That night Mr. Potter slept well. He
T. dreamed that his pigeon asked him to fly
N. dreamed that his pigeon asked him to fly
T. with her, and they soared over a rainbow
N. with her, and they **shoared**[9] over a rainbow
T. in the sky
N. in the sky
T. On the day of the race Mr. Potter got up at
N. On the day of the race Mr. Potter got up at
T. five o'clock and put his pigeon into a
N. five o'clock and put his pigeon into a
T. wicker travelling basket. He looked up at
N. wicker **travel**[10] basket. He **took**[11] up at
T. the mantelpiece
N. the **metalpiece**[12]

looked* up at the **metalpiece**[12]

Go back a bit—not *took* up—
he . . . ?
He looked up at the
MANTELPIECE. Do you have a
fireplace at home? (long
explanation follows)

T. and imagined how a silver
N. and he **managed**[13] how a silver   IMAGINED
T. cup would look beside his father's
N. cup would look beside his father's
T. photograph 'very nice indeed', said Mr.
N. photograph 'very nice indeed', said Mr.
T. Potter as he went down to the station. 'It
N. Potter as he went down to the station. 'It
T. would be nice to win.'
N. would be nice to win.'

The cup

What did he want to see on the
mantelpiece?
And when would he get a silver
cup?

if he wins

T. It was six o'clock when he arrived on the
N. It was six o'clock when he arrived on the
T. platform. The train was due to leave at ten
N. platform. The train was **dr . . . druve**[14] to leave at
    ten
T. past six to take the pigeons on their long
N. past six to take the pigeons on their long
T. journey to the starting place, but Mr.
N. journey to the **start**[15] place, but Mr.

Nadeem

T. Potter waited with his pigeon on his knees
N. Potter waited with his pigeon on his knees
T. until the guard came and put her carefully
N. until the guard came and put her carefully
T. inside and blew his whistle. Mr. Potter felt
N. inside and blew his whistle. Mr. Potter felt
T. that he was losing her again.
N. that he was losing her again.
T. 'She'll be all
N. 'She'll be all
T. right', the guard said as the train left the
N. right', the guard said as the train left the
T. station with a blast of steam . . .
N. station with a bl . . . blast of steam
T. . . . then something
N. . . . then something
T. white glistened
N. white **gessened**[16]

T. near by. She nearly fell out
N. near by. She nearly **flew out—fall out**[17]
T. of the sky with surprise—there was the
N. of the sky with surprise—there was the
T. lighthouse where she had slept, ghostly
N. lighthouse where she had slept, ghostly
T. and familiar in the fog
N. **the family**[18] in the fog
T. familiar in the fog. Now she knew
N. familiar in the fog. Now she knew
T. exactly which way to go, and she flew back
N. exactly which way to go, and she flew back
T. up the river towards the railway . . .
N. up the river towards the railway
T. . . . Mr. Potter sat waiting in his kitchen with
N. . . . Mr. Potter sat waiting in his kitchen with
T. the rain falling down outside. Again and
N. the rain falling down outside. Again and
T. again he peered through the rain but the
N. again he **pared**[19] through the rain but the
T. sky was empty, so he hummed a tune to
N. sky was empty, so he hummed a tune to
T. keep himself calm. 'A watched pot never
N. keep himself calm. 'A watched pot never
T. boils' said Mr. Potter . . .
N. **bowls**'[20] said Mr. Potter . . .

his tea to get ready.

C.W.

What?—er—something white
GLISTENED

Sorry?—GHOSTLY AND FAMILIAR

When you're waiting for
something to happen, it never
does—it's like when you're
waiting for the pot to boil, it
never boils—so he was waiting—
what was he waiting for?

The analysis

No.	Miscue	Level of miscue	Source of miscue	Learner response	Teacher prompt
1.	rubbēd (rubbed)	phonic (Nadeem does not usually give stress to past tense -ed)	**S:** no recognition of past tense function of -ed, i.e. Nadeem is not using syntactic information of text	leaves	leaves
2.	shooked *(stroked)	graphophonic	**slip:** immediately self-corrected	—	—
3.	observade –absorbed (observed)	graphophonic (first attempt non-word)	**Tlit:** unknown word	leaves	discusses possible meaning, then gives
4.	sign (sigh)	graphic/syntactic	**T:** unknown word	attaches meaning of 'sign' to his miscue which does not fit context though his second attempt does (stroke)	discusses meaning, then gives
5.	lookin' (looked)	syntactic:	**L:** possibly due to a tendency to replace -ed form with an -ing form [though there is no evidence of this elsewhere]	leaves	leaves
6.	specially fed (specially well-fed)	omission which results in loss of meaning	**?:** possibly slip	leaves	leaves
7.	climbly (calmly)	graphophonic (non-word)	**T:** unknown word	leaves (not in fact a key word)	asks if meaning known, then gives
8.	softly grey (soft grey)	graphophonic	**?**	leaves	leaves
9.	shoared (soared)	graphophonic (non-word)	**T:** unknown word	leaves	leaves
10.	travel (travelling)	semantic	**S+:** a positive miscue; 'travel basket' is synonymous	—	—

No.	word (text)	graphophonic/graphic analysis	miscue category	leaves initially but gets it following T prompt	suggests backtrack
11.	took *(looked)	graphic (fits preceding context syntactically/ semantically)	**slip**: N. anticipates difficulty with 'mantelpiece'	—	
12.	metalpiece (mantelpiece)	graphophonic (a non-word)	**Tcu:**unknown reference		gives, then long discussion (not included here) to establish what is referred to
13.	managed (imagined)	graphophonic (and fits preceding syntax)	**Tlit:** unknown word	—	gives
14.	druve (due)	graphophonic (non-word)	**S:** Nadeem needs to read ahead; the item is well cued in	leaves	leaves
15.	start (starting)	syntactic	**L:** ? Nadeem possibly not familiar with -ing form as adjective here	leaves	leaves
16.	gessened (glistened)	graphophonic (non-word)	**Tlit:**unknown word	leaves	gives
17.	flew out— fall out (fell out)	first miscue fits previous context syntactically/ semantically; second syntactic variant of 'fell'	**L:** ? possibly due to Nadeem's non-use of some irregular past tense forms—or a slip	leaves	leaves
18.	ghostly the family (ghostly and familiar)	graphophonic (non-structure in English)	**Tlit:** (unpredictable as adjective follows noun referred to— lighthouse)	leaves	gives
19.	pared (peered)	graphophonic	**Tlit:**unknown word	leaves	leaves
20.	bowls (bowls)	graphophonic	**Tcu:**'boils' is not the problem; N. is not familiar with the proverb	leaves	attempts (unsuccessful) explanation

Comments

The text: The text is a 'real' children's book as opposed to a reading book. As such it contains a number of literary expressions and figurative language. The general difficulties for Nadeem are stylistic. He is not familiar with the kind of vocabulary range here, particularly verbs of saying (*observe, imagine*) and verbs describing movement (*soar*). The vocabulary is stylistically appropriate to the text: these features are not gratuitously difficult in that they regularly occur in authentic literature. Indeed the best way to become familiar with them is through reading real children's fiction.

The proverb presents difficulties—possibly culture-specific, though it may well be that many children would not be familiar with it and would, like Nadeem, interpret it literally.

Nadeem: Nadeem is skilful at decoding. However, one suspects that even where decoding appears to succeed he has not understood. This is suggested by his fully stressing both syllables in rub-bēd and wick-ēr. Nadeem's miscues are nearly all graphophonic, and occasionally non-words. On the whole they are left uncorrected. When challenged he tends not to offer an appropriate meaning definition (for it is possible to miscue with a nonsense word to which the learner has nonetheless assigned an appropriate meaning). However, on the credit side Nadeem usually makes even nonsense words fit the preceding syntax. For instance, 'climbly', and 'shoared' are grammatically marked as adverb and verb respectively.

The most interesting part of the reading is where there is no surface miscue at all, in the case of 'whirring'. For Nadeem has 'read' the word just as most people would pronounce it. However, questioning reveals that he attached, initially at least, a meaning that is both syntactically and semantically unacceptable to the immediate context. However, the wider context makes the error very understandable.

At no point does Nadeem, unlike Mark, comment spontaneously on the text, nor does he ask the teacher what an unknown word is or what it means. His reading is fluent but unvaried in pace, suggesting a lack of reflectiveness.

C.W.: As with Mark, I do not give Nadeem credit where it is due. His bid of 'stroke' for *sigh* is a reasonable guess. Similarly though 'worrying' for *whirring* does not fit the immediate context syntactically or semantically, it seems that Nadeem has understood the wider context and the inference contained in 'Lupin . . . especially well-fed'.

I interrupt unnecessarily; 'calmly' is, for instance, not a key word in the story and my intervention is a distraction here.

The long explanation about *mantelpiece* also interrupts the narrative unnecessarily.

3. MAQSOOD

Maqsood is a 10-year-old Pakistani boy who speaks Punjabi, Urdu and Hindi. He reads a little Arabic. He came to England when he was 5, and his English is apparently not significantly different from that of his indigenous English peers. He is reading here from *Meet Harry King* by Anne Oates. Sixteen-year-old Linda is Harry's sister—

The interaction

Maqsood	**C.W.** (Teacher)
T. Linda is 16 and works in a toy shop	
M. Linda is 16 and works in a toy shop	
T. 'Kids' stuff' thinks Harry	
M. **Kids—kinds st . . . kinds staffs**[1] thinks Harry	
T. He wants	
M. He wants	Sorry, I couldn't understand that bit.
Kinds—kinds staffs thinks Harry	What does that mean— 'Kinds staffs'?
Yes 'stuffs'	How do you spell it?
STUFF—stuffs	stuff, yes—kinds of stuff, is it?
kinds of stuff, things . . .	Ah, stuff means?
Lots of things	Could I just have a look? Ah, it's not 'kind stuff'—have another look at that word.
*kid's stuff	What does that mean?
children's stuff . . . thinks Harry	
T. He wants to be a racing driver	
M. He wants to be a racing driver	
T. when he is too old	
M. when he is too old	
T. to play in the English football team	
M. to play in the English football team	
T. Peter and Paul are 10	
M. Peter and Paul are 10	
T. They are twins	
M. They are twins	
T. With their mouth wide open	
M. With their mouth wide open	
T. Dad said they looked like	
M. Dad said they look . . . they looked like	
T. Two little dicky birds	
M. **birds, the twins little doc . . .**[2]	
Miss, I don't know this.	'Dad said they looked like two little dicky birds'—just means birds.
T. sitting on the wall	
M. sitting on the wall	
T. Mum was upset to start with	
M. Mum was upset to str . . . start with	
T. but the names stuck	
M. but the names **struck**[3]	
T. Harry reckons	
M. **Harry Richard**[4]	
T. They have not stopped crying since	
M. They have not stopped crying since	
T. The baby is called John	
M. The baby is called John	

Maqsood   C.W. (Teacher)

T. when they think about it
M. when they think about it
T. but most times they just call him the baby
M. but most times they just call him the baby
T. Linda was a bit upset about him
M. Linda was a bit upset about him
T. Oh, Mum not another boy
M. Oh, Mum not another **baby**[5]
T. Harry does not think about the baby much
M. Harry does not think about the baby much
T. Harry thinks most
M. Harry thinks most
T. about racing cars and football
T. about racing cars and football   What did Linda think about
                                                               having a new baby in the
                                                               family?

        She was upset.
T. And always there is Gran
M. And always there is Gran
T. Gran does not hear very well
M. Gran does not hear very well
T. Harry reckons she does not have to
M. **Harry Richard**[6] she does not have to
T. as she never stops talking long
M. as she never stops **thinking**[7] long   Sorry, I missed that word;
                                                               something she doesn't have
                                                               to—what was the word
                                                               before 'she does not have
                                                               . . .?
                                                               Can I have a look? Ah,
                                                               HARRY RECKONS that is,
                                                               'thinks'.

T. Harry reckons she does not have to
M. Harry reckons she does not have to
T. as she never stops talking long enough
M. as she never stops **taking**[7] long . . .[8]
        Miss, I don't know.   Go back to the beginning of
                                                               the sentence. 'Harry reckons
                                                               she does not have to . . .'

T. Harry reckons she does not have to
M. Harry reckons she does not have to
T. as she never stops talking
M. as she never stops t . . .   Think what we were talking
                                                               about—'she doesn't have to
                                                               hear—to listen to anyone
                                                               because she never stops . . .
        *talking   long . . .?
T. long enough for anyone to talk back
M. *enough for anyone to talk back
T. Gran does not like twins
M. Gran does not like twins
T. Double trouble
M. . . .[9]
        Miss I don't know   DOUBLE TROUBLE
T. Double trouble, she says
M. Double trouble, she says

Maqsood

T. Gran loves the baby
M. Gran loves the baby

Twins are double trouble because they make more noise than . . .
than one.

T. Tonight when Harry wants to hear the football scores
M. **That night when Harry went to**[10] **. . . he . . . to . . . the football soccer**[11]
T. Gran is talking
M. Gran is talking

. . . football scrip . . . scrall . . .

results

T. Gran is talking
M. Gran is talking
T. He turns round to tell her
M. He turns round to tell her
T. and spills Dad's beer
M. and spills Dad's beer
T. Bed shouted Dad
M. Bed shouted Dad
T. just as Harry gets to the door
M. just as Harry gets to the door
T. Linda comes in
M. Linda comes in
T. She has been dancing
M. She has been dancing
T. and she is smiling
M. and she is smiling
T. She smiles more
M. She smiles more
T. when she sees that Harry is in trouble
M. when she sees that Harry is in trouble
T. Harry stamps upstairs
M. Harry stamps upstairs
T. He hates Linda
M. He hates Linda
T. He hates Gran
M. He hates Gran
T. He hates beer
M. He hates . . .[12] *What's this?*

*beer?

yes—he can't hate beer because it aint a living thing.*

C.W. (Teacher)

Do you know why Gran says 'Double trouble'?

than?

'Tonight when Harry wants to hear the football'; could you go back to that? When you—when your Dad watches television, maybe you didn't see the match but you want to hear the football . . .? What's another word? no? SCORES

Well you got that before. 'He hates Linda, he hates Gran, he hates . . .? Do you think that's a strange thing to say?

Maqsood   **C.W.** (Teacher)

T. He goes to the bathroom
M. He goes to the bathroom
T. and sees Gran's teeth in the glass
M. and sees Gran's[13] **tooth**—*teeth in the glass
T. Most of all he hates to see Gran's teeth
M. Most of all he hates to see Gran's teeth
T. Next to Gran's teeth
M. Next to Gran's teeth
T. he sees Linda's eyelashes
M. he sees Linda's eyelashes   What are Gran's teeth doing
                                          in the glass?
Because she's got false teeth.   What about eyelashes?
You put them on your eyes to make your
eyelashes bigger.

Comments

The text: Though the content of the text is interesting, its use of language—more characteristic of speaking than typical writing—creates difficulty for Maqsood. There are cases of ellipsis which do not give him enough information to predict readily. 'Toy shop—Kids' stuff' is one such example (i.e. Harry thought that working in a toy shop was . . .). Colloquialisms and rather coy, outdated expressions likewise create some difficulty. It is not so much that Maqsood does not know the words or is not familiar with colloquial expressions (though baby talk like 'dicky birds' may well not be in Maqsood's stylistic repertory); it is rather that they are not anticipated here. Likewise, the collocation of 'hate' and 'beer' in this context. The text is very culture-specific (cf. false eyelashes), though Maqsood appears to have no difficulty at all with this.

Maqsood: On the negative side, Maqsood does not often self-correct. At times he tolerates loss of meaning, until stopped by the teacher. After any intervention he simply resumes where he left off: good readers tend to back-track to get into the story again.

On the positive side he does ask (tentatively) for the unknown word, though he never asks what the word means. While he tends not to initiate any discussion on the story, his responses to the teacher's questions show a good level of understanding. In particular, Maqsood's comment on 'he hates beer' in the context, i.e. 'it ain't a living thing' provides an interesting insight from a learner on how the language of a text can defeat expectations. And Maqsood is able to offer a very coherent explanation of *why* beer was unexpected here. Moreover, he attempts to impose a meaning on what he reads—having miscued once he reorders the text to give it some meaning, e.g. That night, when Harry went to the football (Tonight when Harry wants to hear . . .) Maqsood is searching for a way to make sense of what he reads.

C.W.: As with Nadeem, I am sitting facing Maqsood. I do not therefore have access to the book and only interrupt him when I cannot make sense of what he is reading. For this reason the miscue 'Harry Richard' (Harry reckons) is not picked up the first time round. Maqsood has made the miscue sufficiently fit the context for me not to take objection (though it might on reflection seem odd for two brothers to be called Harry!)

The analysis

No.	Miscue	Level of miscue	Source of miscue	Learner response	Teacher prompt
1.	Kids—kinds staffs *(kids stuff)	graphophonic (nonsense)	Tco: Maqsood gets 'kids' but is then perplexed by the elliptical and colloquial style	ignores and reads on; tries to reconstruct a meaning—'Kinds of stuff'—when challenged	draws attention to meaning of 'stuff' and closer look at words themselves
2.	birds, the twins little doc . . . . (two little dicky birds)	graphophonic	Tco: colloquial style of text	attempts to impose sense e.g. two → twins, then begins a phonic sounding out, soon abandoned; then asks teacher.	gives with brief explanation
3.	struck (stuck)	graphophonic/ syntactic	Tco: colloquial	leaves	leaves
4.	Harry Richard (Harry reckons)	graphic/semantic (preceding text . . . two names . . .)	Tco: colloquial	leaves	makes some sort of sense in this context, so leaves
5.	boy (baby)	graphic/syntactic	?: a slip	leaves	makes reasonable sense, so leaves
6.	Harry Richard (Harry reckons)	graphic but does not here fit context [cf. 4.]	Tco: colloquial	leaves	gives 'reckons' with definition
7.	thinking/taking *(talking)	graphic/syntactic	T: ellipsis in 'does not have to (hear)' makes 'talk' semantically unpredictable	leaves	draws attention to meaning of sentence, filling out the structure; sends M. back to beginning of sentence

No.	Miscue	Level of miscue	Source of miscue	Learner response	Teacher prompt
8.	— (enough)*	—	**S:** very predictable if one backtracks	asks teacher	backtracks for M.
9.	— (double trouble)	—	**Tco:** colloquial usage unexpected here for Maqsood, but he seems to know the expression	asks teacher	gives and asks for meaning of expression
10.	that night when Harry went to . . . he . . . to . . . the (tonight when Harry wants to hear the)	syntactic?		changes whole structure to impose a meaning	backtracks for M.
11.	soccer (scores)	graphophonic/ semantic	**T:** M. relates 'football' to 'soccer'; 'results' is more familiar to him than 'scores', a less predictable item to collocate with football	leaves	attempts to draw on M's knowledge of the world, but though M. gives 'results', he cannot get 'scores'
12.	*beer	—	**T:** collocation odd to M. in this context	asks teacher	discusses oddness of collocation
13.	tooth–teeth (*teeth)	graphophonic	**Slip:** immediately self-corrected	—	—

4. RAVINDER
Ravinder is 19 and a Punjabi-speaker. He also reads well in Punjabi. He came from India 2 years ago and is attending a language and basic skills class in further education, preparatory to taking a training opportunities course.

The extract being read is from *Back Home* by Ranjit Sumal, about everyday life in India.

The interaction

Ravinder

T. Life in the village began at 4 a.m. waking with
R. Life in the village **begin**[1] at **4 p.m.**[2] **woking**[3] with
T. the sound of
R. the **round**[4] of
T. cattle from the nearby farm. Lying . . .
R. **cettle**[5] from the **nebly**[6] farm. **Laying**[7] . . .
(laughing) *No!*

To read it again.

T. Life in the village began at 4 a.m. waking with
R. Life in the village **begin**[1] at *4 a.m. *waking with
T. the sound
R. the **round**[4]
T. waking with the sound of
R. waking with the er *sound of
T. cattle
R. **cett . . . cheply**[5]

birds.

T. from the nearby farm. Lying there you could
R. from the **n . . .**[6] farm. **Laying**[7] there you could
T. hear the elderly
R. hear the **eldry**[8]
T. women getting up and attending to their work
R. **woman**[9] getting up and attending to their work
T. and the women next
R. and the **woman**[9] next
T. door planning the day as quietly as possible.
R. door planning the day as **quickly**[10] as possible.
T. The clattering of
R. The clattering of
T. utensils made a lot of noise as plates, cups and
R. . . .[11] made a lot of noise as plates, cups and
T. saucers were all
R. s . . .[12]

Ravinder looks puzzled

(*A.* Saucers.)
Ravinder: *Saucers? What is saucers?*

C.W. (Teacher)

Now, did you understand that?
So what is the best thing to do if you don't understand, do you think?
Yes.

Look at that again.

You know what that is. The sound of . . .? What sort of sound do you hear early in the morning?
Yes it could be, but here it's
CATTLE, COWS

NEARBY . . .

ELDERLY

UTENSILS—pots and pans.

Guess: cups and s . . .
What goes with cups?
plates, cups and s . . .
Let's ask Armindo?

Cups and saucers go together (draws quick picture). Don't you have saucers—just cups?

Ravinder

Yes, but we don't call them like that.
We call them plate.

We call this plate—a small plate.

C.W. (Teacher)

Ah, you don't have a special word?

Well, we have a special word—the words are always together, 'cups and saucers', like 'fish and chips' and 'bread and butter'. Start from the beginning of the sentence again.

T. The clattering of
R. The clattering of
T. utensils made a lot of noise as plates, cups and
R. utensils made a lot of noise as plates, cups and
T. saucers were all
R. saucers were all
T. made from metal and not china
R. made from metal and not china

     made from metal . . .
T. As it is still quite dark
R. As it is still **quick**[13] dark
T. most of the family
R. most of the family . . .

T. As it is still quite dark
R. As it is still *quite dark
T. most of the family is still asleep, having
R. most of the family is still asleep, having
T. their usual 10 to 11
R. their usual 10 to 11
T. hours. The men always bathed
R. hours. The men always bath . . .
     What is this? (to himself)
T. bathed in front of the Tubewell
R. bath . . . bathed in front of the tube-well—
     tubewell (said quickly with recognition)
T. The men always bathed in front of the tubewell
R. The men always bathed in front of the tubewell
     It's a water pump.

     No, that's a handpump; a tubewell is a . . . ern . . .
     it takes water from the ground with a motor.

Why did they make a lot of noise?
Yes, good

Sorry to interrupt, but could you read that again?

Is this a picture here? (referring to picture in the book)

The analysis

No.	Miscue	Level of miscue	Source of miscue	Learner response	Teacher prompt
1.	Begin (Began)	syntactic	**L:** not all irregular past tenses yet acquired by R. as an L2 learner	leaves	leaves
2.	4 p.m. (*4 a.m.)	graphic	**slip:** due to inattention	Ravinder goes back to read again; successfully relates 4 a.m. → waking → sound	asks Ravinder how *he* thinks he can resolve loss of meaning
3.	woking (*waking)	graphic (non-word)	**Slip:** due to inattention		
4.	round (*sound)	graphic	**Slip:** due to inattention		
5.	cettle, cett . . . cheply (cattle)	graphic (non-word)	**T:** unknown word to R. as an L2 learner	attempts sounding out at second reading	tries to get R to predict from 'morning' and 'sound', but word unknown, so gives
6.	nebly (nearby)	graphic (non-word)	**T:** unknown word	leaves on first reading	gives at second reading
7.	laying (lying)	syntactic:	**L:** replacement for 'lying' (also native-speaker usage)	leaves	leaves
8.	eldry (elderly)	graphic (non-word)	**T:** unknown word	leaves	gives
9.	woman (women)	syntactic	**L:** irregular plurals still uncertain in R's own speech	leaves	leaves
10.	quickly (quietly)	syntactic/semantic/graphic	**S+:** makes sense; a good reader might miscue with this replacement	leaves	leaves
11.	— (utensils)	—	**T:** unknown word	—	gives word with quick explanation
12.	cups and s . . . (cups and saucers)	—	**Tcu:** unknown collocation—readily predictable by native speakers but presents some cultural difficulty for R.	—	talks of collocations (mentions others to give idea that words 'go together')
13.	quick (quite)*	graphic	**slip** **?:** gets it unhesitatingly at second attempt	—	asks R. to read again

Comments

The text: The content of the text is familiar to Ravinder. He comes from a rural part of the Punjab in India, so much of the vocabulary is predictable. Some difficulty is presented by formal, literary words such as *elderly*, though they are either well cued in or not crucial to an overall understanding. Because the general content of the text is more familiar to Ravinder than to myself, this offers a valuable opportunity for him to describe to me what various culture-specific items and behaviour are. This helps Ravinder both to feel at home with the text and also to take the initiative in our relationship. It also offers him an opportunity to extend his oral language.

Ravinder: Ravinder starts this part of the extract with a string of graphophonic miscues. The sense is quickly lost. He has been reading for some time, so he may be tiring. The reason, I felt, was loss of attention rather than inattention to meaning. He hits on just the right strategy to get back on course, namely back-tracking. Feeling at home with the content here has given him confidence. He volunteers the explanation as to what a waterpump is—he does not wait to be asked. Many of Ravinder's miscues are attributable to the fact that he is still acquiring English.

C.W.: I ask Ravinder himself how best to resolve the loss of understanding in the first two lines. This strategy might have helped Maqsood, for instance, to be more independent in his reading.

Not wishing to intervene too much, I simply give Ravinder words which are almost certainly unknown to him, such as 'nearby' and 'elderly'; inconsistently, I sometimes offer a quick gloss as to meaning, sometimes not. I do not correct miscues which I judge to be attributable to Ravinder's use of English, such as 'woman' (women).

The lengthy digression about *cups and saucers* is possibly a distraction—after all, the text does not centre around an understanding of this collocation. Moreover, I impose on Ravinder my own culture-specific set of collocations rather than drawing on what might function as collocations for him.

5. YASMEEN

Yasmeen is 19 and from Pakistan. She has been 11 months in England and is very much still a second language learner of English, in that her English is developing and changing continually. She reads fluently in Urdu. The text presents some particular difficulties of vocabulary, but Yasmeen chose it as it was about going to the Careers Office, and Yasmeen herself had had an interview with the Careers Officer a few weeks previously, as the preamble to the reading indicates:

CW. Where is Maria—tell me the story.
Y.   She gone to career office you know and she's er . . . interview you know.
CW. Who interviews her?
Y.   Maria er . . . Career Office—Officer.
CW. You had an interview didn't you a few weeks ago? What did he say to you?
Y.   Er . . . two three months ago. I can't remember. He says you learn English.
CW. Was it a woman or a man?
Y.   Woman she say . . . but I can't speak English.
CW. She said she couldn't get you a job?
Y.   Because she's can't speak English.
CW. Because *you* can't speak English.
Y.   Yes.
CW. You *can* speak English quite well, but you must become better.
Y.   Yes.

The interaction

Yasmeen	C.W. (Teacher)
T. So I went to the Careers	
Y. So I went to the Careers	
T. I asked about the college course	
Y. I asked about the college course	
T. They said they were waiting	
Y. They said they were waiting	
T. for the results of the tests	
Y. for the results of the tests	
T. that they did at the hospital	
Y. **they**[1] they did at the hospital	
T. I said 'How do you know about the tests?'	
Y. I said 'How do you know (repeats quickly 'how do you know') about the tests?	
T. She said, 'We knew a few weeks ago'	
Y. She said, 'We knew [hesitates slightly] a few	Yes, 'knew'
What's a few?	one or two
Oh yeh, medium weeks ago	
T. They must have known before I did	
Y. They must have, **must have know . . . none**[2]	KNOWN
T. before I did	
Y. before I did	
T. So they said	
Y. So they said	
T. Come back in three weeks' time	
Y. Come back in three weeks' time	
T. When we know the results of the tests	
Y. When we know the results . . . the results of the tests	
T. Then we'll soon find you a job	
Y. Then **we will**[3] soon find you a job	

Yasmeen	C.W. (Teacher)

T. She said she's still trying for the college
Y. She said she's still trying for the college
    What's 'trying'?

Well, I think it means she's trying to get to college.

T. After, I went into hospital
Y. After, I went into hospital
T. I've been going to hospital
Y. **I have been**[4] going to hospital
T. ever since I was three months
Y. **ver in since**[5] I was three months

EVER SINCE, so she's been going to hospital since she was three months old.

T. I'm eighteen now
Y. **I am**[6] eighteen now
T. I've got thalassaemia
Y. **I have good**[7] thalassaemia

Yes, 'thalassaemia', it's a strange illness of the blood.

T. I've got too many white cells
Y. **I-ve**[8] got too many white cells
T. and not enough red cells in my blood
Y. and not . . .[9]
    Enough—F or G?
    Oh dear!

ENOUGH
It isn't spelt like that, though. 'She's got too many white cells and not enough red cells in my . . .?

    blood
T. Every month I go into hospital
Y. Every month I go into hospital
T. to have blood transfusions
Y. to have **trans -fusion**[10] transfusion

(explains what transfusions are)

T. I've also got too much iron in my blood
Y. **I-ve**[8] also got too much iron in my blood
T. I have to have injections for that daily
Y. I have to have **in . . .*injection**[11] for that daily

IN

T. Sometimes I have to have a pump
Y. Sometimes I have to have a **pum**[12] *What?*
T. to get rid of the iron
Y. to get **right off**[13] the iron
    I don't know what's this?

(long explanation given about the purpose of the pump)

T. I have penicillin
Y. I have penicillin
    Yes, medicine
T. vitamin C and folic acid
Y. vitamin C and **follis**[14]

You know what penicillin is.

FOLIC ACID—just another medicine 'cause she's ill.

T. I came out on April 30th
Y. I came out on April 30th
T. I missed signing on that week
Y. I must signing[15] (pronounces hard g)

Signing, you know, when you sign your name

    Yes, I know.
T. On the Thursday after that
Y. On the Thursday after that

Yasmeen	**C.W.** (Teacher)
T. I went to sign on	
Y. I went to sign on	What does it mean 'to sign on'?
Yes, yes I know 'sign' but spelling wrong!	No, its spelt like that.
G?	You know, English spelling is very funny.
Yes, very funny 's-i-g-n'	
(attempts phonic sounding out)	
Too hard.	

Comments

The text: The text presents some very specialist vocabulary, which is bound to be new for most readers. It is not so much the difficult words, however, that create difficulty for Yasmeen—after all the content can be explained—but the structure and style of the text. Some structures are in advance of her competence in English, e.g. 'Must have known' and 'I missed signing on'. Elsewhere difficulty is created by contracted forms and colloquial expressions, such as 'she said she's still trying for the college'.

Yasmeen: Yasmeen is very skilled at phonic decoding; this is occasionally to her advantage, in that she can sometimes decode an unknown word where phonetically regular; more importantly, she asks for the meaning of the word, either directly or through a rising intonation. Many skilled decoders do not employ this crucial additional strategy to learn new words and meanings through their reading. We see her in the process of learning or checking English grammar, e.g. 'What's "a few"'? and then translating it into her own interlanguage, 'Ah medium'. Occasionally decoding principles do not work, however, and she is frustrated that English does not show the close graphophoneme correspondences that Urdu does. Hence her outraged reaction to the English spelling system!

In general, Yasmeen expects to get meaning from what she reads. Her positive reading strategies and her willingness to ask for help compensate for as yet limited knowledge of the language system of English. She is to a much greater extent than Nadeem and Maqsood, for instance, engaged in an interaction with both the teacher and the text.

C.W.: I concentrate rather over-much on the content of the text itself, which is not of great interest to either Yasmeen or myself. Time is spent in explaining the meaning of specialist words rather than drawing on Yasmeen's existing knowledge of the world. Time might usefully have been spent, too, in discussing more fully some of the features which create difficulty in this text, in particular the use of the contracted forms.

The analysis

No.	Miscue	Level of miscue	Source of miscue	Learner response	Teacher prompt
1.	they . . . they did (that they did)	syntactic	**T:** 'that' as relative pronoun creates difficulty [frequently omitted in this context]	Y. hesitates but leaves (miscue does not affect sense of text)	leaves
2.	must have know—none (must have known)	graphophonic	**L:** tense form of modal + perf. aspect (must have known) unfamiliar to Y.	Y. is aware that there is a breakdown here (though her attempt is phonically close); rising intonation signals uncertainty	gives KNOWN
3.	we will (we'll)	syntactic	**T:** contraction creates difficulty **S+:** Y. restructures text (maintaining sense)	leaves	leaves
4.	I have been (I've been)	syntactic	**T:** contraction **S+:** restructures text	leaves	leaves
5.	ver in since (ever since)	graphic	**L:** syntax unknown to Y. cf. 3 and 4 above	leaves	gives and glosses the sentence
6.	I am (I'm)				
7.	I have good (I've got)	graphic	'Good' is a slip; Y. is looking ahead at the real difficulty 'Thalassaemia' which she decodes with little hesitation	leaves	leaves

No.	Word (target)	Cue	Analysis	Reader action	Teacher action
8.	I-ve (I've got)	graphophonic (rhymes with 'Ivy')	T: cf. 3, 4 and 6	this time Y. fails to recognize reduced structure and falls back on decoding strategy	leaves
9.	— (enough)	—	L: highly predictable for native speakers—less so for L2 learners	Y. queries spelling F or G?	gives and back-tracks into text for Y.
10.	trans-fus-ion (transfusions)	graphophonic	Tsp: word not known	Y. decodes word (though omitting pl. -s marker); querying intonation signals uncertainty as to meaning	explains meaning
11.	— *(injections)	—	Tsp: word not at first recognized	picks up initial syllable prompt (but omits plural-s)	gives first syllable
12.	pum (pump)	graphophonic	Tsp: highly unpredictable	requests help with 'what'?	explains process in which pump used
13.	right off (rid of)	graphophonic syntactic	Tco: colloquial style unfamiliar to Y	leaves	leaves
14.	follis (follic)	graphophonic	Tsp: unknown word	querying intonation	gives with quick explanation
15.	must signing (missed signing)	graphophonic	L: Y. does not know the pattern miss + ing (to fail to do something); S: strategy of sounding out confuses Y here.	attempts sounding + comments on English writing system	explains meaning of 'sign'

6. SARLA: DEVELOPING STRATEGIES

Sarla is 11. She has lived in Britain for 5 years. She speaks Gujerati at home to her parents, neither of whom know any English at all. She sometimes speaks English as well as Gujerati to her brother and sisters. She is currently learning to read and write in Gujerati. Her everyday spoken English, unlike that of Maqsood, for instance, shows some non-native features, such as occasional omission of tense markers and the article, e.g. 'he was in army'.

Sarla has chosen the book herself, like Nadeem and the others, and the preamble is included:

Session 1

C.   OK Sarla, we'll carry on. What's this book about that you've got here?
S.   *The Running Man.*
C.   What do you think it's about. Any idea?
S.   Children.
C.   Children, yes. Anything else? I mean, have you had a look at the pictures or anything. What sort of story does it seem to be?
S.   They must be playing hide and seek—hiding behind the bushes . . . that man is after him.
C.   What's it called again?
S.   *Running Man.*
C.   *Running Man*—Part 2, it says. Is there a Part 1? Don't you want to read Part 1 first?
S.   It isn't here.
C.   All right, if that's the one you want to read.

The interaction

Sarla	C.W. (Teacher)

T.   Harry King and Nick Hardy are hiding
S.   Harry King and Nick Hardy are hiding
T.   in the clump of bushes in the park
S.   in the clump of bushes in the park
T.   They can see the park keeper waving a broom
S.   They can see the park keeper waving a broom
T.   at Steve Box and Tom Crooks
S.   at Steve Box and Tom Crooks
T.   Harry and Nick can't help laughing
S.   Harry and Nick can't help laughing
T.   They are the ones who raced their bikes
S.   They are the ones who **reach**[1] raced* their bikes
T.   across the park. Steve and Tom
S.   across the park. Steve and Tom
T.   have only just come through the gate
S.   have only just come through the gate
T.   'Good ghost film on the tele
S.   Good ghost film on the tele
T.   last night' says Nick
S.   last night says Nick
        He must have saw a film on TV about ghosts.   What does he say?
T.   'If you believe in ghosts', says a voice
S.   If you believe in ghosts says a voice
T.   behind them. Steve and Tom have escaped
S.   behind them. Steve and Tom have s . . . s . . . escaped

Sarla   **C.W.** (Teacher)

T. and crept into the usual

S. and crept into the **sh** . . .[2]

                                            Why don't you go back and start
from the beginning of the
sentence again? Sometimes that
helps.

No, I'm stuck on this one (indicating unknown
word)
                                            Yes, I know, but sometimes if
you go back a bit it can help you.

T. Steve and Tom have escaped

S. Steve and Tom have escaped

T. and crept into the usual

S. and crept into the . . .[2]   I'll give it to you—it's USUAL

T. usual hiding place

S. usual hiding place   What does the 'usual hiding
place' mean?

Where they used to hide before . . . in the bushes

T. 'I think I do', says Harry. 'I felt a bit funny

S. I think I do says Harry. I felt a bit funny

T. last Saturday anyway'

S. last Saturday anyway

T. He looks at Nick. This is the first time

S. He **looked**[3] at Nick. This is the first time

T. they have spoken of the old house

S. they have spoken of the old house

T. Nick nods. 'Sort of creepy feeling up your back', he
says

S. Nick **nod**[4]. Sort of creepy feeling up your back he
says

T. and then of course

S. and then of **c** . . .[5] (tries to sound out)   What do you usually do when
you find a word you don't know?

Try to work it out.   How do you work it out?
Like this (she covers part of the word) *She* (the
class teacher) *said you should cover up two letters
and then a few more.*   Yes, you can do that, but
sometimes it helps you to . . .

Go back   Yes, go back. So, '. . . sort of
creepy feeling up your back
then of . . .?'

*course   Yes, good; you see sometimes if
you go back you get the whole
meaning altogether. And then,
of course . . .

T. they have to tell the others

S. they have to tell the others

T. about the Running Man

S. about the Running Man

T. Steve and Tom roll about laughing

S. Steve and Tom roll about laughing

T. 'Funny feeling, smell of burning.

S. funny feeling, smell of burning

T. Load of rubbish', they scream

S. **loud**[6] rub-bish—rubbish they scream   LOAD OF

T. This makes Harry and Nick mad

S. This makes Harry and Nick mad

Sarla   **C.W.** (Teacher)

T. 'OK come and see for yourselves'
S. OK come and see for yourselves
T. 'Yes, and we will stay till it is dark
S. Yes, and we will stay till it is dark
T. Got to be a big devil to frighten us'
S. Got to be a big devil to frighten us

1. . . . If they are going to stay till it is dark
S. . . . If they are going to stay till it is dark
T. they need lights. And some food—
S. they need lights and some food
T. They might miss supper
S. They might **be supper—surprised**[7]   No, start again.
T. They might miss supper
S. They might *miss supper
T. Harry dashes into the house
S. Harry **dashed**[8] into the house
T. He gets his torch and then looks in the pantry
S. He gets his torch and then **look**[9] in the pantry
T. A packet of biscuits goes down his shirt front
S. A peck—a packet of biscuits goes down his shirt
      front
T. and then he sees some candles and matches
S. and then he sees some candles and matches
T. That is Gran's
S. That is Gran's
T. Gran can remember the war and the power cuts
S. Gran can remember the war and the power cuts
T. so she makes sure that Hitler
S. so she makes sure that . . . that . . . that **Hitle**[10]
      (tries to sound out but comes to a stop)   Oh, Hitler, Do you know who
                                                            Hitler was? (Long explanation
                                                            follows)

T. so she makes sure that Hitler will never
S. . . . so she makes sure that Hitler will . . . never
T. put her in the dark again
S. put her in the dark again.
T. No use telling Gran the war is over
S. No use telling Gran the war is over
T. . . . they hurl themselves
S. . . . they (Steve and Tom) **hurr . . . hurr**[11]   HURL THEMSELVES
T. forward and storm inside
S. forward and storm inside
T. 'Devil, devil, come and get me', they chant
S. 'Devil, devil, come and get me' they **cant**[12]   CHANT
T. chant
S. chant
T. and smash out the wooden shutters
S. and smash out the wooden **stutters**[13]   SHUTTERS (+ explains meaning)
T until one falls off and crashes to the floor
S. until one **fall**[14] off and **crash**[14] to the floor . . .
T. They rush round the other rooms upstairs
S. They rush round the other rooms upstairs
T. Tom finds a little dry furry
S. Tom **found**[15] a little dry furry
T. thing on the window sill
S. thing on the window sill

Sarla

T.	He chucks it at Harry
S.	He **chocked—checked**[16] it at Harry
	Checks
	Check it
	Chuck*

Kicks it or throws it.

T.	... it at Harry
S.	... it at Harry
T.	Harry gets that cold feeling again
S.	Harry gets that cold feeling again
T.	Just for the second
S.	Just for the second

scared

T.	'Downstairs. Downstairs. Find the devil'
S.	Downstairs, downstairs, find the devil,
T.	Steve and Tom chant
S.	Steve and Tom **chat**[17]
T.	It is getting dark now and they need torches
S.	It is getting dark now and they need torches
T.	to see the round pattern
S.	to see the round pattern
T.	on the floor of the great hall
S.	on the floor of the great hall
T.	'Magic', says Steve
S.	Magic says Steve
T.	'These are like those star things in the paper
S.	These are like **other**[18] star things in the paper
T.	When Mum sees how lucky she's going to be
S.	When Mum sees how lucky she's going to be

Singer and that

T.	She reckons reading them made her marry Dad
S.	She re ... reckons reading them made her **marriage**[19] dad
T.	and there isn't much magic in that'
S.	and there isn't much magic in that

T.	... on Sunday morning Mrs. Crooks shouts
S.	... on Sunday morning Mrs. Crooks shouts
T.	across the fence
S.	across the fence
T.	'My Tom is proper peaky this morning.
S.	My Tom is proper **p ...**[20] this morning
T.	Dunno what they were doing at Nick Hardy's
S.	**Dun ... dun ...**[21] what they were doing at Nick Hardy's

T.	'Funny, Harry looks a bit off colour too'
S.	Funny, Harry looks a bit off colour too
T.	Harry thinks it will be a long time
S.	Harry thinks it will be a long time
T.	before he watches another ghost film on tele
S.	before he **watch**[22] another ghost film on tele

C.W. (Teacher)

What does he do?
What does that mean?
Look again, there's a U there.
Yes, chucks it at Harry—do you know what that means?
Yes, it's 'throw' actually.

What do you think that cold feeling is?
Yes, good.

Do you know what it means—the stars in the paper? What are the stars in the paper?
Yes, good, stars are singers sometimes but ... (long explanation follows)

PEAKY—it means very ill
DUNNO, another way of saying 'I don't know'.

The analysis

No.	Miscue	Level of miscue	Source of miscue	Learner response	Teacher prompt
1.	reach *(raced)	graphophonic	slip: immediately corrected	—	—
2.	[sh] (usual)	—	T: 'usual' as adjective relatively unpredictable item of structure	attempts sounding; initially resists T. prompt to backtrack	suggests backtrack gives
3.	looked (looks)	graphophonic/semantic	T: we expect simple past tense for narrative; S. occasionally shifts into this tense	leaves	leaves
4.	nod (nods)	syntactic	L: S. occasionally omits third person -s (cf. 14 and 22) as this is sometimes omitted in her own speech	leaves	leaves
5.	of . . . [k][r] *(of course)	—	S: predictable if whole of preceding text taken together	attempts sounding	discusses S's strategy back-tracks for S
6.	loud (load)	graphophonic	Tco:colloquial style	—	gives
7.	they might be supper . . . surprisec *(they might miss supper)	graphic (supper/surprised)	Tcu:'supper' is cultural item? (though cued in by 'food')	restructures to make sense—surprised . . . be surprised; gets it immediately when back-tracks	suggests backtrack
8.	dashed (dashes)	graphophonic/semantic	T: we expect simple past tense for narrative (cf. 3 and 15)	leaves	leaves
9.	look (looks)	syntactic	L: S. occasionally omits third person sing s (cf. 4, 14, 22)	leaves	leaves
10.	Hitl . . . (Hitler)	—	Tcu:reference to unknown person	attempts sounding	explains reference

No.	Text (target)	Type	Comment	Response 1	Response 2
11.	hur . . . (hurl)	—	T: unknown word	attempts sounding	gives
12.	can't (chant)	graphophonic	T: unknown word	—	gives
13.	stutters (shutters)	graphophonic	T: unknown word	—	gives
14.	one fall off . . . crash (one falls . . . crashes)	syntactic	L: cf. 9 and 22	leaves	leaves
15.	found (finds)	graphophonic/semantic	T: cf. 3 and 8	leaves	leaves
16.	chocked—checked *(chucks)	graphic (first attempt non-word)	Tco: colloquial style	S. does not initially respond to request for a meaning, though eventually does so	asks for meaning / draws attention to look of word
17.	chat (chant)	cf. 12			
18.	other (those)	graphic	slip ?: S. anticipates coming difficulty with 'star things'	—	explains cultural reference (of stars)
19.	marriage (marry)	graphophonic	L?: structure 'made her marry' unfamiliar to S	leaves	leaves
20.	[p] (peaky)	—	Tco: both items particularly difficult for L2 speakers	attempts sounding, in both cases unsuccessfully	
21.	dunn (dunno)	—			
22.	watch (watches)	syntactic	L: cf. 9 and 14	leaves	leaves

Comments

The text: Cultural references to persons, events and phenomena create some difficulty for Sarla, e.g. 'Hitler' and 'the stars' in the paper. Attempts to convey colloquial speech create difficulty, too, e.g. 'dunno'. Likewise the regional (northern English) expression 'proper peaky', which is quite unfamiliar to most Londoners, let alone a second language learner.

Sarla: On the whole Sarla expects to read for sense, and the few graphophonic miscues she leaves do not obscure the meaning significantly. Typically, she shows that a phonic sounding out will often only help where the word is already known and readily predictable from context. 'Rub-bish' is broken down into syllables—Hitler and 'dunno', both readily decodable (in fact the latter is as close as one gets to a phonetic realization of speech), defeat Sarla. She gets very close to a plausible rendering but a rising intonation and reluctance to continue indicate difficulty with meaning. Sarla's case illustrates the point made by Meek *et al.* (1983):

> when a word should be easy to sound out yet the pupil cannot 'make it mean' the reason lies in the fact that the word is unfamiliar and not in the pupil's lack of skill'.

C.W.: My handling of the pre-reading discussion is rather perfunctory. I could have led Sarla into the content and sense of the book more helpfully.

I am anxious to encourage Sarla to use more of the text to predict difficult items, but do not want to undermine the advice of her other teacher. Hence the lengthy exchange about Sarla's usual strategies.

My questions remain too close to the detail of the text, e.g. 'What does the "usual hiding place" mean?' rather than encouraging a wider exploration of character, motives and implications, or relating the story to Sarla's own experience.

Session 2

It seemed to me that Sarla was reading with greater fluency and confidence just a few weeks later. Noticeable on listening to her, but difficult to convey in the transcript, is the way she is intoning the text, that is, adding appropriate stress and intonation. Stress has been conveyed by italicizing stressed words.

On this occasion Sarla brought her own book from home into the reading lesson—about a talking horse. As Sarla makes few miscues, Sarla's rendering is given without the text.

The interaction

Sarla	C.W. (Teacher)
Mike got off the school bus with lots of other children but he didn't walk home with any of them because he wanted to see if he could find some good rocks for his [k][1] (tries to sound out)	
	What do you think is the best thing to do when you come across . . . ?
Go back.	Yes, mind you, you might not know this word—you know when people have a hobby like stamps, what do they have?

Sarla

collect

[shun]

rock collection

So nobody was with him when he saw the horse. The horse was just standing there and Mike was surprised because he had never seen a horse anywhere near the house before. Mike got out of the ditch where he had been looking for rocks and he and went over to the horse. 'Hallo horse, where did *you* come from? he asked. '-Well', the horse said, 'I was just there waiting for the school bus. 'Hey, was that you talking', Mike asked. 'Of *course*' said the horse. 'You don't see any *other* horse round, do you?' 'Well no' Mike said. The horse bent over to eat some grass. Fin . . . finally Mike said 'I didn't *know* horses could talk **thought**[2]' (stops knowing that 'thought' doesn't fit context) . . . 'Have you ever talked to a horse'? 'No', **said Mike**[3]—no Mike said. 'Well then', the horse said. Mike wondered what he meant by that remark but he waited a while and then he said, 'Why were you waiting for the school bus?' 'I was hoping some boy would take me home to live with him. You see, I don't have a boy'
The donkey—the horse.

I saw a film on the TV.

Not a horse, it was a mule. (comment from other student in group)
A donkey, he was in army.
Yes he help people.
I wish you could live with me but we don't have a . . .
burn[4] or anything.
burn
He doesn't have a place for a dog or cat or anything like that. 'Nobody round here does'. 'A garret will be alright'. 'Really you mean you will come with me and be my own horse'? 'No you will be *my* boy'. 'Will **you . . . your**[5] my mother be surprised?' (read as question, not exclamation) 'Oh I never talk to grown ups'. 'My mother won't mind that', Mike said. 'In **fence . . . feast**[6]

I think she had just as soon she didn't. *Wow* I have a horse,' Mike shouted. 'What's your name' the horse asked Mike, '**b . . . b . . .**[7] and I have a big sister **g . . .**[8] '. . . What's *your* name?' The horse thought for a minute. 'I guess my name will be Mike.' 'But that's *my* name'. 'Don't you like it?' 'Sure but I feel really funny calling you Mike.' 'Alright, then my name will be **g . . .**[8]

C.W. (Teacher)
So that's collect (drawing attention to word) it's got something on the end, collect
. . .
So he hasn't got a stamp collection but he's got a . . .

THOUGH

Who's this talking now?
Have you ever heard a horse talking?
Did you? In which a horse was talking?

The donkey was in the Army.

What's that word again?
What does that mean?

Yes. Um.

Start again . . . My mother won't mind that. In f . . . IN FACT—do you know that expression? It means . . . she might not mind.
So IN FACT

BRADFORD, GLORIA

GLORIA

Sarla	C.W. (Teacher)
'That's my *sister's* name; besides its for a *girl*. Do you like any other name?' 'Well' said the horse you . . . you certainly are fussy. Let me see. I know my name will be Mr. Bradford'. 'That's my *father's* name . . . Come on please listen you can have any other name in the whole world. I mean **that**[10] Mrs. Bradford . . .[11]	I'll give you that—CERTAINLY
	I MEAN NOT—I MEAN NOT MRS. BRADFORD—see if it works if you go back again. 'You can have any other name in the whole world.
I mean not Mrs. Bradford* either but any other name, I promise.'	Good.

Comments

The text: The question/answer nature of the dialogue makes the progression of the text predictable. This only breaks down in the case of the rhetorical question: 'Will my mother be surprised!' Sarla at first miscues *your* here simply because she has got into the rhythm of the question/answer exchange—all the other questions are real questions with the 'you' pronoun.

The major difficulties are not the content but the structure words, such as *though, in fact, certainly*. These are characteristic of rather literary formal dialogue and not very familiar to Sarla.

Sarla: In several ways Sarla shows that she is a more confident reader, for example:

—she nowhere leaves uncorrected a nonsense miscue. One doubtful case—*burn*—is resolved when, whether the word is new or not, Sarla shows that she has attributed an appropriate meaning to it (unlike Nadeem's explanation of 'whirring' for example (p. 173));
—she is now apparently aware that 'going back' in the text can help (when she suggests it here, unfortunately, the strategy does not work, but she saw it work for her on a previous occasion);
—although she does not ask questions or very readily volunteer information, she does elaborate a little more in drawing on her own experience, e.g. in the TV story of the talking donkey;
—she 'acts out' the text, playing the respective parts and using contrastive stress to highlight the important content;
—syntactic miscues show Sarla drawing more effectively on her knowledge of the language system of English, as for example the slight restructuring 'said Mike/Mike said' and the understandable miscue 'thought' (she anticipated 'thought Mike'—then was confused because the reporting verb has come earlier: 'Mike said'). Equally 'I mean that', where 'that' is by far the most likely item to follow 'I mean'.

The analysis

No.	Miscue	Level of miscue	Source of miscue	Learner response	Teacher prompt
1.	[k] *(collection)	—	**Tcu:** semantically unpredictable (cultural phenomenon?)	attempts sounding out; suggests going back (though prompted by T.)	discusses strategy gives semantic cues, e.g. hobby—stamps, draws attention to look of word
2.	thought (though)	graphic	**Tco:** difficult item of structure; characteristic of speech	pauses, knowing that a verb is not required here	gives
3.	said Mike *(Mike said)	syntactic	**S+:** synonymous structure	Sarla immediately self-corrects—unnecessarily, as the initial restructuring is a positive sign	—
4.	burn (barn)	graphic	**T?:** word unknown or **L?:** Sarla's pronunciation of word?	leaves but teacher prompt shows that S. has assigned an appropriate meaning; she goes for a meaning explanation rather than phonic similarity (cf. Nadeem 'whirring')	asks what word is asks what word means

#	Item		Analysis		
5.	you . . . your *(my)	syntactic	**T:** Q and A of text leads one to expect second person pronoun	Sarla immediately self-corrects but intones text inappropriately here	—
6.	in fence . . . feast (in fact)	graphic	**T:** connector unfamiliar	—	suggests backtrack finally gives
7.	[b] Bradford	—	**Tcu:** unfamiliar word	attempts sounding	gives
8.	[g] Gloria	—	**Tcu:** unfamiliar word	attempts sounding	gives
9.	— certainly	—	**T:** formal language	—	gives
10.	that (not)	fits preceding context syntactically/ semantically	**T:** elliptical = I mean that you cannot	—	gives
11.	— *either	—	**T:** reference item—creates difficulty	S. picks up the back tracking prompt started by T. and is successful	backtracks for S.

Conclusion

The Case Studies have aimed to focus on the reading process itself, with all the difficulty this involves. The attributing of a likely source to each miscue, for instance, is bound to be speculative. However, some kind of charting of learner-reader strategies and their change and development in response to different kinds of texts and different teachers would seem one way of attempting to see the learning to read process in context.

Bibliography

Ajitsaria, A. (1984) *The Tiger and the Woodpecker*, (ed. Ingham, J.). Middlesex Polytechnic on behalf of the Reading Materials for Minority Groups project

Albrow, K. H. (1972) *The English Writing System: notes towards a description*. Longman

Applebee, A. (1977) *The Child's Concept of Story*. University of Chicago Press

Arnold, H. (1982) *Listening to Children Reading*. Hodder and Stoughton

Barr, P., Clegg, J. and Wallace, C. (1981) *Advanced Reading Skills*. Longman

BBC (1975) *BBC Adult Literacy Handbook*. BBC Publications

Bennett, J. (1979) *Learning to Read with Picture Books*. The Thimble Press

Brewster, J. (1983) *Developing Language Awareness in Hambrough Middle School: A Case Study*. Paper presented for NCLE working party on Language Awareness

Brice-Heath, S. (1982) What no bedtime story means: narrative skills at home and school, in *Language and Society*, vol. 11, no. 1, pp. 49–76

Buck, C. (1979) Miscues of non-native speakers of English, in *Miscue Analysis* (ed. Goodman, K.). ERIC Clearinghouse on Reading and Communication Skills

Carrell, P. (1983) Some Issues in Studying the role of Schemata or Background Knowledge in Second Language Comprehension, in *Reading in a Foreign Language*, vol, 1, no. 2, pp. 81–92

Chomsky, C. (1970) Reading, writing and phonology, in *Harvard Educational Review*, vol. 40, pp. 287–309

Clark, H. H. and Clark, E. V. (1977) *Psychology and Language, an introduction to psycholinguistics*. Harcourt Brace Jovanovich

Clark, M. (1976) *Young Fluent Readers*. Heinemann Educational Publications

Corder, S. P. (1973) Error Analysis, in *The Edinburgh Course in Applied Linguistics*, (ed. Allen, J. P. B. and Corder, S. P.), *vol. 3: Techniques in Applied Linguistics*. Oxford University Press

Corder, S. P. (1981) Idiosyncratic Dialects and Error Analysis in *Error Analysis and Interlanguage*. Oxford University Press

Cummins, J. (1979) Linguistic Interdependence and the Educational Development of bilingual children, in *Review of Educational Research*, vol. 49, no. 2, pp. 222–251

Dakin, J. (1973) The teaching of reading, in Fraser, H. and O'Donnell, W. R. (eds.) *Applied Linguistics and the Teaching of English*. Longman

Davies, A. and Widdowson, H. G. (1974) Reading and Writing, in Allen, J. P. B. and Corder, S. P. (eds.) *The Edinburgh Course in Applied Linguistics, vol. 3: Techniques in Applied Linguistics*. Oxford University Press

Davies, F. (1982) Paper presented at a seminar on *The Effective Use of Reading*, National Association for Remedial Education, Chester College of Higher Education

DES (1975) *A Language for Life* (The Bullock Report). HMSO

Dixon, B. (1978) *Catching them Young, vol. 1: Sex, Race and Class in Children's Fiction*. Pluto Press

Donaldson, M. (1978) *Children's Minds*, Fontana/Collins

Edwards, V. (1979) *The West Indian Language Issue in British Schools*, Routledge and Kegan Paul

Fishman, J. A. (1965) Who speaks what language to whom and when, in *La Linguistique*, vol. 2, pp. 67–88; revised as 'The relationship between micro and macro sociolinguistics in the study of who speaks what language to whom and when,' in Pride, J. B. and Holmes, J. (eds.) *Sociolinguistics*, Penguin

Freire, P. (1972) *Cultural Action for Freedom*. Penguin

Gardner, K. (1978) Reading Comprehension, in *The Teaching of Comprehension*, ETIC Occasional Paper, The British Council English Teaching Information Centre

Goodman, K. S. (1964) A linguistic study of cues and miscues in reading, in *Language and Literacy: The Collected Writings of Kenneth S. Goodman, vol. 1: Process, Theory, Research*, edited and introduced by Frederick V. Gollasch, 1982. Routledge

Goodman, K. S. (1967) Reading: a Psycholinguistic Guessing Game, in Gollasch, *op. cit.*

Goodman, K. S. (1973) Miscues: Windows on the Reading Process, in Gollasch, *op. cit.*

Goodman, K. S. and Burke, C. L. (1973) The Goodman Taxonomy of Reading Miscues, in Gollasch, *op. cit.*

Goodman, Y. and Green, J. (1977) Grammar and Reading in the Classroom, in Shuy, R. (ed.), *Linguistic Theory: what can it say about reading?* International Reading Association

Grant, D. W. and Moony, A. (1980) *Improving the reading comprehension of Spina Bifida children: a preliminary account of a pilot remedial teaching programme using cloze procedure*. Report to Ealing College Research Committee

Grice, H. B. (1975) Logic and conversation, in Cole, P. and Morgan, J. L. (eds) *Syntax and Semantics, vol. 3: Speech Acts*. Academic Press, pp. 41–58

206

·Griffin, P. (1977) Reading and Pragmatics: Symbiosis, in Shuy, R. (ed.), *Linguistic Theory; what can it say about reading?* International Reading Association

Halliday, M. A. K. (1973) Relevant models of language in *Explorations in the Functions of Language*, Edward Arnold

Harris, R. (1979) *Caribbean English and Adult Literacy*. Adult Literacy Unit, London

Harrison, C. (1980) *Readability in the Classroom*. Cambridge University Press

Hewison, J. (1981) Home is where the help is, in *Times Educational Supplement*, 16 January

HMI (1980) A View of the Curriculum, in HMI documents *Matters for Discussion*, no. 11.

Hoffman, M. (1976) *Reading, Writing and Relevance*. Hodder and Stoughton

Holt, J. (1969) *How Children Fail*. Pelican

Johns, T. and Davies, F. (1983) Text as a vehicle for information: the classroom use of written texts in teaching reading in a foreign language, in *Reading in a Foreign Language* vol. 1, no. 1, pp. 1–19

Kellie, P. (1982) *A study of peergroup reading in a multilingual classroom*. Unpublished project presented for CNAA Postgraduate Diploma; Language in the Multiracial Community, Ealing College of Higher Education

Kohl, H. (1974) *Reading How To*. Penguin

Labov, W. (1969) The Logic of non-standard English, in *Georgetown Monographs on Language and Linguistics*, vol. 22, pp. 1–31; reprinted in Giglioli, P. P. (ed.) 1972 *Language and Social Context*. Penguin

Labov, W. (1972) Some sources of reading problems for speakers of the Black English Vernacular, in *Language in the Inner City*. Blackwell

Laishley, J. (1972) Can comics join the multi-racial society? *Times Educational Supplement*, 24 November

Lakoff, R. (1974) *Language and Women's Place*. Harper and Row

Langer, J. (1981) Pre-reading plan (PReP): facilitating text comprehension, in Chapman, J., (ed.) *The Reader and the Text*. Heinemann Educational Books

Linguistic Minorities Project (1983) *Linguistic Minorities in England*. A report from the Linguistic Minorities Project. University of London Institute of Education, July 1983

Lunzer, E. and Gardner, K. (1979) *The Effective Use of Reading*. Heinemann Educational Books, for the Schools Council

Mace, J. (1979) *Working with Words, Literacy Beyond School*. Writers and Readers Publishing Cooperative in Association with Chamelion

Mackay, D., Thompson, B. and Schaub, P. (1970) *Breakthrough to Literacy Teachers Manual: the theory and practice of teaching initial reading and writing*. Longman, for the Schools Council

Mandler, J. M., Scribner, S., Cole, M. and Deforest, M. (1980) Cross-cultural invariance in story recall, in *Child Development*, vol. 51, no. 1, pp. 19–26

McNally, J. and Murray, W. (1962) *Key Words to Literacy*. The Schoolmaster Publishing Co.

Marland, M. (1977) *Language Across the Curriculum*. Heinemann Educational Books

Martin-Jones, M. (1984) The Newer Minorities; literacy and educational issues, in Trudgill, P. (ed.) *Language in the British Isles*. Cambridge University Press

Meek, M. with Armstrong, S., Austerfield, V., Graham, J. and Plackett, E. (1983) *Achieving Literacy: Longitudinal Studies of adolescents learning to read*. Routledge and Kegan Paul

Mellish, D. (1982) *Reading: Some of the problems faced by children whose mother-tongue is not English, with reference to commonly used Readers*. Unpublished project for LMRC, Ealing College of Higher Education

Milner, D. (1983) *Children and Race: Ten years on*. Penguin

Moon, B. C. (1974) *Individualized Reading*. Reading Centre for the Teaching of Reading, University of Reading School of Education

Moy, B. and Raleigh, M. (1981) Comprehension: bringing it back alive, Part Three. *English Magazine*, no. 6, Spring, pp. 33–38

Page, E. N. (1977) *The Vocabulary of Chemistry—A Problem?* Unpublished MSc thesis. University of Reading

Perera, K. (1979) The language demands of school learning, in OU PE232 *Language Development, Supplementary Reading, Block 6*

Perera, K. (1981) Some language problems in school learning, in Mercer, N. (ed.), *Language in School and Community*. Edward Arnold

Raleigh, M. (1981) *The Languages Book*. The English Centre, ILEA

Reid, J. F. (1958) A study of thirteen beginners in reading, in *Acta Psychologica*, vol. 14, no. 4, pp. 295–313

Reid, J. F. (1966) Learning to think about reading, in *Educational Research*, vol. 9, pp. 56–62

Rosen, C. and Rosen, H. (1973) *The language of Primary School Children*. Penguin

Rosen, H. and Burgess, T. (1980) *Languages and dialects of London Schoolchildren*. Ward Lock Educational

Schank, R. C. and Abelson, R. P. (1977) Scripts, plans and knowledge, in Johnson-Laird, P. N. and Watson, P. C. (eds.) *Thinking. Readings in Cognitive Science.* Cambridge University Press, pp. 421–32

Skutnabb-Kangas, T. and Phillipson, R. (1983) *Inter-communicative and Inter-cultural Competence.* Paper presented at the BAAL Annual Meeting

Smith, F. (1971) *Understanding Reading: A psycholinguistic analysis of reading and learning to read.* Holt, Reinhart and Winston

Smith, F. (1977) Making sense of reading, in *Harvard Educational Review*, vol. 47, pp. 286–395

Smith, F. (1978) *Reading.* Cambridge University Press

Smith, F. (1983) *The promise and threat of microcomputers for language learners.* On TESOL '83: The question of control. Selected papers from the Seventeenth Annual Convention of Teachers of English to Speakers of other Languages, Toronto, Canada

Soderbergh, R. (1981) Early reading as language acquisition, in *System*, vol. 9, no. 3, pp. 207–212

Southgate Booth, V., Arnold, H. and Johnson, S. (1981) *Extending Beginning Reading.* Heinemann Educational Books

Steffenson, M. S., Joag-Dev, C. and Anderson, R. C. (1979) A cross-cultural perspective on reading comprehension, in *Reading Research Quarterly*, vol. 15, no. 1, pp. 10–29

Stewart, W. (1969) The Use of Negro dialect in the teaching of reading, in Baratz, J. and Shuy, R. (eds.) *Teaching Black children to Read.* Washington, D.C. Centre for Applied Linguistics

Stubbs, M. (1980) *Language and Literacy, the Sociolinguistics of Reading and Writing.* Routledge and Kegan Paul

Studdert, J. (1980) *Reading Development: the use of Cloze procedure as a small group activity.* ILEA, Centre for Urban Educational Studies

Sutcliffe, D. (1982) *British Black English.* Basil Blackwell

Target, F. (1982) *A report on the provision for mother-tongue maintenance in the Borough of Ealing.* Unpublished project for LMRC, Ealing College of Higher Education

Taylor, D. (1981) The family and the development of literacy skills and values, in *Journal of Research in Reading*, vol. 4, no. 2

Trudgill, P. (1974) *Sociolinguistics.* Penguin

Trudgill, P. (1975) *Accent, Dialect and the School.* Edward Arnold

Walker, P. (1980) Whole Schools reading. *English Magazine*, no. 4, Summer 1980, pp. 28–29

Warham, S. (1981) A linguistic perspective on reading skills, in Chapman, J. (ed.) *The Reader and the Text.* Heinemann Educational Books

Watkins, O. (1981) Active reading and listening, in Sutton, C. (ed.) *Communicating in the Classroom.* Hodder and Stoughton

Weaver, C. (1980) *Psycholinguistics and Reading: from process to practice.* Winthrop Publishers Inc.

Widdowson, H. G. (1979) Discourse and text. Paper presented at Ealing College of Higher Education Conference on the Reading Skill

Wight, J. (1976) How much interference? *Times Educational Supplement*, 14 May

Wight, J., with Hunt, P., Sapara, S. and Sinclair, H. (1978a) *Make-a-Story.* Reading through Understanding project, ILEA Learning Materials Service

    (1978b) *Share-a-Story.* Reading through Understanding project, Holmes McDougall in collaboration with ILEA Learning Materials Service

    (1978c) *Explore-a-Story.* Reading through Understanding project, Collins, in collaboration with ILEA Learning Materials Service

Wiles, S. (1981) Language issues in the multi-cultural classroom, in Mercer, N. (ed.) *Language in School and Community.* Edward Arnold

Wilkinson, A. (1971) *Foundations of Language. Talking and reading in young children*

Williams, R. (1981) Lexical familiarisation in content area textbooks, in Chapman, J. (ed.) *The Reader and the Text.* Heinemann Educational Books

Zimet, S. (1980) *Print and Prejudice.* Hodder and Stoughton, in association with the United Kingdom Reading Association

Index